ED PAULSON

INSIDE CISCO

THE REAL STORY OF
SUSTAINED M&A GROWTH

JOHN WILEY & SONS, INC.

New York • Chichester • Weinheim • Brisbane • Singapore • Toronto

ISBN 0-471-41425-5

Printed in the United States of America.

10 9 8 7 6 5 4 3 2 1

ACKNOWLEDGMENTS

As with any major project, this book is the final product of a team effort with the author as the central conduit for information and analysis. I foremost want to thank Cisco Systems for creating such a great company and set of acquisition practices such that this book was warranted in the first place. Next my special thanks go to Mario Mazzola of Cisco Systems, Barry Eggers of Lightspeed Venture Partners, Kim Niederman of LongBoard, and Dave Newkirk of SS8 Networks for submitting themselves to my detailed questions and being willing to go on record about Cisco and its practices. Additional thanks go to a large number of friends, colleagues, and acquaintances who shared their stories about Cisco, acquisitions, and life in Silicon Valley. A special thanks is in order for those authors, writers, reporters, and analysts whose previous work helped frame much of what is included in this book. Every reasonable effort was made to make sure that attribution was given to you all as applicable. I hope that a part of this work returns the favor to you someday. My mother, Jean, an ex-professional secretary and excellent editor, deserves special thanks for her rapid and meticulous editing of the initial drafts. The folks at Cape Cod Compositors warrant a thank-you for their professional and detailed editing of the final versions of this book, making sure that the quotes, footnotes, and countless other details wound up in the right spots. Thank you, Mary Daniello, Associate Managing Editor at John Wiley & Sons, for demanding from us the best we could deliver. Thank you, Jeanne Glasser at John Wiley & Sons,

Acknowledgments

for believing in this book and helping to make it a better product for our readers. Thank you, Lisa Swayne, my agent, for handling the business and legal side of things so that I could write. A most special thank-you goes to my wife, Loree, who listened for hours about Cisco, acquisitions, writing, valuations, Silicon Valley, and any number of other topics when, doubtless, she would rather have been watching HGTV. Finally, a heartfelt thank-you goes to you, the reader, without whom none of this would be possible.

E.P.

CONTENTS

INTRODUCTION

Cisco is a business giant and truly one of the most astounding success stories of modern times. This is a company with historical annual revenue and income growth rates of between 30 percent and 100 percent or more with annual revenues in the tens of billions of dollars. A large, established company, with one of the largest market capitalizations in the world, Cisco acts in many ways as though it is a start-up. The firm reinvents itself based on marketplace demands and technological advances while avoiding the stagnation and dogma that often accompany large size and huge success. Independent of the difficult times that Cisco and the entire networking industry are experiencing in 2000 to 2001, you have to give credit to Cisco for its past successes. I personally expect that Cisco will come out of these depressed economic times stronger, leaner, and more competitive than it was going in, which will make it an even more formidable adversary than before. And, whether that happens or not, understanding the key management ingredients that provided its historical success is valuable for any manager looking to grow a business in a dynamic marketplace.

A confluence of many factors contributed to Cisco's historical success, including the growth of the Internet, the influence of its leaders such as John Chambers and the original founders, the incredible Nasdaq run of the 1990s, and the technological advancements associated with networking technology. Another area that must be considered—and is viewed by many to be the most critical component of Cisco's outstanding historical performance—is a well-tuned acquisitions process. Cisco has acquired more than 70 companies since 1993, acquiring 26 companies in fiscal 2000 alone, and has

1

constantly refined its acquisition process along the way. In fact, the company has been so successful with its acquisitions that the industry created a new term for Cisco's type of research and development (R&D) approach: acquisition and development (A&D).

Buying a company is easy. Making that purchased company succeed in the postpurchase environment is something else altogether. Just as anyone can get married, anyone can buy a company. But not everyone can make a marriage successful, and many companies wind up selling (divorcing themselves of) the very companies they initially enthusiastically acquired, often selling for a fraction of the original purchase price. Not only has Cisco acquired 70+ companies, but it has retained almost all of the acquired personnel while improving Cisco's revenues derived from the acquired firms' products and technologies—sometimes increasing the acquired company's revenue stream over 50 times in as little as 18 months. All of this was done while also maintaining the dignity of Cisco's and the acquired company's personnel. That kind of acquisition success warrants additional investigation and understanding. Understanding the management essence of that kind of acquisition success prompted my interest in writing this book.

Inside Cisco takes a detailed look at the very processes that make the Cisco acquisition engine work so well. It first analyzes the Cisco way of doing things and, when applicable, the rationale for doing it that way. It then presents the assumptions associated with the Cisco way of performing acquisitions along with an assessment of how applicable or portable the Cisco approach is to other companies and industries.

The intent of the book is to deliver the merger and acquisition (M&A) gospel according to Cisco—the company that has become the gold standard of M&A practices, both strategically and operationally. My hope is that readers will be simultaneously entertained and informed, gaining insight into Cisco's acquisition philosophy and practices, as well as how its process might be applied to the reader's company.

Let's face it: The vast majority of acquisitions fail to meet the expectations set by the buyer and seller at the time of the purchase. The shattered dreams, aspirations, financial goals, and personality conflicts arising from these failed acquisitions are the stuff of evening television dramas but nothing that any professional wants in his or her life. However, acquisitions have been, and continue to be, a powerful technique not only for growing a company but also for keeping it from stagnating as it grows. The constant infusion of talent, technology, products, and personnel that accompany a successful acquisition program keep the buyer vibrant as it grows into its future success.

Cisco has figured out a process that works. Its processes provide an excellent starting point for any business manager intending to use acquisition to its full advantage. Its track record sets the backdrop of success against which any other acquisition program can be compared. Every professional should be interested in using acquisitions as the potent strategic tool that they can be, and not the company-stalling nightmare they have often become. These professionals are well-served by first learning the practices of the best. And the best practices are those of Cisco Systems.

Inside Cisco starts out presenting some background information about Cisco Systems, its incredible financial and operational success history, an overview of the basic Cisco acquisition process, and an introduction to the key people who helped mold Cisco Systems into the company and culture that it is today—a culture, by the way, designed to acquire and assimilate other companies.

The middle chapters (4 through 9) present the minimum criteria that any Cisco acquisition candidate must meet even to get to the due diligence stage. In essence, these are Cisco's initial show stoppers. Readers will find this emphasis on intangibles intriguing in that Cisco places its heaviest emphasis on the technology, products, and employees of a target company. It considers financial analysis and pricing as a final stage of the process, after it has been determined that the rest of the company is a good fit. Back to the marriage analogy—it is silly to talk about a prenuptial agreement if the fact that one party wants kids and the other doesn't is enough to derail the marriage plans altogether. Work out the details that are of paramount importance with the belief that, for the right situation, the right financial arrangement can be made.

The next set of chapters (10 through 14) takes a detailed look at the mechanics of the Cisco process from target selection, to due diligence, to personnel, product, and manufacturing assimilation, along with the Cisco rationale for setting the purchase price.

The chapters close with a summary analysis of the feasibility of a growth-by-acquisition strategy (Chapter 15) and a somewhat objective assessment of the overall Cisco acquisition and development (A&D) approach to product line enhancement (Chapter 16). These chapters will make more sense to the readers after having read the preceding chapters.

Included in the appendixes is various pertinent information excerpted from my book, *The Technology M&A Guidebook* (John Wiley & Sons, 2001) such as a simple due diligence checklist, some general background information about company buyer types and their motivations for purchasing companies, and a listing of Cisco's acquisitions to date. Not all of the information presented in the background appendixes applies to Cisco directly, but it is included to provide a framework for understanding what is unique about the highly focused and refined approach that Cisco has cultivated.

Throughout the book you will find sidebars that refer to various aspects of Cisco Systems. When the comments are from someone who has worked for or currently works for Cisco Systems or one of its acquired companies, the sidebar is called "From Inside Cisco." If the comments are from a third party but related to Cisco, then the sidebar is called "About Cisco." General Silicon Valley background information or comments are presented in the "Inside the Valley" sidebars.

The information presented comes from any number of sources. My intention was to distill the superfluous facts from those critical to an understanding of the Cisco M&A methodology. Much of the information comes directly from my personal interviews with current Cisco executives, ex-Cisco executives, published interviews, and comments from colleagues within high technology in general or Silicon Valley in particular. It was amazing to me the number of people I know in Silicon Valley who have worked for, are working for, or are in some way attached to Cisco Systems. Cisco is a large company that casts a wide net within Silicon Valley, and it has directly touched the lives of tens of thousands of people. Their stories are presented here as well when applicable.

My sincere wish is that you find this book as enjoyable to read as I found it to write; that the Cisco A&D methodology presented makes an impression on you; and that you carry the presented information with you in a way that perhaps transforms an acquisition that you may become involved with from one of number-crunching and fiefdom conflicts into one of integration and exhilarating success. Being part of a growing business that is truly changing the way people live their lives converts work from something we do to make a living into something that we passionately pursue with a high level of motivation. Acquisitions, handled effectively, keep a company dynamic. Acquisitions, handled effectively, ward off the unfortunate stagnation that comes with success. Cisco knows acquisitions. Read this book and learn what Cisco knows. Learn how you can turn acquisitions into your powerful strategic weapon. Prosper and enjoy!

CHAPTER 1

SO WHAT'S THE BIG DEAL?

In this business, if you are acquiring technology, you are acquiring people. That is the reason large companies that have acquired technology companies have failed. If you look at AT&T and NCR, or IBM and ROLM, the acquirer did not understand that it was acquiring people and a culture. If you don't have a culture that quickly embraces the new acquisition, if you are not careful in the selection process, then the odds are high that your acquisition will fail.
——John Chambers, President and CEO, Cisco Systems

Within the networking and communications industry, Cisco Systems is the 800-pound gorilla to beat. This is not a new company although people sometimes think of it as such. On the contrary, this company has been around since 1984 when two Stanford University employees decided that this newfound networking technology they had just implemented for Stanford needed wider exposure. The company was initially based on highly technical, and mostly invisible, products called routers, which determine the directions in which Internet-based communication will be transmitted. Pretty esoteric stuff on which to build a multibillion-dollar business powerhouse, but Cisco did it.

The normal person on the street doesn't typically own a router, but because of Cisco they know that routers exist. Ask your neighbors, whether in technology or not, if they have ever heard of Cisco Systems and you will likely find that they own or have owned Cisco stock. Ask them what Cisco does, and they will say something like, "They are on the Internet and make routers." Dig any deeper and there won't typically be much more there, but they will still own the stock—although of late they will lament the amount of money they have lost. (By the way, I have tried this any number of times and the results are fairly consistent.) People tend to think of Cisco as "new" technology but treat it like an old standard like GE or IBM from an investment perspective. Some people love Cisco. Some people hate Cisco. But most people know of Cisco. That in itself is quite an accomplishment, particularly since the company had done practically no advertising up until very recent times. Other notable achievements attributed to the company and its performance are that because of Cisco:

- Many early owners of Cisco stock have made tremendous gains on their portfolio holdings and bettered their personal way of life.
- Several thousand Cisco employees go to work as millionaires.
- John Chambers, Cisco's president and chief executive officer (CEO) is asked to meet with the president of the United States and with leaders of foreign countries and to speak to some of the greatest minds in the world today.
- Over 70 companies that used to be stand-alone corporations have been taken into the Cisco family with acquired people staying on as Cisco employees, defying the industry turnover norms.

Cisco Systems has refined the use of acquisitions as a strategic business weapon. Where other companies acquire organizations with the ensuing results being stalled growth or further restructuring in a frantic attempt to make the acquisition profitable, Cisco increases the revenues of its acquired companies and fully integrates new employees into its culture. Cisco looks for acquisition target companies that can simultaneously address customer needs and increase Cisco's revenue. Cisco does not make it a practice to do acquisitions as a financial exercise—the company is too busy growing its markets and taking market share from others to bother with those types of financial shenanigans.

Perhaps Standard & Poor's (S&P) can say what I am trying to say more succinctly and with a higher level of objectivity, as stated in one of the S&P Industry Survey reports dealing with Computers: Networking.

> Cisco Systems continues to dominate the enterprise gear market. The company's well executed acquisition strategy has positioned the company as the largest and fastest growing among its peers. . . . In a business defined by continuing price declines, Cisco has been able to keep its gross margins above 60 percent—sharply higher than its competitors—aided by steady introductions of new products and implementation of cost cutting initiatives.[1]

By the way, this is said about a company that grew its revenues 56 percent from fiscal 1999 ($12.154 billion) to fiscal 2000 ($18.928 billion) while maintaining excellent (52 percent) net income growth as well.

Some people contend that Cisco is on a decline since its stock dropped precipitously in calendar years 2000 and 2001. Certainly the stock has dropped, like many others on the Nasdaq, but this does not mean that Cisco, the operational company, is in decline. It is incredi-

---

About Cisco

Given the kind of pressure they [Cisco] are under from the shareholder community, it's like they've done it backward and in high heels with the whole world watching.[2]

—Virginia Brooks, analyst with the Aberdeen Group, commenting on Cisco's ability to maintain a high state of readiness and focus

---

bly cash rich and continues to maintain a solid cash position, while sustaining 40 percent revenue growth. Clearly this company is doing something right. This chapter presents background information providing a little more perspective on this incredible company's accomplishments.

ACQUIRE AND GROW

Cisco buys companies as an integral part of its operation. It doesn't buy companies because these companies sometimes appear on the radar screen. It does not buy companies because it feels that its financial muscle could be more efficiently used, gaining a higher return, if invested in the purchase of a company with no operational benefits. It buys a company because that purchase will expand Cisco's product offerings, enabling it to offer a wider array of products and services to its customers. Cisco intensely believes that if you do the things that are right for Cisco's customers, it will benefit Cisco. And, so far, its history bears this out as a solid approach.

There are a number of important contributors to the success of the Cisco acquisition strategy, not the least of which is the high-technology industry that Cisco shares with such industry leaders as Nortel Networks, 3Com, Lucent, and hundreds of other smaller players. Technology is not going away. Sure, the Nasdaq took a huge hit in the 2000 to 2001 time frame, but this does not mean that customers no longer need technology or the benefits derived from its use. There is a solid case to be made that technology in general and networking in particular will do nothing but increase in importance to both business and general public consumers. Cisco is positioned smack-dab in the middle of the Internetworking revolution that continues to expand our reach globally. The world is a little closer and smaller because of Cisco and its technology partners, and we, the consumers, will continue to find new ways of using this Internet-connected world.

And technology continues to evolve at a mind-boggling rate. Instead of quoting Moore's Law, again, let me simply use a term passed on to me by one of Cisco's engineering vice presidents: "perishable." Yes, technology is perishable. Just like that head of lettuce you bought last week at the store that is no longer edible, much of the technology purchased 12 to 18 months ago is no longer viable. It is too slow, or not compatible, or it is simply too much hassle to get and keep working. And why hassle with it when you can purchase a replacement part that is likely smaller, more reliable, less expensive, and faster than that clunker you are hanging on to? In short, technology is perishable, although with a shelf life a little longer than that of a head of lettuce.

My point here is that technology continually advances, and these advances are in demand by network users, most of whom are already Cisco's customers. Is Cisco always going to properly anticipate and design the right products for the right customers at the right price at the right time? Not likely, as evidenced by Cisco's lackluster performance in early 2001. That is simply not realistic. But can Cisco keep in touch with its customers, keep tabs on the start-up marketplace, and design a process by which that start-up's technology can be offered to customers when both the customers and the products are ready? Now, that is doable! And that is just how Cisco traditionally approaches its business, both strategically and operationally.

MONEY, INTERNET PROTOCOL, TIMING, LUCK, AND MORE MONEY

What makes a Cisco a Cisco? Or a Microsoft a Microsoft? Why can certain companies have these nearly meteoric rises while others remain flat or, even worse, disappear completely? Any successful entrepreneur who is being honest with you will let you in on a little secret: Planning is great, but add a little luck to it and you have a highly successful start-up. Luck is important in any venture, but there is also a good case for saying that we make our own luck as well.

FROM INSIDE CISCO

Certain things have happened that have been very lucky for Cisco along the way, but I think that in a lot of ways you create your own good luck. It was a unique combination of the right place, the right time, good management, and mistakes by the competitors.

—*Barry Eggers, former Cisco executive and current Silicon Valley venture capitalist*

Al Shugart, founder of a number of well-known start-ups such as Shugart Associates and Seagate, has a plan for success in Silicon Valley. He says that if you plan and are unlucky, you will likely survive but not explode; if you are lucky without planning, you might survive but your chances are slimmer. Don't plan and don't be lucky, and you are out of business; but plan and then be lucky, and the sky is the limit. Cisco appears to have fallen into this last category.

"First of all, they [Cisco] were in the right market at the right time," says Barry Eggers, former Cisco acquisitions leader and a general partner with Lightspeed Venture Partners, a venture capital firm in Menlo Park, California. "They were there at the beginning [of the Internetworking market] as were a couple of other players, like Proteon. They executed fast [and] took advantage of that market. . . . That market turned into a larger networking market that they were able to control. So part of it was right place, right time."

Okay. That is the luck part of it combined with the ability to have recognized the opportunity and quickly acted on it. But there was more to their success, according to Eggers.

"Part of it is in the execution along the way. They have had a lot of important people who have done a lot of great things. Terry

[Eger] is one of them. John Morgridge. John Chambers. A lot of people one layer down, even down to the individual engineer who has done a lot of key things to help Cisco along the way. They have been able to hire the best in the industry along the way [and] keep them around."

It's also useful if your competition helps you out by making blunders. That was the case with Cisco and several of its primary competitors according to Eggers.

"Another thing that has benefited Cisco is that some of its competitors made major mistakes along the way. A good example is the Wellfleet-Synoptics acquisition, a merger of equals that formed Bay Network. For a couple of months it created a company bigger than Cisco, but only for a couple of months. After that, Bay Networks ended up being a very minor player in the market." (See more on the dangers associated with a merger of equals in Chapter 9.)

I agree with Barry's assessment. There are a lot of talented people in Silicon Valley specifically and in high tech in general. Something was, and still is, special about Cisco that enabled it to outperform its competition, provide excellent working conditions for its employees, and provide high value to its customers while also providing excellent investment returns to its shareholders.

I contend that what differentiates Cisco from other companies is that it not only knows the way it wants to operate, it actually operates that way. In other words, Cisco walks the talk. From John Chambers on down to the lobby receptionist, Cisco is a company of people dedicated to providing excellence. Cisco is a highly motivated and competitive company that is determined to be the number one or two market share leader in every market space within which it competes. It is intent on maintaining a high degree of communication with its customers and being the first vendor to provide its customers with the solutions they are looking for.

Cisco is a company that not only sells Internet technology, it uses that technology for its own internal operation. (It eats its own dog food!) In fact, by some estimates Cisco has the most active electronic commerce site in the world, and encourages its customers to place orders for Cisco equipment over the Internet. Over 90 percent of all

Cisco orders are processed over the Internet. There is an internal intranet that connects all Cisco sites into one electronic village. Cisco has the goal of tying the entire world together using Internet technology. Now, how is that for a grand, world-class goal?

FROM INSIDE CISCO

The Industrial Revolution of 200 years ago divided society by creating a gap between "haves" and "have-nots." Today's Internet Revolution has the potential to unite everyone by combining the strength of the Internet and education, the two great equalizers in life. By applying what we've learned in business to all aspects of society, we have the power to use technology to create an Internet gateway that has the potential to positively change people's lives.

*—From the Cisco Systems Fiscal 2000
Annual Report*

IT'S ALL IN THE NUMBERS

Enough talk about high-level management perspective stuff. Let's take a look at some hard facts that reinforce, in a numeric way, my assertions. This section first looks at Cisco's financial history and then presents some summary information about its acquisitions at the time of this writing. It is important to remember that what Cisco did in the past worked. The company grew at alarming rates and treated its people and acquired company personnel with dignity and opportunity along the way to its success. Perhaps Cisco of 2001 and forward will not enjoy the financial or stock market success of the Cisco of past, but this does not negate the fact that what Cisco did back then worked. It worked for all of the right reasons, and those reasons were more than simply being in the right industry.

Remember that Cisco had plenty of competition back in the early 1990s, such as Cabletron, Synoptics, Wellfleet, Proteon, and others. Those companies have not fared nearly as well over the same years in the same marketplace as Cisco has fared. When a marketplace or an economy takes a drop, companies within those industries or economies also take a hit. That is, in large part, what happened to Cisco in the late 2000 time frame continuing into 2001. Cisco is, and continues to be, one of the best-run companies in the world, but it must also operate within the existing market conditions. A serious drop in orders within the networking marketplace is going to have a negative effect on all companies in the space, with those that are less efficiently run suffering the most serious, if not fatal, blows. Well-run companies will weather the downturn and may even come out the other side stronger than when they went in. This is a true test of the management of a company—surviving, and even thriving, through a serious downturn in the economy and/or a marketplace. It might have gotten caught believing some of its own public relations releases, but it is also taking substantial steps to reinvent itself within a difficult marketplace.

If anyone can excel in a given marketplace with a specific set of market conditions, good or bad, it is Cisco. Look to the past as an indicator of what has worked and why it worked. From this analysis, look for ways to apply this information to your own situation so that we can someday write a book about your company.

Cisco's Financial History

Cisco was founded in 1984 as a California corporation. It was a small company with only a handful of employees until the late 1980s. It received its first round of venture capital funding in 1987 from Sequoia, $2.5 million. Cisco had 10 employees at the time.

Cisco went public on February 16, 1990, with an initial public offering (IPO) of 271.2 million shares that went out at $18 and closed the day at $22.50. Since then, Cisco has split two for one seven times and three for two twice. A single share of Cisco stock purchased in 1990 and held until today would have split so that the shareholder now owns 288 shares of Cisco stock for each share purchased. And that single share of stock purchased at $20, for example, is now worth $5,000 (assuming a current stock price of at least $17 per share). Are you starting to see why investors who discovered Cisco early on are so happy with this company?

The company was long-term debt-free as of October 28, 2000, and had $6.391 billion in cash on hand. For those accountants among you, its current assets were $13.059 billion and its current liabilities $5.802 billion, providing a current ratio of 2.25. As mentioned earlier, it did this while increasing revenues by 56 percent from $12.154 billion in fiscal 1999 to $18.928 billion for fiscal 2000. Net income for the same period increased by 52 percent. Cisco does not now and never has paid a dividend to its shareholders. As of July 28, 2001, as reported at the Cisco web site, Cisco still had $4.9 billion in cash, $12.835 billion in current assets, and $8.096 billion in short-term liabilities, which still provides a current ratio of 1.58—not bad for a company experiencing a serious downturn.

Take a look at Table 1.1 for a summary of Cisco's financial performance since its IPO in 1990.

It can be seen from this table that Cisco has had some incredible financial and operational years since its IPO. Remember that it is one thing to grow a company at 30 to 50 percent when the company generates only a few hundred million dollars in revenue. It is something completely different to grow at those same rates when the company has a revenue level of tens of billions of dollars.

Growing at these rates while maintaining high profitability and low debt is a tricky business that Cisco has managed well. But it has also managed something else well that brings us to the topic of this book. Cisco has maintained its agility while becoming at one point the largest company in the world by market capitalization. Cisco has been able to maintain this nimble nature while still growing huge

Table 1.1 Summary of Cisco's Financial Performance since 1990 Initial Public Offering

Year	Stock Splits	Revenues	Revenue Percent Growth	Income	Income Percent Growth	Earnings per Share	Number of Employees
1990		$ 69,000,000			n/a	—	254
1991	2 for 1	$ 183,000,000	165%	$ 43,200,000	n/a	$0.01	506
1992	2 for 1	$ 340,000,000	86%	$ 84,400,000	95%	$0.02	882
1993	2 for 1	$ 649,000,000	91%	$ 172,000,000	104%	$0.04	1,451
1994	2 for 1	$ 1,243,000,000	92%	$ 314,900,000	83%	$0.07	2,262
1995		$ 1,979,000,000	59%	$ 479,200,000	52%	$0.10	3,479
1996	2 for 1	$ 4,096,000,000	107%	$ 913,300,000	91%	$0.15	8,259
1997	3 for 2	$ 6,440,000,000	57%	$1,414,000,000	55%	$0.23	10,728
1998	3 for 2	$ 8,459,000,000	31%	$1,872,700,000	32%	$0.29	14,623
1999	2 for 1	$12,154,000,000	44%	$2,567,000,000	37%	$0.38	20,657
2000	2 for 1	$18,928,000,000	56%	$3,914,000,000	52%	$0.53	34,617
2001		$22,293,000,000[1]	18%	$3,086,000,000[2]	−21%	$0.41[3]	30,000[4]

[1]As reported on Cisco web site, year end.
[2]Pro-forma reported results.
[3]Met Street estimates.
[4]An approximation based on several reports and notification of a reduction of approximately 6,000 regular employees as stated in the June 1, 2001, 10-Q filing.

from the influence and infusion of acquired companies, their products, technologies, and personnel.

M&A Buying Spree

Starting in 1993, with Cisco's purchase of Crescendo Communications, Inc., Cisco has pursued a series of acquisitions as a way of moving quickly into product areas that customers demanded and Cisco did not yet supply. Cisco contends that Silicon Valley is its research lab, and Cisco prefers to let the Valley entrepreneurs and the venture capitalists take the initial validation risks on any new technology. Once products are proven technologically and from a customer demand perspective, Cisco moves in and buys the company and its products. It then proceeds to assimilate completely the acquired products, technology, personnel, and customers into the Cisco culture and operational model. In short, the acquired typically completely disappears once purchased by Cisco.

Cisco's core belief is that great technology run through the Cisco sales and manufacturing operation will leverage the purchase to much higher revenue levels than the start-up could ever have done on its own. John Chambers regularly refers to the leverage that Cisco achieved with the Crescendo purchase as a validation of this process. Chambers claims that the $95 million paid for Crescendo, a company with around a $10 million revenue run rate, was justified in that Cisco's switching products sales, derived directly from the Crescendo purchase, grew to a $500 million revenue run rate within 18 months of the purchase. In essence, the Cisco operational model leveraged Crescendo's products to generate 50 times the revenue stream. Sounds like leverage to me.

FROM INSIDE CISCO

When something changes faster than we anticipated or we make some other mistake, then we adjust very quickly and don't spend a lot of time with the "not invented here" syndrome, trying to protect our decision of two years ago.

—*John Chambers, Cisco president and CEO, commenting on the need to quickly move past and recover from mistakes*

Cisco started out slowly with its acquisitions and eventually picked up steam so that in calendar year 2000 alone Cisco purchased 22 companies, for a grand total of 70 acquisitions finalized between 1993 and 2000. Total spent on the 70 purchases equals nearly $35 billion, with around 7,000 employees being acquired in the process. (See Appendix D for a chart detailing the important financial aspects of the acquisitions.)

By the way, it is difficult to find any sales information for most of the acquisitions since they were privately held companies before being purchased by Cisco. As a result, it is not possible to determine accurately the total amount of leverage gained from the acquisitions. Suffice to say that LightStream Corporation, acquired by Cisco in 1994 for $120 million, sold $1.5 million worth of products the year before the Cisco acquisition and is reported to have generated $45 million in Cisco sales revenue a year later. LightStream produced high-end asynchronous transfer mode (ATM) technology products and had 60 employees, which put it right into the Cisco sweet spot with respect to number of employees. Whether all of the Cisco acquisitions performed to this standard as to the sales leverage is difficult to ascertain precisely, but looking at Cisco's sales history it is clear that Cisco did something right.[3]

LightStream was doing well from a revenue perspective but was put on the road to obsolescence shortly thereafter by Cisco's purchase of StrataCom in 1996 for around $4.6 billion. There must have been strong motivation for making such a move, and there was, according to Chambers.

"We began to notice that wide area networking and local area networking were coming together more rapidly than we had thought. . . . [Customers] were telling us that while they liked our direction with LightStream and liked our next-generation product, we were not going to have the market share that they needed to feel comfortable with in the next 12 to 18 months. So, even though LightStream was on a tremendously successful run rate, we literally ate our own young and acquired StrataCom for $4.6 billion—getting a much bigger player in the ATM business—because the market changed quicker than we thought."[4]

Not all of Cisco's acquisitions have been a success—or "grand slam," as Chambers puts it. But those that have performed well within Cisco have generated large revenue gains and brought Cisco into new markets. Most importantly, the acquisitions kept Cisco in the running for customer business, which is Cisco's most important business objective.

In many ways, Cisco's acquisition and development (A&D) investment processes are a lot like a venture capital firm's. A venture firm does not expect each of its acquisitions to make it gobs of money, although it doesn't buy in expecting to lose. Out of a mix of companies, the firm expects that 40 percent to 60 percent will maintain their own and stay afloat. Another 20 percent to 40 percent will be dismal failures, and another 20 percent to 40 percent will be whopping successes. The ones that succeed will make all the rest of them worthwhile. Cisco operates in much the same way. It does not expect all of its acquisitions to be stellar, but those that are will contribute to Cisco's revenue stream in a huge way. Those that do not make it are not a total loss since the acquired people are now part of Cisco. And the others that maintain themselves are also wins in that the people are acquired and Cisco maintains a presence in those chosen markets. For Cisco, there is strategic value in this.

WHAT'S NEXT?

Chambers is regularly asked for his version of the successful company of the future. Here are some of his thoughts on this subject.

- The fast will beat the slow any day. Be first and work quickly to get a dominant market share in your chosen areas. "If you can't be fast, you're going to get left behind."
- Have intense customer focus. "Any company that does not have its finger on the customer will get left behind."
- Use a horizontal business model. "Horizontal companies will win. They always have in any industry."
- Use open standards. "It will be a single data-voice-video world underneath a packet-cell infrastructure."

20

- Create a company that attracts and maintains talent. "This is an area where a handful of really bright engineers will outproduce a thousand other engineers."

- Use the Internet technology within your own organization. "Otherwise, you can't get the profitability or productivity or the capability to move with the speed to take on the large competitors, or the capability to create the profits which will allow you to have the market cap which allows you to acquire."[5]

One of the more difficult issues facing Cisco as its revenues increase is finding new marketplaces that can sustain the types of revenue growth that are needed to fuel the Cisco 30+ percent annual revenue growth rate. A 30 percent growth rate for a $20 billion company requires that Cisco add $6 billion in annual revenue. There are not many markets that can sustain that type of growth, and if it is a mature market Cisco must take that revenue share from another already established vendor to meet those goals. That is a much more difficult process than selling new products into a hot new market that everyone agrees must be expanded. Time will tell if Cisco can compete in new markets. I fully expect that it will succeed, with success defined as maintaining profitability while acquiring market share. But, I also fully expect that given Cisco's size, the new markets it is entering, and the existence of a serious economic slowdown it may be that Cisco's future revenues will not grow at historical levels. Perhaps this is the reason for the sharp decrease in the stock price in late 2000 and early 2001.

Yet, Cisco will continue to add products to its price list, and the more advanced technology products will likely be acquired instead of developed in-house. This acquisition strategy has worked for Cisco in hot times and will continue to work for it in depressed marketplaces as well. In short, acquisition and development is a viable business expansion strategy that will surely be adopted by other companies as they begin to understand the business wisdom associated with the approach. As usual, Cisco got there first!

■ THE FINAL ANALYSIS

As you work your way through this book you will see that Chambers is continuously reshaping and molding the company to meet performance benchmarks. As usual with Chambers (and Cisco), if it sounds like a good idea for someone else, it is an equally good idea for Cisco and should be implemented. Cisco has every intention of continuing its acquisition and development product creation strategy into the future, although with a more targeted approach that concentrates on key market segments instead of a broader-brushed approach. This approach will likely not involve as many acquisitions per year, as indicated by the lack of a new acquisition in the entire first half of calendar 2001. In some ways, the depressed stock market may present buying opportunities for Cisco that would not be as readily available in a robust stock and IPO market. Remember that Cisco is cash-rich and has a stock that is currently priced at a much lower level than it has been within the past 24 months. A lower-priced stock has an easier time moving up in price, whereas the previous lofty stock price levels were more likely to come down instead of increase.

The Internet and its related technologies will survive because it has a viable, useful purpose for its users. The Internet is bigger than Cisco but Cisco is in large part synonymous with the Internet, and if the Internet survives so will Cisco. If the Internet has some unforeseen problem that makes it less viable from a business perspective, then Cisco will likely move on to the next opportunity emerging from its customers and will continue to acquire those companies needed to fuel that success. It may stumble as part of that transition, but Cisco will survive. The recovery process may not always be pretty and its actions may not always seem reasonable to the general public, but Cisco has a legacy of survival and adaptation in an industry that treats adaptation as a requirement. Paranoia is a common thread within Cisco, and that paranoia sets Cisco enough on edge to keep it from falling an unrecoverable distance when it stumbles.

CHAPTER 2

BUYING THE CISCO WAY

If you buy a company with customers, product flows, and entrenched enterprise resource systems, you have to move very gingerly. Otherwise, you risk customer dissatisfaction. Figuring out how to integrate this type of company could take nine months.[1]

— Mike Volpi, Senior Vice President, Cisco Systems

The incredible growth experienced in the networking industry has manifest amazing successes for some companies and dismal failures for others. John Chambers refers to the current networking phenomenon as the "fourth evolution of computers." The first was mainframes, dominated by IBM; the second was minicomputers, which had a number of major players with none being clearly dominant; and the third was personal computers and local area networks (LANs) driven by Intel and Microsoft.[2] There is a solid case to be made for this assertion. The end user's need for computers has driven the proliferation of user workstations. Early users connected directly to a mainframe that existed on their local site. Today, users do not exist at a single location as was initially seen with the mainframe computer. The more mobile users became, the greater the need was for networked communication from outside of the company site, requiring the extension of the LAN to a more wide-area-networked (WAN) approach. The Internet with its standards and business-political neutrality offered the most acceptable approach for cost-effective and high-speed connections between geographically remote sites.

Many experienced industry participants, including Bill Gates, admit to having underestimated the amazing rate of acceptance that the Internet and its associated Internet Protocol (IP) technology would achieve. With the right technology and a vision for the Internet, Cisco was positioned perfectly to capture this emerging market.

The rapid acceptance of the Internet also spawned numerous technologies designed to increase bandwidth, management control, and customer-perceived performance while decreasing cost. The generalized version of Moore's Law that technologies have approximately an 18-month life span before being challenged by the next generation of technology has never been more true than within networking. Cisco Systems realized early on that managing this technological evolution while also managing explosive corporate growth may require more resources than Cisco could produce on its own.

CISCO'S BUSINESS GOSPEL

Cisco Systems has a fundamental philosophy that drives its overall business direction and decision making: "Customers today are not just looking for pinpoint products, but end-to-end solutions. A horizontal business model always beats a vertical business model. So you've got to be able to provide that horizontal capability in your product line, either through your own R&D or through acquisitions."[3] Partnering is another strategy that Cisco uses for meeting customer requirements. An end-to-end networking solution is defined by Cisco Systems as "one that provides a common architecture that delivers consistent network services to all users."[4] As part of this emphasis, Cisco divides the marketplace into three target markets: enterprises, service providers, and commercial customers.

1. Enterprises are large organizations that require connectivity over multiple locations and various computer types. Typical enterprise customers include government agencies, educational institutions, utilities, and large corporations.

24

2. Service providers are those companies that provide information services such as telecommunication carriers, Internet service providers (ISPs), wireless communication providers, and cable companies.

3. Commercial customers are those needing data networks that connect not only to internal locations, but potentially also to the Internet and/or business partners.

Perhaps it was Chambers' sales background that fostered the intensely customer-driven focus that already existed upon his arrival and is still practiced by Cisco Systems today. Coming from a sales background myself, I can admit to having been frustrated numerous times in my life as I relayed to skeptical engineering personnel the various customer direction information I would uncover in customer discussions. What I would hear from customers regarding their future plans and product/service features would get no further than that meeting since engineering and marketing departments would take the view that they knew more about what the customer needed than the customer did. Most frequently the customers were right (What a surprise, no?), much to the later chagrin of the company that did not have the required future products or services to compete with those companies that did listen.

Listening to customers can rarely be wrong; ultimately they are the ones who will spend the money that purchases future generations of products and services. Many companies give lip service to this belief, but successful companies such as Cisco Systems turn customer relationships, listening, and attention into a passion. From this passion comes the critical input needed to steer Cisco's next generations of products and services.

THE MARKET AND CUSTOMERS DECIDE

Companies have a tendency to think that their way of doing something is the right, and the only, way of doing it. They tend to believe that the stories that they tell their customers in a competitive selling situation reflect the way things really are. But that is often not the case.

Cisco practices what it calls "technological agnosticism" in that it strives to remove the "religious mind-set" from technology decisions. Cisco's initial success as a router company was incredible, and it would be a natural outgrowth of that success to believe that routers were the best, and only, way to solve networking problems. If Cisco had maintained that viewpoint in spite of customer feedback, it would likely never have pursued its first acquisition in 1993 of Crescendo Communications, a switching company. This acquisition was important to Cisco and represents an excellent example of a company reevaluating its practices in light of customer feedback. More about the Crescendo Communications purchase is presented throughout this book.

CISCO CRYSTAL BALL

Predicting future trends is clearly an art form that requires a unique blend of experience, industry insight, and data. Cisco's approach is to:

- Listen closely to its customers.
- Monitor technology advances.
- Attend trade conferences.
- Monitor trade publications.
- Listen to the venture capital and investment banking community.

Located in a technology hotbed like Silicon Valley offers frontline information on the latest technology developments, and Cisco's reputation for acquisition and investment acts as a magnet for the typically cash-starved start-up looking for a major corporate financial partner or purchaser. Of these information sources, Cisco places great emphasis on the feedback it gets from its major customers.

"Successful companies all crash and burn for the same reason or slow down for the same reason: They get too far away from the customers and employees and they lose their ability to move fast. So we are fanatical about staying close to the customers—paying every one of our managers on customer satisfaction. I spend 50 percent of my time with customers," says Chambers in a 1999 interview.[5]

Cisco plans on a one-year horizon with the assumptions associated with the plan evaluated for accuracy on a quarterly basis. When a company knows that its market moves on "Internet time" where one calendar year equals seven Internet technology years, evaluating quarterly is roughly the equivalent of evaluating annually for other industries.

Are other companies privy to the same marketplace information? With regard to the publicly available information, the answer in general would be "Yes." Then what is it that makes Cisco Systems able to avoid stagnation as part of its culture? As anyone who has performed market analyses can attest, the significance of the information found is filtered through the preconceived notions and expectations of the persons performing the analysis. Generally what we are looking for we tend to find, and if we want to support a specific viewpoint, then information can be interpreted in such a way that it supports that viewpoint. Obtaining a truly objective viewpoint is often difficult, which is why the technological-agnosticism philosophy practiced by Cisco is instrumental to its continued success.

If a company has a strong political or personal interest in a particular business practice, philosophy, or technology, it can filter everything it sees through this belief system, tainting a gold mine of market information to the point that the future trend "gems" are lost in the interpretation. Using future customer acceptance as a benchmark for decision making may force a company to abandon past doctrines, policies, or technologies for those presented by customers as their primary areas of interest. Having a large enough customer base provides a solid statistical basis on which to make future product and services development decisions.

Microsoft has honed its customer feedback mechanism to a fine edge such that a large number of new Microsoft product features are directly derived from customer recommendations. Customer feedback is treated as a valuable company resource instead of as a source of annoyance. Really soliciting and listening to customers is almost always solid business advice and Cisco has integrated this not only into its spoken philosophy but also into its practices.

Should the marketplace change faster than Cisco had earlier anticipated when prior decisions were made, it adjusts quickly to the change once it is recognized, and avoids the "not invented here" trap of protecting political decisions that were made years earlier. This is proven by Cisco's reducing its workforce by around 6,000 people during its recent rough times, a move that directly conflicts with Cisco's previously expressed "no layoff" philosophy. Cisco chose to make what it believed was the right move for the overall company instead of holding on to its past "no layoff" philosophy, possibly weakening its future competitiveness.

In the past, Cisco has acquired companies for a technology that would make obsolete a technology acquired only a brief time earlier. Chambers contends that Cisco would rather "eat its own young," referring to already existing Cisco technology that is destined for obsolescence, before a competitor with a better offering does so instead.

CREATE A PLANNING MATRIX

Based on the feedback from the various internal and external information sources, Cisco puts together a planning matrix that acts as a map for determining development or acquisition direction.

This matrix tracks various market segments of interest. It lists whether Cisco either owns or can obtain a leadership position in that market area and the technology sources required to obtain that leadership. Possible sources for obtaining that technology are defined as either internally developed or acquired products and technology. Leadership à la Cisco translates into a number 1 or number 2 position in each market segment of interest, or it chooses not to compete in that segment. Cisco sets an objective to have a 50 percent market share in every market where it participates and doesn't even enter the market unless it expects to get 20 percent market share "right off the bat."

And, if that position cannot be achieved using internally development resources, then Cisco looks for a way to buy into that leadership position.[6]

From this matrix, Cisco personnel then either begin internal development projects or go on the search for a target company that can provide Cisco with a more rapid entrance into that market segment. The company strives to have 70 percent or more of Cisco's new product offerings developed internally, with the balance coming from external sources (i.e., acquisition).

SYSTEMIZE THE ACQUISITION PROCESS

Once acquisition was determined as an integral part of the Cisco product development methodology, it was then treated as simply another operational aspect of the company. To this end, the acquisition process was systemized, with guidelines established for determining targets, opening up discussions with the companies, and performing due diligence. Executive management is brought in only during the final stages, except in rare cases. Board approval is not required for the majority of the acquisitions. Establishing a process means that acquisition becomes more of a routine with specific expectations since the processs has a clearly defined input and output.

In this case, the input is the need to find and acquire a company with the resources needed to provide Cisco with the market position and share desired. The output is the complementary integration of the target's personnel, technology, and customers into Cisco's. The subsequent achievement of the market share goals outlined in the planning matrix within desired time frames is a valid benchmark for acquisition success.

The unique and excellent aspect of Cisco's approach is that turning acquisition into a process enables a larger number of Cisco personnel to acquire expertise in the acquisition methodology, which then makes it less personnel dependent and more repeatable. Like any excellent corporation with an excellent operational record, Cisco has taken as much of the guesswork out of the acquisition process as possible; this increases its reliability and decreases its associated risks. Cisco understands its marketplace and the demands of that marketplace, and has structured its entire organization around successfully satisfying these marketplace demands. Acquisition as an occasional or opportunistic process, which is the exception instead of the rule, does not apply to Cisco Systems. At this company, acquisition is simply one of the activities it pursues as intrinsic to its continued success. As such, it is fostered, cultivated, streamlined, and continually improved just as any critical business process would be for any top-notch company.

At Cisco Systems, acquisition is simply another business decision and process.

THE PRIMARY TARGET EVALUATION CRITERIA

Fundamental to the Cisco acquisition approach is the belief that acquiring a company's technology without acquiring the future efforts of its people is a formula for an unsuccessful purchase. As a result of this basic tenet, Cisco spends a lot of time evaluating a company before any purchase agreement is reached. In essence, Cisco treats an acquisition as something like a marriage with both partners evaluating the other before vows are exchanged. Blending this requirement for personnel retention and the need for a systemized acquisition approach requires the establishment of five primary evaluation criteria that remain almost completely inviolable.

These basic criteria are:

1. The target and Cisco must share a compatible vision of the future from both an industry and a product perspective.
2. The acquisition must produce a quick win for Cisco shareholders, preferably within 12 months of the purchase.
3. The companies must share a complementary culture, or what Chambers calls the "right chemistry."

4. There have to be long-term wins for the four major constituencies—namely, shareholders, employees, customers, and business partners.

5. For large acquisitions, the target must be geographically located close to a Cisco office.

FROM INSIDE CISCO

In addition to having complementary technologies and a shared vision of future networking architectures, Cisco and StrataCom are both entrepreneurial, fast-growing Silicon Valley companies that thrive on the dynamic networking market. There's an excellent fit of cultures, values, and personal chemistry.[7]

—*Dick Moley, former CEO of StrataCom, commenting in a press release announcing the Cisco-StrataCom merger*

All of the five criteria are sufficiently important that a special chapter of this book is dedicated to each, and these areas are covered in detail in their respective chapters (Chapters 4 to 8). A target company must meet at least three of the primary evaluation criteria or Cisco will pass on the acquisition ("red light"). If the company meets all five criteria, the target is actively pursued ("green light") with a higher likelihood that purchase will occur but with the clear understanding that Cisco may still later choose to not make the purchase. Should only four of the five be met, then a judgment call is made ("yellow light") by the team in determining whether the areas of incompatibility are such that the longer-term likelihood of a successful acquisition is compromised.[8] By some reports, Cisco acquires only one out of every ten companies that it considers, with the other nine simply not meeting Cisco's acquisition criteria.[9]

According to Chambers, walking away from a deal is a difficult thing to do. "We've killed nearly as many acquisitions as we've made. . . . I believe that it takes courage to walk away from a deal. It really does. You can get quite caught up in winning the acquisition and lose sight of what will make it successful. That's why we take such a disciplined approach."[10]

▬ NO MERGERS OF EQUALS

An interesting assertion of Chambers' is that a merger of equals cannot work. By this he means that two companies with equally strong cultures, personnel, and resources cannot effectively merge since inevitable power and cultural clashes will occur. Cisco makes a point of acquiring only companies that are substantially smaller than Cisco; given Cisco's market capitalization and annual revenues, there is a large pool from which to choose.

A merger between large players in the same industry is appealing in that the combined entity might be substantially larger than any other and shift the dynamics of an entire industry. The companies' customer base broadens; effective management teams are expanded, providing additional management growth capacity; distribution channels grow; and competitors are required to adjust their future strategies due to the radical shift in the competitive landscape caused by the merger. It is likely that a merger of industry-leading equals would cause additional mergers on the part of competitors as a way of increasing their own market size. These "forced" mergers disrupt their operations as well. If these subsequently merged companies combine in an ineffective way they may find themselves in a worse competitive position than they were in before the merger.

A major problem with a merger of any size is that a certain amount of disruption is inevitable as the two entities digest the changes associated with the new, combined entity. When two large, rapidly growing companies merge, their growth rate will have to slow as structural and other administrative issues are dealt with. Business momentum is lost, which can be costly in a highly competitive, dynamic industry like networking.

A merger of equals adds the additional complexity of merging equally strong and successful cultures. Agreement on the clear leader is a possible area of contention. Factions can form within the companies as each business culture struggles to protect its prior way of business life, which can further complicate the difficult integration period. Should these problems not be worked out quickly and amicably, the merger can actually cause the combined entity to suffer a serious business slowdown that may take a long time to remedy.

FROM INSIDE CISCO

In a merger of equals, you stand a very good chance of stalling out both companies. . . . It can be a major distraction to both.[11]

—*John Chambers, commenting on the dangers associated with a merger of equals*

"RESISTANCE IS FUTILE—YOU WILL BE ASSIMILATED"

Just as the value of any business is substantially determined by its future ability to generate a profit, so is the value of an acquisition. Otherwise the acquired company is simply worth what it historically brought to the table at the time of the acquisition. Cisco makes a purchase with the complete belief and knowledge that the value of the acquisition is substantially based on the target's future potential as a part Cisco. The future is what Cisco purchases; minimal value is placed on the target's historical performance. Planning to integrate the target into Cisco's operation and culture successfully and quickly is an integral, critical, and mandatory part of the Cisco acquisition methodology.

There is an expressed intention from the beginning of any acquisition discussion that the acquired company's personnel, products, and technologies will be integrated into the Cisco culture. There is a respect provided for what was there before that made the target successful, but also a conviction on Cisco's part that the target must integrate seamlessly into Cisco's operation or the acquisition will not meet expectations. Cisco intends and works toward having the customer see a uniform front in all dealings, which makes rapid integration an important goal. For this reason, a great deal of up-front time is spent on the cultural and personnel aspects of the target; special emphasis is placed on determining the level of compatibility between the target's and Cisco's culture. As one Cisco executive so directly put it, "We don't let them believe that the acquisition will happen without changes to their operation. We let them know that we will come in and change everything."

An acquisition that loses the majority of the target's employees while transferring the existing products is considered, by Cisco standards, a failed acquisition. A special effort is made to retain the top management since the employees of a start-up tend to be incredibly loyal to their founders, who are also typically the executive management team. Special effort is also made to retain the technical personnel such as engineering since they are the creators of the intellectual property (technology) that is of primary interest to Cisco in the first place. Cisco's historical success rate at retaining its own hires along with acquired company personnel is truly one of the remarkable achievements of the Cisco methodology. And this retention success is being accomplished in Silicon Valley, a location notorious for its lack of employee loyalty and the resulting high employee turnover.

Personnel retention is an earmark of a successful Cisco acquisition and is covered in detail in Chapter 12.

THE FINAL ANALYSIS

Cisco Systems has made acquisition an integral part of its engineering development program. Given the special importance placed on acquisition as a strategic weapon, Cisco has systemized the acquisition process so that it is treated as a standard part of business operation. Acquisitions do not typically need to receive board approval, since the procedures for determining a viable acquisition candidate are clearly defined so that those performing the acquisition itself clearly understand the parameters within which the acquisition is feasible.

Cisco develops a matrix that charts likely industry segment trends and delineates Cisco's level of participation in each of those segments. If Cisco can quickly become a leader in a particular segment using internally developed products, then acquisition is not needed. If not, then acquisition is pursued as an alternative to internal development. In other words, acquisition is not pursued for its own sake but as a tool for furthering Cisco's market penetration in the particular target segments required in pursuit of its overall vision of being the end-to-end supplier for its networking customers. Industry trends are determined substantially from customer feedback, which is constantly solicited, monitored, and assessed. If Cisco Systems has a dogma it is to provide the customers with what they will want, when they will want it, and listening to customers about what they want is the best way to find out what they want. Technology agnosticism keeps Cisco from locking itself into a technology fixation that misses otherwise obvious industry trends.

A clearly defined set of primary evaluation criteria is in place against which all acquisition candidates are compared. If the target does not meet at least four of these criteria it is simply not pursued, no matter how attractive it may otherwise look. If it meets all five of the criteria, then the acquisition is pursued to the next stages of extensive due diligence, synergy estimation, pricing, and the other myriad actions that are involved with a company acquisition. Cisco also ensures that any acquisition is not a merger of equals, that the target company knows that it will become part of Cisco Systems, and that everything the target currently does and knows will likely be changed in the integration process. A merger of equals is specifically avoided since it will interfere with this seamless integration.

Of particular importance in this qualification criteria listing is the need for a culture and an overall vision that are compatible with Cisco's. Just as one would not knowingly marry someone with whom one is incompatible, Cisco treats an acquisition candidate and its employees as potential business "marriage" partners. There is an expressed intention of never getting a "divorce" in the form of a major layoff resulting directly from the acquisition nor anticipating substantial discord that could seriously interfere with the future co-operation needed for success. Cisco makes no bones about letting the target know that it will be assimilated and that the management and its personnel should come to peace with this as a reality because it will become their reality after the acquisition is finalized. And it will become a reality quickly, with most of the integration happening within 90 days of the purchase.

CHAPTER 3

THE COMPANY THAT SANDY, LEN, DON, JOHN, AND JOHN BUILT

We believe that Cisco has the potential to be the most influential and generous company in history. We are in the fortunate position to be at the center of the Internet economy, and we recognize that although this position gives us confidence, we must balance this confidence with healthy paranoia. We are proud of our accomplishments and want to thank our shareholders, customers, employees, partners, and suppliers for their continued commitment and confidence in our ability to execute.

—Cisco Systems Fiscal 2000 Annual Report

Cisco's success has been earned. To treat its success as anything less than excellent execution combined with a fair share of luck would be doing the people of Cisco's history and its current stakeholders a disservice. Its success was earned from the confluence of various distinct and timely events that, taken as a whole, afforded Cisco the incredible success that it has enjoyed. That success is, in no small part, a direct result of the cultural norms that Cisco as an organization operates within; and John Chambers, Cisco's CEO and president, goes to great pains to ensure that this culture is not corrupted in any substantial way.

People say that the Internet is what made Cisco. They say that Cisco was "just lucky." If that were the case, then 3Com, Bay Networks, Cabletron, and any number of other companies with great products and a relatively equal footing at the time that the Internet was taking off would be sharing equally in the Cisco limelight, when the fact is that they have struggled simply to maintain their beachheads against Cisco's full-press market assault.

John Chambers has become somewhat of a soothsayer for the modern business community. The same people who listen for Alan Greenspan to talk about the state of the economy from the Federal Reserve's perspective listen for John Chambers to talk about his view of things from the corporate perspective. And well they should. When you are the CEO of one of the world's largest market capitalized companies, one that is continually driving the "new economy," and one that has a dominant market share in almost all of its chosen market areas, you have a platform and the credibility to say what you see to be true. Chambers has the proven track record and recognized believability that earns respect from industry and national leaders from around the world. Yet, when he talks you don't get the bravado that often accompanies being a person of influence. He is straightforward in his approach and seems really to care that his message gets across. Not a lot of attitude with a whole lot of sincerity.

This chapter takes a closer look at John Chambers as a CEO with a special emphasis placed on how his personality type and the personalities of the people around and before him have shaped not only Cisco's culture but its way of transacting its merger and acquisition activities.

THE INITIAL PLAYERS—SANDY, LEN, AND DON

Sandy (Sandra) Lerner and Leonard Bosack are the two who got Cisco started. They were working with Bill Yeager, another Stanford employee, on developing the initial router technology while working for the Stanford University information technology department. The routers were needed to optimize their internal network and, once

---

About Cisco

The company name, Cisco, is said to be purloined from the tail end of San Francisco which also explains the logo that looks like the Golden Gate Bridge, for those of you who may have never seen either the logo or the bridge. There is another story that Cisco came from the name of a town in the Sierra foothills, Cisco, where Sandy's aunt had a ranch.

---

operational, Stanford didn't want any part of commercializing the product. So, Sandy and Leonard took things on themselves and, with a few Stanford colleagues, started Cisco Systems.

Early on, Cisco was a company of just a few people. In fact, Cisco had only 10 employees at the end of the 1987 fiscal year, roughly three years after its founding. When a company is this size, the founders have incredible influence on the culture of the company, and Cisco adopted some traits from Sandy and Leonard that carry on to this day. So what were those founder personalities that helped shape a company like Cisco?

Sandy had an intense interest in customer satisfaction. She believed that making the customer happy was the most important thing that Cisco could do. And she never really expected Cisco to grow larger than a few million dollars annually in sales.

According to Kim Niederman, former Cisco sales executive in the early 1990s and now CEO of LongBoard, Len and Sandy's aspirations were not anywhere near as grandiose as the company turned out.

"I asked [them] what they thought they were trying to do when they thought of the company," recalls Niederman. "I know that at one time they said, 'You know, what we're trying to do is build a nice little $10 million company.' That's all they were trying to do."[1] Surprise, surprise! Sandy confirms this viewpoint in a *Forbes* article where she, "It was not my intention to get rich. My intention was not to be poor."[2]

Sandy has been described many ways, and some of them are not very flattering. Selected attributes are that she was opinionated, bossy, short on interpersonal skills, smart, and outspoken. Len, on the other hand, is almost always described as a great programmer and great guy who was easy to get along with. They were married while still at Stanford and remained married while both were working at Cisco. They divorced shortly after leaving Cisco in August 1990, just a few months after the IPO. Rumor has it that they are still close friends to this day.

Sandy and Len had a difficult time getting venture capital funding in the mid-1980s when Silicon Valley venture capital was really a game run by blue bloods, mostly all men who had made their money from Fairchild Semiconductor, National Semiconductor, and other silicon-intensive manufacturing monsters. To be a venture capitalist, you had a BSEE (bachelor of science in electronic engineering) from a top school (e.g., Stanford) and an MBA. You came from the right background and had the right pedigree. Style and presentation were important in the venture capital climate in the mid-1980s. Sandy just didn't fit the bill. As stated in one publication, "Sandy's performance did not play well in the pampered, hushed, well-heeled, and exceedingly gentlemanly world of West Coast venture capitalism."[3]

Sandy and Len were turned down by as many as 75 venture capital firms before finding Don Valentine, a founder and general partner

---

Inside the Valley

Venture capital has changed since the 1980s. I was recently visiting some venture capital firms in Menlo Park, California, and found the environment to be professional, sometimes glacially polite, but the surroundings to be pretty basic. The people I found to be all business and intent on their work. The offices of many of the partners may not have even had pictures on the walls. And no ties or suits could be found unless, as one friend put it, "You are Japanese or working with the Japanese." I guess it helps to have a lot of young people with a lot of money to invest, and thank goodness for it, I say.

with Sequoia Capital. Imagine what those other 75 are thinking to-day as they look back at this really big one that they simply let pass through their fingers. At any rate, Valentine seemed to have the right personality mix not to be put off by Sandy's forceful approach (which perhaps stemmed from his experiences as a Marine during the Korean conflict). Or it might have come from having spent years in the Valley working for National Semiconductor, which, by the way, had made him wealthy enough to start funding other start-up ventures. Perhaps he was also willing to look past the presentation since he had previously himself dismissed an idea pitched him by a young, shaggy-haired kid who wanted money to fund his and a buddy's computer firm called Apple. Valentine simply didn't think that the kid had the stuff to make it work, and passed on the venture. See, we all make mistakes, even the really good ones among us.

Valentine agreed to put up $2.5 million in return for one-third of the company's stock ownership, along with a provision that he would have ultimate say-so on how the company would be run or Sandy and Len would have to sell their shares to Valentine. They agreed, and Cisco got its money. By the way, it was never spent. This one, Valentine got right.

"[Cisco's] one of those rare companies that was started at a moment in time where the problem was so vital that customers would pay in advance," says Valentine. "Cisco in 1987 filled a desperate need. Customers were tearing the hinges off the door to get the products. I never met a company that entered the market in such a timely way with no competition."[4] Luck?

Valentine knew that Sandy's and Len's management styles could not take Cisco to the levels needed for maximum return. They were primarily engineers who had a solid business sense, but they were not managers first who knew how to manage a company through the perilous times that accompany meteoric growth and success.

At the time, Len was the chief technology officer of the company, and Sandy was the vice president of customer service. Valentine had sanction to fill the executive management slots with people of his choosing. His first major choice was John Morgridge, formerly with Grid Systems, to become the president and CEO.

Notice that at that time, Cisco was known for having great technology, innovative products, an intense customer satisfaction focus, and an open, if not really confrontational, management style. Sandy was also the pioneer of "IP everywhere," having seen in the 1980s that Internet Protocol (IP) technology had a very real potential for taking over communications in just the way that it has today. Sandy clearly understood that connecting remote locations over the public or private networks would present huge benefits to technology users. There is no question that Cisco Systems has been, and still is, a leading evangelist in the benefits associated with a ubiquitous IP-based network. This, I believe, is also an integral part of the current Cisco gospel with IP tacit in almost everything that Cisco does.

Sandy believed that Cisco should be using the technology that it was selling and that Cisco would benefit from the technology's implementation just as Cisco's customers would benefit. Since Cisco's customers were also technically oriented, it made sense to use the technology as a major means of communication. Cisco started out selling its products over the Internet as it existed in 1984, and Cisco continued to cultivate its online ordering functions. In fact, Web-based sales of Cisco's products accounted for over 90 percent of Cisco's customers' orders in fiscal 2000, with Cisco maintaining a corporate commitment to having that percentage number creep higher every year. In 1989, Cisco went live with its customer service site that enabled Cisco customers to download software and software upgrades. It then was expanded to include a bug reporting system so that customers could troubleshoot their own bugs or report ones that they found themselves. The implementation of this technology is estimated to have saved Cisco from hiring as many as 10,000 additional engineers who would otherwise be needed to answer these service calls.[5] This commitment to using the Internet as an integral part of Cisco's operation started with the original founders and has been enhanced ever since by subsequent generations of Cisco employees.

Cisco was not very big at this time, having only 48 employees at the end of fiscal year 1988 when John Morgridge, 54 years old, came on board.

Some key elements of the current Cisco culture were already in place when Morgridge took over leadership of Cisco Systems.

"From day one we cared more about customers than anything. We were fanatical. Always have been," says Barbara Beck, senior vice president, Cisco's initial and current human resources manager. Fanatical customer service. Always had it. Always will, thanks initially to Sandy Lerner and the follow-on continuation of this policy first by John Morgridge and currently by John Chambers.

MORGRIDGE'S CHALLENGES

Experience is a good thing in business, and when risk is involved it is often handy to have had experience with failure. Perhaps having been there before, you can smell it when failure's possibility once again raises its head. It helps to know how to make things work properly, but it is also important to be able to recognize, early on, when things are not working well and need changing. Perhaps failure adds a healthy paranoia that keeps you on your toes as you bask in success.

FROM INSIDE CISCO

Some think that Cisco's calendar-year 2001 struggles are the first litmus test for its management since it had never experienced a serious business downturn in its history, whereas companies like Sun, Microsoft, and Oracle have weathered these before and still thrive. If Cisco makes it through, which I fully believe it will, then its management team will be just that much stronger as a result. It is the tough times that temper the management stuff of dynamic organizations.

Morgridge, prior to joining Cisco, was the president and CEO of Grid Systems, manufacturer of a portable computer. In my Wang Laboratories days, I had a Grid computer that I used when traveling. By today's standards it was a boat anchor, but at that time it was way better than the Compaq luggables of the period. What I do remember is that one day I had this really cool portable computer from Grid with a trick flat plasma display. Then suddenly, what seemed like the next day, I had a problem in that Grid as a company started to crash and burn. Grid's remains were sold to Tandy, also a Texas company. Around this time frame (1988), Morgridge left his two-year stint at Grid to go to Cisco, obtaining options worth about 6 percent of Cisco's stock in the process.

What drew Valentine and Morgridge together were a few common points that to this day play a strong part in Cisco's daily management and acquisition procedures.

- Morgridge had been through several failed ventures and had earned his stripes with respect to risk taking. Cisco looks for risk taking and some mistakes on the part of an acquisition candidate as a way of showing that the management is not too conservative.

- Morgridge was frugal and would keep Cisco spending to a minimum, a practice that remains prevalent at Cisco today. Morgridge flies coach, has a small office, and does not look for frills in his Cisco involvement. A tight rein on spending is an attractive trait in any potential Cisco acquisition candidate. Having expensive offices while still operating from venture funding is a red flag to Cisco when getting to know a candidate. Don Valentine says, "John Morgridge is the only president we've ever financed who is cheaper than I am. I am very cheap. One of the things I was warned about when we were doing reference checks on him a long time ago was that when you have dinner with him, don't let him choose the wine. I've always carefully heeded that advice."[6]

- Morgridge was ex-military, having done a three-year stint in the Air Force after graduating from the business school at the

University of Wisconsin. Processes and procedures are what make the military run and are a necessary component of any efficient company, especially one that plans to expand rapidly. The creation of replicable procedures is a necessary integration step for any Cisco acquisition.

- He had spent many years as a salesperson with Honeywell and had been a vice president of marketing at Stratus Computers before moving to Grid, and as a result had a strong sales and marketing background. A strong sales emphasis is important when Cisco evaluates an acquisition candidate.

- Morgridge was direct and tough with his communication, which was needed to handle Sandy. This communication mode is still prevalent at Cisco today, and honesty is a necessary requirement for any Cisco acquisition candidate.

FROM INSIDE CISCO

You can always quit and see if we rehire you.[7]

—*John Morgridge, Cisco CEO at the time, responding to a Cisco employee's complaint that his stock options were now worth less than those of people being newly hired*

Morgridge started hiring professional managers to fill key slots within the company, much to the dismay of Sandy, who didn't like the fact that nongeeks were taking over her company. And she made no bones about expressing her displeasure with the way things were going. The resulting personality conflicts between Sandy and the newly installed staff eventually led to an insurrection. The senior management finally went to Morgridge and presented the ultimatum that either Sandy left or they would all leave. Sandy was asked to leave, and did so in August 1990. She and Len sold their stock back to Cisco in December 1990 for around $170 million.

The founders may no longer be with Cisco, but their DNA is integral to Cisco's providing the great technology products, the intense customer focus, and the direct communication mode that lives on to this day. John Morgridge added his unique stamp to the company culture in conjunction with that of Don Valentine, and this combination was obviously working well since Cisco closed out fiscal 1990 with $69 million in revenue and would nearly triple revenue in 1991 by closing the year at $183 million.

JOHN CHAMBERS—BANKING ON A&D

In early 1991, John Chambers was the senior vice president for sales at Wang Laboratories, in Lowell, Massachusetts. He had just finished laying off over 5,000 Wang employees as the company tried to recover from any number of prior setbacks, including the death of its founder and chairman, Dr. An Wang, in 1990.

FROM INSIDE CISCO

The most impressive man I've ever known, other than my father, was An Wang. It was the trust that he put into me, that he gave me, the belief he had in me, that I'll never forget.[8]

—John Chambers, Cisco CEO, remarking on his being put in charge of Asian sales while working at Wang Laboratories

Having personally met Dr. Wang on several occasions, I can say firsthand that he was not only one of the premier technology visionaries of his time but also a great man who exerted a positive, powerful influence over Wang Laboratories. His loss, although likely not the primary reason that Wang eventually faltered, may well have been one of the final straws that broke Wang Laboratories' already frail back. Dr. Wang had promoted Chambers in 1990 to the position of executive vice president for sales just before passing away from cancer. The responsibility for cleaning up a lot of the mess fell to Chambers.

Chambers frequently remarks about the personal anguish he experienced during the Wang Laboratories layoffs. The layoffs were accomplished in the period just before Christmas of 1990, and Chambers left Wang shortly thereafter. This period of his life was difficult for Chambers and provides a foundation for understanding much of what drives him and Cisco's culture today. Having had close friends at Wang during this period I can attest to the atmosphere of gloom that seemed to pervade the Wang Towers in Lowell. No doubt this was a difficult time for Chambers, especially given his intense personal feelings of loyalty to Dr. Wang.

"It about killed me," says Chambers whenever asked about the experience. Others say that for Chambers personally the Wang experience was a defining moment in his character and one that shaped his values profoundly. Perhaps this is why he also vows that he would do almost anything to avoid causing another disaster for shareholders and investors like the one he inherited at Wang.

FROM INSIDE CISCO

Chambers contends that the best way to avoid a divorce is to be picky about the person you decide to marry. The best way to avoid layoffs after an acquisition is to make sure that the people and culture you acquire are people you want to work with after the acquisition. Then make sure that the acquisition pays for itself so that you can afford to keep those people around.

A positive that did come out of the Wang experience was that Morgridge and Valentine, on the West Coast, were watching Chambers' handling of the Wang situation and thought highly of him as a result. So, when Chambers was no longer with Wang in early 1991, Cisco offered him the job of senior vice president of worldwide operations, making him Morgridge's right-hand man and likely successor. Chambers, 42 at the time, accepted. Cisco closed out fiscal 1991 with revenues of $183 million and around 506 employees. To put this in context, remember that Chambers had just laid off over 5,000 Wang employees, an almost 10 times differential. Cisco was a very small company compared to Wang and required Chambers to relocate to the opposite end of the country, raising a question about why he would be willing to make such a move. According to some reports, Chambers had sent out several dozen letters looking for a job after leaving Wang, and only Cisco responded. Funny how fate has a way of entering into things, isn't it?

CHAMBERS—PRIOR TO WANG

John Chambers was raised in Charleston, West Virginia, a city of around 50,000 residents and the state capital. His mother was a psychologist and his father a physician, obstetrics/gynecology. His grandfathers were a bank president on one side and a builder on the other. In short, the Chambers family was well off, especially for a city the size of Charleston. The only son of the family, John Chambers had to struggle with school because of dyslexia; but instead of giving in to the condition, he decided to work his way to academic success. He did just that by spending more hours studying than his peers, and eventually worked his way through undergraduate school and then law school at West Virginia University.

To me this says something about Chambers, the man, and his intense competitive nature. A number of dyslexic people I have known chose fields that did not require much reading, such as art, photography, video production, and other graphically oriented professions working with images instead of words. Chambers chooses and successfully completes a law curriculum, arguably the most word- and reading-intensive field you can find. Most people suffering from dyslexia would avoid it at all costs. This is the earmark of an intensely competitive individual who, from all reports, does not like e-mail and who has an incredible memory for anything said or heard in his presence.

Realizing that he did not want to be a lawyer, Chambers decided to make a change. He took his high school sweetheart, Elaine, now his wife, to Bloomington, Indiana, where he attended and graduated from Indiana University with an MBA specializing in finance and management.

He took a job with IBM in 1976 as a salesperson and did pretty well at it, finally ending up in China selling IBM equipment to a people who really didn't see the need for it. Seven years into his IBM experience Chambers realized that his lack of engineering background was hurting him in the heavily technology-driven IBM, and perhaps greener pastures should be pursued. Wang Laboratories presented that next employment opportunity, and in 1983 he joined Wang in charge of around half of Wang's overseas business, specifically in the Asian marketplace. By the way, this change made a lot of sense for Chambers since Wang was arguably an extension of IBM from a technology perspective. Dr. Wang was the single largest shareholder of IBM stock in the world, resulting from his having sold a patent to IBM for early core memory designs. Wang Laboratories was also one of the largest, if not the largest, non-IBM supplier of IBM Systems Network Architecture (SNA) compatible equipment in the world. Having been with IBM, Chambers understood the selling of SNA equipment, and that experience carried directly over to Wang.

A few important characteristics carry over today at Cisco that are related to Chambers' IBM days. IBM was known at the time as being intensely customer driven and practiced a multilevel sales strategy whereby account access was gained at the executive levels of a company as an integral part of the sale process. Chambers believes that IBM forgot about selling its equipment to the smaller accounts and focused a lot of its sales effort on the larger customers. This provided a market foothold on which smaller companies like Wang and Digital

Equipment Corporation (DEC) could enter the market, eventually growing to substantial sizes in their own rights. This shift from IBM can be construed in some ways as having opened the door for any number of smaller companies—including, eventually, Cisco—to enter the marketplace, taking business away from IBM.

FROM INSIDE CISCO

We're paranoid. A lot of companies are arrogant. They're on top, and they believe they belong there. We've got almost the reverse attitude. We've got tremendous fear of failing. We make Andy Grove at Intel look relaxed.[9]

—John Chambers, commenting on Cisco's
healthy paranoia of missing the next
change that could put Cisco out of business

"People like us [Cisco] came in and took the bottom away from them [IBM]. Having been there and learned from it, it offers a strong reminder on why you have to do it differently,"[10] says Chambers. Cisco, Microsoft, and others took a huge chunk out of IBM's market shares. Why can't someone new do the same thing to Cisco and Microsoft? Now that reality will make you paranoid but also keep you on your toes.

Another aspect of his IBM days that carries over today at Cisco, and was a direct complement to the Cisco culture already in place on his arrival, was IBM's intense customer satisfaction focus at the time.

"My team [at IBM] would move heaven and hell not to let our customer down, and we were rewarded very well for it from that perspective. We would spend time with the president talking about where he or she was going strategically, but we balanced our role throughout [the company]," says Chambers.[11] Cisco still practices this multilevel contact method when selling its major customers and also when determining the next direction in which Cisco's product offerings must move. Cisco's customer satisfaction focus has grown in importance under his leadership.

It was the company's desire to provide its customers with what they wanted, and listening to directions provided by customers that led Cisco to pursue an acquisition and development (A&D) strategy. If Chambers had believed that Cisco engineering knew better what customers needed than the customers themselves did, then the Crescendo purchase may never have happened and Cisco may not even be here today.

A side note is also appropriate at this point regarding the economic environment within which John Chambers was raised, which likely had a profound impact on his maintaining his personal equilibrium in the midst of Cisco's overwhelming success and personal adulation.

Charleston and West Virginia went through some difficult economic times in the 1960 to 1980 time frame, and the local population dropped by 15 percent over that period. Even though he came from what was locally a privileged background, perhaps the small-city atmosphere, struggling with his reading disability, and the later depressed economic status of West Virginia uniquely combined to keep Chambers in touch with his modest West Virginia values. He is well known for listening to those around him and for having a common-folk presence about him, not typical of a man running a $20 billion+ company and having a personal wealth of over $500 million! Certainly he cultivates that image, but this doesn't mean that the image is far from the man himself.

In 1993 Cisco was faced with a major decision. Synoptics, a data switching products company located in Silicon Valley, was interested in a merger with Cisco. Both were about the same size and from the same industry. Chambers had concerns about the potential success of a merger of equals and, some people claim, he also needed some type of project that would enable him to politically and managerially earn his stripes on his own merit within Cisco. Chambers decided that buying another, smaller switching products company was the better approach for Cisco and proposed that Cisco purchase Crescendo, a start-up company located in Sunnyvale, California, instead.

FROM INSIDE CISCO

An interesting side benefit befell Cisco when Sandy and Len sold their shares back to the company at the end of 1990, the year of the IPO. These shares were now available to the company to use for funding of acquisitions in which Cisco's stock would be traded for the target's stock. Sandy and Len's shares constituted around two-thirds of the issued Cisco stock at the time.

The initial interest in Crescendo Communications came from a Cisco customer, Boeing, which told Cisco that Boeing was about to issue a $10 million order to Crescendo for its switches. Cisco also heard from another major customer, Ford, that it was also interested in switching. Intense customer satisfaction meant that Cisco had to provide switching products. It could merge with Synoptics to get access to the products or buy Crescendo. Chambers convinced Cisco's board that the Crescendo purchase was the right approach. (See Chapter 10 for additional information about this internal decision process.)

Using some of the stock obtained from Sandy and Len, Cisco purchased Crescendo, a company with $10 million in revenue, for a whopping $95 million! The press had a field day with the amount Cisco paid, but the last laugh was had by Cisco as the switching market in general, and Cisco's switching products revenues in particular, exploded through the roof. Crescendo had been a grand slam that made Cisco a lot of money, validating the concept of acquisitions as a business strategy and establishing Chambers as a business leader in his own right.

"In fact, the most fortunate and important thing that happened in all of Cisco's M&A history is that the first one was a grand slam," reflected Barry Eggers, former Cisco M&A leader and now general partner with Lightspeed Venture Partners, a venture capital firm in Menlo Park, California. "Without that first one having a lot of success, it might have slowed down the pace at which they did everything else. It [Crescendo] is the best acquisition that they have ever done, bar none. When you have one like that to start out with, it makes it a lot easier to do all the others."[12]

The Mario Rule came from this acquisition and has carried over to all subsequent Cisco acquisitions. The Mario Rule, named after Mario Mazzola, founder and CEO of Crescendo at the time of the acquisition, states that no employees from the acquired company can be laid off or substantially reassigned without the joint approval of both CEOs. Mario was concerned about the layoff of Crescendo personnel resulting from the acquisition and elicited a written agreement with Chambers that outlined the Mario Rule. Little did the two of them know how similar their respective views were on protecting their employees from layoffs—Chambers from his experiences at Wang Laboratories and Mazzola from his experiences at DAVID Systems, a company he cofounded and managed as vice president of engineering through very turbulent times.

"For me the world was this," says Mario when referring to the time of the Crescendo sale. "The experience of DAVID was [difficult]. . . . I was involved in two layoffs and I tend to be on the side of the people. Okay. [At Crescendo] we are making money, and people had been enjoying and believing in us—and now they would go to a new environment. I wanted to be reasonably confident that at least the same things financially that they were expecting from Crescendo, including a stable job, were going to be the case for [them at] Cisco. And I didn't know the Cisco management very well. Knowing more [today about] the people in Cisco, I know that all this would have been a marriage in a really good way."

We once again see that like attracts like. Crescendo was not looking to be acquired at the time that Cisco and Chambers offered to make the purchase. Yet, circumstances were such that the marketplace and people involved had arrived at just the right point for this acquisition to occur. As we now know, the purchase was an excellent move for both Cisco Systems and Crescendo's personnel, most of whom are still at Cisco.

If Mazzola had not had his experiences with the layoffs at DAVID Systems he might not have requested the no-layoff commitment that is now a part of the Cisco acquisition policy. Without Chambers' Wang layoff experience he might not have responded well to Mazzola's no-layoff request. This refusal would have likely forced Mario and Crescendo to decline the acquisition offer, substantially changing Cisco Systems' history along with that of the entire industry. Without the incredible success of Crescendo, Cisco and Chambers might not have had the internal Cisco management and board support to pursue additional company purchases. And this book would likely not exist.

Once Crescendo turned out to be a grand slam in all ways, Chambers and Cisco had the validation to further pursue additional acquisitions. No doubt all kinds of people within Cisco, Crescendo, and even the customer community helped in making the Crescendo purchase a success. But it was Chambers' insight regarding the liabilities of a merger of equals and his willingness to take a risk on a start-up company, while also being highly sensitive to the protection of acquired personnel, that moved Cisco into the direction of A&D. From that point on, it was a matter of making the right people responsible for acquisitions, standardizing the process as much as possible, and ensuring that the target's personnel would mix with the Cisco culture. People like Ed Kozel, Barry Eggers, Mike Volpi, and Ammar Hanafi have all helped maintain a standard of acquisition excellence that has given Cisco the outstanding reputation it enjoys with respect to acquisition success.

Other companies have tried using acquisitions as a competitive weapon. Cisco made it work, much to the chagrin of its competitors but to the joy of the thousands of millionaires who now go to work every day at Cisco Systems.

THE FINAL ANALYSIS

Cisco today is a different company than any other in large part because of the people who helped define its culture. It might be Sandy

Lerner promoting "IP everywhere" back in the mid-1980s, or her early adoption of the Internet not only as a place to sell products but also as a tool to be used inside Cisco itself. Or it might be the frugal nature of Don Valentine and John Morgridge that not only kept Cisco on a sound fiscal path but also created a culture where excessive consumption is not condoned. Perhaps it was Lerner's intense customer focus that was carried on by Morgridge and which is now heavily promoted by Chambers. You could also consider Chambers' and Mazzola's deep commitment to their employees and their desire to never again have a layoff. Then there was Len Bosack's geek tendencies that simply created the greatest technology products just because they needed creating.

What is clear when talking to any of these people is that no one person at Cisco created the successes and that the Cisco DNA is truly a composite of many inputs. And this DNA is bigger than any single person, including Chambers even given his incredible influence over the organization. One thing has become plain, however, about Cisco: It has been and continues to remain true to the values and principles that created this dynamic, adaptable, and challenging company and this focus is, in large part, due to the strong Chambers influence. In an industry where change is the norm, it is possible not only to survive but to prosper when a company adapts to the industry changes while remaining true to itself, its values, and its major stakeholders.

CHAPTER 4

VISION COMPATIBILITY MUST EXIST

You must have agreement about where the industry is going and the role each partner wants to play in that regard. If the roles don't complement each other, you will be fighting all the time. You have to look at the visions of both companies. If they are dramatically different, you shouldn't touch it.[1]

—John Chambers, President and CEO, Cisco Systems

Cisco Rule #1

The management of the target company must have a vision of the industry and its products that aligns well with Cisco's industry and product vision.

THE VISION THING

Vision is perhaps one of the most important success tools available. Without it the future can turn into a series of activities that do not seem to lead to any particular goal or end point. Success is a relative item that is obtained when specific goals are reached, and only with a clearly defined vision of those goals can one determine when they are reached.

Companies without a stated vision per se that practice a strong culture of excellence are still working toward a vision whether explicitly stated or not. Popeye's Restaurant, a great restaurant in Lake Geneva, Wisconsin, for example, promotes the end result of a successful customer visit as one where the customer, when leaving the restaurant after a meal, feels that he or she got great food at a good price along with great service and wants to come back again. The industry vision in this case is that restaurants thrive that successfully meet this total success equation. Everything that exists within the restaurant's operation is designed to ensure that the customer has this experience, and any lack of commitment on behalf of the employees with respect to making this final outcome, or vision, a reality is simply not tolerated. The culture clearly says to employees that they must share and act on behalf of the total satisfaction vision or leave. It is just that simple.

This vision must be shared with and by employees, or a company must continually monitor employee activities to ensure that they lead toward management's intended goal. Clearly defining a vision that is also clearly communicated to employees, on the other hand, enables employees to work on their own with responsibilities that they know lead in the optimal direction for the company as a whole.

A Chicago suburban high school soccer team near my home recently won the Illinois high school state soccer championship. This is a small school that beat much larger schools to win this championship. It was composed of students who had played together for several years and had traditionally done pretty well. The level of teamwork was high, as was the level of enthusiasm about playing soccer. When the recent school year started, the students decided among themselves that they were going to go undefeated for the season, which meant, by implication, that they would win the state championship. On the face of it, this was a highly irrational act—the odds were clearly against this smaller school winning, given the much larger schools against which it would have to play. Internal squabbles between players and their parents got resolved as the team aligned itself behind this goal. Even the coach had to be won over to the team members' vision of winning the state championship, which eventually happened.

FROM INSIDE CISCO

You need to feel that you can establish a good working relationship, that the chemistry is there, that the vision is there.[2]

—*Mario Mazzola, senior vice president, Cisco Systems, commenting on the importance of vision compatibility between Cisco and a target*

When this team played, they played as a team. They had a common goal that was clearly defined in the vision of going undefeated and winning state. And they did just that. The team was composed of predominantly the same players as in prior years, but they had never won state before. Is it possible that the difference between winning and losing once the basic talent is there is simply the difference between a team that works toward a clearly defined, completely shared vision? I contend that there is a lot to be said for this common-vision approach to management being the most effective, most enlivening method of business management. People's lives change when they experience working with a group of people that truly functions as a team. Anything less than teamwork is less than adequate, and is often a wasted effort. Most businesses do not function with that type of teamwork, as one or more departments or agencies or team members typically pull for their own best interest over that of the team. This fragmentation tends to diffuse common efforts, causing the team to now work in smaller splinters. Only through commonly shared goals and visions can all members be working autonomously yet in the best interests of the team.

A major difficulty in defining a corporate vision is that it must not only meet the company's goals but must also be shared by the employees who must make this vision into a tangible reality. The employees must feel personally motivated to take actions that move the company toward the goals. Cisco Systems is one of many companies that has successfully turned this shared vision into a business reality that not only acts as a rallying point for employees but actually defines the values that make Cisco Systems the success that it is.

CISCO'S VISION

Cisco Systems has a clearly defined vision of what it takes to succeed in the networking industry. Here are a few vision points that drive Cisco's overall strategy and specific actions:

- Customer expectations change rapidly, with the changes continually redefining the value-added, commodity products, and services thresholds.
- Customers are looking for end-to-end solutions instead of "pinpoint" products that deal with only one particular segment of the overall connection.
- A horizontal business model always beats a vertical model, and providing that horizontal capability in a company offering is a requirement.
- Compliance with open standards is a requirement. Proprietary standards are gone.
- Voice, data, and video will all eventually travel over a packet-cell network infrastructure.
- Time to market with new products and technology is critical, with the fast beating the slow every time. And if you are slow, you will be left behind and will likely eventually disappear.

Cisco establishes its organizational structure, procedures, and policies to enhance its position in each of these industry vision areas. And it is now large enough and has enough industry influence that it can define de facto standards just as Microsoft has done for years in the software arena.

Chambers is quoted as stating, "We got very bold. We made the conscious decision that we were going to attempt to shape the future of the entire industry. We decided to play very aggressively and truly attempt in the networking industry what Microsoft did with PCs and IBM did with mainframes."[3]

Here is a company with a mission. It intends to establish itself as the dominant leader in its selected industry segments, as determined by customer demand, and then either adhere to existing industry standards or define its own, which it intends to become the de facto standards for that segment. A grand vision, to be sure.

SEEING THINGS THE SAME WAY

Picture two people considering marriage. They are in love. They believe that they can create a wonderful future together and begin to talk about what that future looks like to each of them. The groom expects to live simply in a modest house, have a few children, coach Little League and retire in his mid-50s. The bride, on the other hand, is particularly interested in running a Fortune 1,000 company and believes that she needs to retain her freedom to keep that a reality. Secondarily she is interested in international travel and is enamored with the prospect of living in a Manhattan high-rise. Children, in her view, would get in the way of her professional aspirations and are certainly out of the question for at least 5 years, and more likely 10 years. And, she fears, 10 years from now is when she will likely have the chance to make her jump to the top, which would certainly put kids off for another few years at least.

It is clear that this couple needs to have a no-nonsense discussion regarding their future aspirations and combined life goals. Based on the information presented, this couple appears to have very different visions of future married life, and most parents or friends would recommend that they take a serious look at whether these differences might even be enough to warrant postponing or canceling the marriage. Otherwise, this couple could be looking at a miserable married life that would not make either one of them happy.

Two companies looking to merge have a similar decision facing them as they endeavor to combine personnel, technologies, and vendor and customer bases. Any buying company that assumes it can simply purchase the other company and "work things out later" will most likely be sadly disappointed that things don't resolve themselves easily in the future. Acquired founders who feel that their company should have gone in one direction when the buyer intends to take it in another can seriously disrupt future development plans and cause headaches for the buyers. More than one acquisition has been scuttled by the lack of endorsement from acquired company management, which in turn infects the attitudes of acquired employees, who are usually dedicated to the prior founders. If the founders say that things are bad, they must be bad, and previously enthusiastic employees can become recalcitrant at best and disruptive at worst. It is critical that the target's management be on board with respect to the future direction of the combined entity, or the buyer may have to take extraordinary steps to remedy the situation—with a substantial time delay being the almost inevitable outcome of the problems. And time delay is a primary enemy of any acquisition in a technology field. Should the buyer's efforts be delayed, competitors will have an advantage that would not have been theirs otherwise—simply from lack of performance on the part of the merged entities.

Perhaps the buyer will require that acquired personnel behave in a way that is completely inconsistent with the target's prior culture, or may simply treat the acquired personnel as second-class citizens within the acquired company's culture. (The second-class citizen treatment is a common "buzz" complaint expressed regarding Microsoft's attitude toward acquired company employees.) In either case, the acquired personnel will be unmotivated in their new environment, which will seriously hamper future cooperation.

This in itself may not seem like a big problem until the buyer recognizes that the seller's personnel will be required to create product enhancements effectively and quickly that will not only integrate the target's products with those of the buyer but also drive the products into their next generation. If the loss of a few key personnel stalls new product developments for a year or more as the buyer's personnel learn the seller's technology, the market opportunity that precipitated the purchase in the first place may be filled by a competitor, making the buyer now a market follower instead of the leader that it initially intended.

The lack of complementary vision between buyer and seller can turn a viable acquisition into one that not only does not meet expectations, but also creates bad personnel blood along the path toward reaching that unfortunate failure state. The buyer now has a situation where the acquisition not only did not meet expectations, but has actually spawned personnel conflict issues that did not exist prior to the purchase.

Ensuring complementary visionary goals does not ensure success, but it surely removes a major stumbling block in the way of achieving that success. Marriage is difficult even when the spouses agree on where they are headed. It is nearly impossible when each spouse is pulling the relationship in a direction that the other does not desire. Business mergers should move forward from the same understanding.

UNCOVERING A COMPANY'S VISION

It is one thing to say that vision compatibility is important. It is another to confidently, and accurately, discern a company's vision. Here are five recommendations that may help you in this regard.

1. Review the annual report of the target company. It is here that company management will present its view of the industry to shareholders. The annual report will also present the ways that the company is preparing itself to address the current and future industry conditions.

2. Look for keynote speeches or other public presentations made by key target company management. In these speeches, much of the company's vision will often be outlined.

3. Review the trade journals for articles written by either key management or engineering personnel. Once again, these articles will often outline overall perceived trends and the steps that the company is taking to capitalize on these trends.

4. Simplest, and likely most straightforward, is simply to have a few detailed discussions with the key management personnel who set the strategic vision for the company.

5. Talk to the venture capital or other financial partners of the company. More than likely these people have detailed information about the past, current, and future vision perspective of the key management personnel.

Be aware that the management and financial partners may present their versions of the vision and culture in such a way as to complement what they believe to be the buyer's vision. Sellers often adapt to the needs of their buyers, and buyers are well advised to perform a little extra due diligence by reviewing past information and comparing it to the information being presented. If there is concordance, then buyers can take this consistency as a positive sign. If there is a significant difference between prior information and that being currently presented, then buyers are well served to delve more deeply into any discrepancy. In any long-term relationship you are always better off learning early on the truth about the other partner. The truth will eventually come out, and if it is an unwelcome discovery, it may arrive to the detriment of those intending to have their expectations successfully met.

VISION, TECHNOLOGY, AND RELIGION

Technology fields are a lot like religion in that much of what happens today is determined by the perceived future outcomes of industry participants. Integrated Services Digital Network (ISDN) was the technology of choice in the mid-1980s. Much attention was paid to the dramatic future impact ISDN would have on the industry in particular and society in general. I remember making sales presentations to customers relaying the values of purchasing "ISDN-compatible" systems so that they could ensure that their purchases did not become prematurely obsolete.

In reality, at that time ISDN was a technology in search of a need to fulfill. It has today come somewhat into common use, but a little late when compared with other technologies such as digital subscriber line (DSL) and cable modem, among others.

My point here is that if one believed in the mid-1980s that ISDN was *the* technology and moved all company activities in that direction, then talking to a company that contended that X.25 was the preferred technology would have likely caused heated discussions regarding future industry and product directions. If these differences could not be worked out to everyone's satisfaction, then discord would likely result along with the unfortunate personnel factioning that can follow.

Technology is designed by engineers, who design based on their vision of how the final product will perform. Special software and hardware features are often built into the product to accommodate the next generation of technology evolution, which is in turn based on the engineer's vision of what the future will hold. Some technologies are designed to accommodate a high degree of flexibility, while others are designed to meet a specific technical outcome.

Buying a company with the expectation of incorporating acquired technology into the buyer's own requires a close look at the industry and design philosophies incorporated into the products. What on the surface may appear a nominal difference may actually require a major redesign effort to bring a product into alignment with the buyer's design goals.

The detailed design decisions are usually derived from a set of pre-conceived notions about product evolution from one generation to the next. And these notions are usually based on a belief regarding the overall industry trends and how the company intends to participate within those trends. Understanding the vision of the target company founders, management, and personnel provides an understanding foundation against which design engineering, manufacturing, marketing, and policies can be interpreted. Mapping the uncovered vision against that of the buying company provides an excellent basis for determining the level of existing vision compatibility and provides a means for assessing the level of expected future compatibility.

CISCO'S ASSUMPTIONS

Implicit in the vision rule is the belief that the acquired personnel are an integral part of the transaction and that vision conflicts that arise between key personnel will eventually undermine any future value that is expected from the purchase. The intellectual property aspect of the acquisition is the underlying critical component of value to Cisco in an acquisition transaction.

If the assets of value for another buying company in another industry could be acquired and effectively transferred without the people, then the need for future vision compatibility would not be as demanding. For companies that are more infrastructure oriented such as banking, cable television, telephone, or other industries where the number of customers and geographic presence are the primary assets being acquired, with the personnel being secondary, then vision compatibility may not necessarily be a potential deal stopper. In general, however, vision cannot be overemphasized as an area warranting intense review for all acquisitions in any industry, since much of the target's daily operation will be oriented around supporting success as defined by the company vision.

Only from a thorough understanding of the company's historically espoused vision can a buyer make an accurate assessment of its level of transferability to the new, postacquisition, merged environment. Products, vendors, customers, and especially management and employees will carry the vision legacy with them and must be aided in the transition to the new environment.

If a reasonable degree of confidence is present that they can effectively make the transition, then the acquisition should be treated as having passed the vision rule test. If the transfer confidence is not there but vision is deemed a noncritical part of the acquisition, then it is likely that a large number of employees may be lost in the process of the transfer. They may be lost because the buyer simply builds in a complete personnel overhaul as part of the acquisition overhead or because the acquired employees will leave for what they deem more suitable working conditions than those offered by the buyer. Under these circumstances, a buyer should strongly consider taking a proactive stand on employee replacement and quickly, up front, let acquired personnel know that they need either to get on board with the new vision or promptly submit their resignations. If vision is deemed important and is also evaluated as being incompatible and personnel retention a key acquisition goal, then there is a strong case to be made for passing entirely on the acquisition, just as Cisco would likely do under these circumstances.

Implicit also in the vision compatibility requirement is the contention that people in general and professionals in particular do not work well where their personal beliefs are continually in conflict with those of the overall organization. Just as it is difficult to swim against the current of a river, so is it difficult to work effectively in an environment where one's beliefs are continually being challenged or, even more damaging, discounted completely. People simply won't remain employed for long in this type of environment; future turnover of personnel will be the almost inevitable result. Even worse is the case where people remain employed but simply cease to perform their jobs at anywhere above minimal requirements. In this second case, both the employee and the company suffer along with shareholders, customers, and other employees.

I have an executive-level colleague who was employed by a company that was recently acquired by one of its competitors. My colleague's attitude about the company was one of distrust. He dreaded the purchase knowing that he would likely not continue working for the buying company long after the purchase. They offered him large sums of money to stay with the merged entity but to no avail. In the end, no amount of offered money was enough. He simply did not want to work in an environment that did not share his industry visions or personal values. He left the company to work for a competitor.

Vision and values often become intertwined, especially in smaller companies where the founders can have a profound impact on daily operations and the overall culture. I clearly want the reader to separate the vision aspect of the Cisco rules from the value aspect, which is covered in Chapter 6.

A final assumption that is tacit with each of these elimination rules is that there will always be another company to pursue that will provide the same types of benefits as the one currently under scrutiny. Just as some people settle for a marriage partner who is not their ideal simply because they feel no others may come along, companies pursue poor business relationships, whether mergers, acquisitions, or alliances, with other highly incompatible companies simply because they feel that nothing better will come along. Cisco, by its actions, believes that it is better served by avoiding a cumbersome business relationship than by taking the risks associated with entering into a business relationship that it knows is incompatible from the start. In the technology fields, there is usually some other company that is developing an alternate form of the technology of interest to Cisco at the time of the potential acquisition. Places like Silicon Valley have a readily available supply of engineers, venture capitalists, and social networks that ensure that any new technology is rapidly discussed, evaluated, and often cloned within a short period of time. And if the technology is based on an industry standard, then the method of implementing compliance with the standard is what is really being purchased. This takes the proprietary edge off of the development process and opens up the very real possibility that another company is already developing an alternate technological method for providing standard implementation.

In other words, given Cisco's proximity to high-technology hotbeds (such as Silicon Valley, Boston, and Research Triangle), the networking industry's dependence on standards, Cisco's prominence as an industry leader, and its reputation for continual acquisition activity, it is natural for Cisco to assume that another acquisition target will appear that will meet its initial qualification criteria. Companies in other industries that are less dynamic or less heavily dependent on the rapid implementation of intellectual property may find that they cannot be as selective in their choices of acquisition targets. Even better for these companies, they may find that they do not need to be as selective in their choices of targets, as the assets being purchased are more tangible, such as buildings, airplanes, customers, or geographic presence.

PORTABILITY EVALUATION

Vision is a human trait and not one limited to a particular business segment or technology. In my opinion, the presence of a complementary vision from the pre- to postacquisition environment can greatly improve the likelihood of the acquisition meeting all parties' future expectations. The lack of a consistent vision can only hurt future success prospects. Having a complementary vision should be considered a highly desirable aspect of the purchase under almost any circumstances. Value should be attached to its presence since it will likely decrease time to market for future products and decrease future employee turnover, as two major desirable outcomes. If these items are important to the acquisition, vision compatibility should be heavily weighted on the positive side.

Even in a retail environment, vision compatibility may be an important consideration. Assume, for example, that a specialty retailer purchases a general merchandise retailer with the primary interest in obtaining the real estate locations as a rapid way of expanding the specialty retailer's retail presence. These stores must be staffed by salespeople who will likely initially come from the acquired chain's personnel. If they are continually ruing the loss of the general lines and feel that the current specialty line is too limiting, then sales will likely suffer as a result. If, on the other hand, the locations purchased had personnel already in alignment with a specialty store temperament, then the transition will likely go more smoothly and new store sales will likely show a more rapid increase.

THE FINAL ANALYSIS

Rule #1 requires that the target company have a product and industry vision that is compatible with Cisco's and treats this compatibility as a necessary condition for pursuing the acquisition. This rule treats personnel and their vision of the future as an integral part of the acquisition and contends that lack of vision compatibility will simply create future problems as personnel work out the details of future product and service offerings.

Cisco takes the time to ensure that key management's vision of the industry and their desired place within the industry are clearly defined. Once vision is defined, a determination is made on both sides to see if a complementary accord can be reached between the acquired management's view and Cisco's because, after all, Cisco's is the only one that matters once the purchase is completed. Managers who do not share the Cisco vision are often asked to leave as part of the acquisition with the intent of the parting being amicable and in the interest of protecting the futures of the acquired company's products, services, employees, customers, and legacy.

Products are evaluated to ensure that the underlying visions that created the existing product set have not created any technological incompatibilities that cannot be easily and quickly overcome in the postpurchase environment.

Vision is not the same as the values and culture of the company, and these areas are evaluated on their own merits, and with equal weighting.

Any buyer who is interested in retaining the target company's enthusiastic personnel in the postpurchase environment must consider vision compatibility as part of its evaluation. It is difficult to place too much emphasis on the importance of clearly understanding the vision and values of an organization; this importance is clearly indicated by Cisco's making these two areas of investigation potential deal stoppers.

CHAPTER 5

WIN IN THE SHORT TERM

If we did not produce a win with Crescendo in the first year, our share-holders would have been all over us.[1]
> —John Chambers, President and CEO, Cisco Systems

Cisco Rule #2

Shareholders must see a short-term win from an acquisition, or their support for the purchase, and the management who performed the acquisition, will erode.

It seems obvious when stated: The merger of two companies must create a win for the buying company's shareholders. The share-holders deserve for the acquisition to create a shareholder win since, after all, the buying company is using shareholder money to facilitate the purchase. This chapter takes a detailed look at this important area of acquisition activity that Cisco makes a centerpiece of its qualification strategy but which is frequently given secondary consideration by other buying companies.

SHORT-TERM WINS FOR SHAREHOLDERS

Corporate managers are working with other people's money. Share-holders entrust corporate management with money that the managers then invest. Managers don't own the company; the shareholders own the company. Yet, some managers act as though their interests are the same as those of the shareholders without regard for how their actions are going to affect the shareholders' view of investment return. Naturally, if the managers are also majority shareholders they have a natural way for treating the company as their own.

Shareholders traditionally look for the best place to put their money, always on the lookout for the best return on investment. They leave their money in a particular company's stock because they believe that this particular company has a higher likelihood of providing a larger percentage return on invested capital than the investment alternatives. Should that perception change, then the shareholders can easily change their stock ownership position from one company to another. If this selling activity happens in large quantity, there will be enormous selling pressure on the stock that then drives down the stock price, further exacerbating an already bad situation. Preserving and increasing shareholder value while growing a company in a dynamic marketplace are what top managers get paid large amounts of money to do. Cisco has historically demonstrated a proven ability to walk this fine line while simultaneously implementing an aggressive acquisition strategy.

Acquiring a company adds a second area of complication to the shareholder value equation in that the buying company's stock is often used to fund the purchase. Using stock to fund the purchase preserves valuable cash for later investment in areas such as marketing, research and development (R&D), or expansion. But using stock to fund an acquisition purchase requires the issuance of stock to the selling company's owners, which then dilutes the stock positions of existing buying company shareholders. When shareholders see additional company stock being issued and their current stock positions being diluted, they had better believe that the stock issuance is in their own best investment interest, or management can expect to be subjected to intense questioning regarding motivations and rationale for the purchase.

Chambers contends that shareholders must see some type of short-term win from the acquisition or the target company does not fit the Cisco acquisition profile. When a company acquires a number of other firms representing billions of dollars in valuation per year, keeping shareholders happy with increased returns makes a lot of sense. This also helps to explain the decrease in acquisition activity on Cisco's behalf during the first half of 2001. Other operational issues dragged down corporate financial performance, and absorbing debt or further diluting stock with acquisitions would only have exacerbated an already difficult situation. The company is still committed to performing acquisitions but on a more selective basis.[2]

LOOK TO FUTURE VALUE

The current activities of a purchased company are of interest to Cisco, but mainly for the future potential of those activities when processed through Cisco's operation. The future value of the acquisition is what Cisco purchases, not the current value.

"Our ideal acquisition is a small start-up that has a great technology product on the drawing board that is going to come out in 6 to 12 months from now. When we do that, we are buying the engineers and the next-generation product. Then we blow the product through out distribution channels and leverage our manufacturing and financial strengths,"[3] says Chambers. Credibility is a problem with any start-up and the more integral a start-up's offering is to a customer's operation, the more important that credibility becomes. Overcoming that credibility issue is necessary for the start-up to expand its presence nationally or internationally. By selling through established distribution networks, the start-up can provide cutting-edge technology while also enabling the customer to purchase with some degree of support confidence.

The Cisco approach of purchasing a start-up and offering its cutting-edge technology through the Cisco "mill" provides an excellent blending of technology and customer service. The customer feels more comfortable trying newer technology since it is being offered, and supported, by Cisco instead of a financially strapped start-up with a limited support network. The start-up gets to see its technology adopted more quickly than it ever would have experienced using its own limited financial resources. Cisco reaps the financial benefits associated with the technology's rapid adoption while simultaneously putting the acquired engineers to work developing the technology's next generation of products. Showing a 12-month return to shareholders on the purchase is feasibly done under these circumstances, and, even better, a longer-term return is provided as follow-on products are introduced. (See Chapter 7 for additional information on longer-term impact of acquisition decisions.)

Referring to the 1993 Crescendo purchase for $95 million (Crescendo's annual revenues at the time of purchase were $10 million), Chambers noted these specifics: "We took a device like Crescendo's networking product, and within 18 months, we had a $500 million run rate. No small-scale company could go from $10 million to $500 million in 18 months. They just can't handle the scale. But we could scale because of our distribution, financial, and manufacturing strengths."

Applying the standard Cisco gross margin of 65 percent to the 18-month revenue performance achieved shows that Cisco gained $325 million (65 percent of $500 million) in gross margin within an 18-month period after deal closure. This represents a gross margin that is 3.42 times the purchase price which was achieved without any initial cash outlay since Crescendo was purchased with issued stock alone. Not a bad return on investment by almost any measure. The Crescendo purchase brought Mario Mazzola, the founder and president of Crescendo, to Cisco. Mario is still with Cisco at the time of this writing and serves as the senior vice president of new business ventures.

A&D CREATES SHAREHOLDER VALUE

Companies that continue to grow revenues must continually feed new products and services into their offerings. These products or services can be either internally developed or obtained from outside sources. These external sources can themselves be obtained by the licensing of technology, through partnerships or alliances, or through the direct acquisition of the company that produces the technology. This technology can itself be in the early stages of development or it may be mature. Managing the variety of options in a way that maximizes the likelihood of a successful later market offering requires vigilance and a clear understanding of company goals.

Research and development (R&D) is usually treated as a cost center in that the engineers involved with the research draw cash and other corporate resources from the corporation during the period of technology development, which will likely involve years. Once the technology is proven, it will then take additional time to turn the technology into a viable product offering. This offering must then be formalized, marketed, sold, and installed before it actually turns into a recognizable revenue stream by the offering company. There likely will be several years between the time that a technology goes into R&D and when that technology actually generates company revenues. And not all of these R&D projects will later turn into successful product offerings, which in turn adds another level of financial risk to the situation.

The networking industry within which Cisco operates is one built on standards and optimization. As the need for network traffic grows, customers are continually on the lookout for better ways to utilize existing infrastructure while simultaneously decreasing costs and increasing end-user performance perceptions. Faster, cheaper, and more reliably are the driving forces behind market evolution in the networking arena.

Leaps in networking technology provide excellent ways for optimizing the use of existing infrastructure, such as was initially experienced with the introduction of the router. As network usage increased along with the larger data traffic demands associated with image and multimedia applications, so did the need for expanded network traffic capabilities. Data switching and optical networking represented technological leaps designed specifically to meet this increased market demand.

FROM INSIDE CISCO

In periods when the industry ran slower, and different business models worked, the vast majority of product development came from internal teams. As the market begins to accelerate, you can't keep up with the customer requirements; everything moves too rapidly. . . . Companies who are going to be leaders will have to have a new focus totally on acquisition as a core competency.[4]

—John Chambers, commenting on the need to move away from internal development in a rapidly changing marketplace

A company like Cisco can fund its own advanced R&D projects. Optical and switching technologies represented advanced developments years before becoming functionally and financially viable. The danger associated with doing this type of internal research is that early-stage technology often does not turn into a viable technology or product offering for any number of reasons. Years of time and money may be invested before the approach is shown not to be viable. Waiting until a smaller company proves the technology to be viable while also installing a few test (beta) sites to validate the customer need and product design takes a substantial amount of risk out of the R&D process. This is a primary motivation for the Cisco R&D through acquisition approach.

Look at the situation from this perspective. Assume that Cisco decides to develop its own switching products as it views a potential market need several years into the future. Assume also that for any number of reasons Cisco is unsuccessful with its internal development effort. The future market eventually becomes ready for a switching product, and Cisco's competition is already offering working switching products. At this point, Cisco has one of four choices if it wants to offer end-to-end solutions to its customers—which, by its own business objectives and vision statement, it must do:

1. Cisco can try to leverage its older technology for a little bit longer lifetime through more aggressive selling efforts of its existing products (knowing that this is a short-term solution at best).

2. It can partner with another company that offers the newer-technology products and have a strategic segment of its offering exist at the whim of an outside company.

3. It can license the technology from a third party and once again have an important part of its offering exist at the whim of another company.

4. It can purchase a company that offers the needed technology in the form of a proven product. Doing so takes much of the risk out of offering the technology. The purchase allows Cisco to maintain its customer account relationship credibility while also eliminating the possibility of having its product offerings affected by, or even disrupted by, an external company.

The smaller company pushing the technology envelope, of which there are many in Silicon Valley, Research Triangle, and other high-tech gardens, can be treated as an outsourced R&D lab of sorts. The smaller companies get venture funding from any number of sources to develop and validate a technology in the form of a proven product. Once proven, that company either may grow on its own market-reception merits or may be sold to Cisco or one of its competitors.

Cisco wins with the acquisition in that the technology is far less risky to introduce to its customer base since the products are now proven from both an engineering and a marketing perspective. The smaller company wins in that its initially risky venture has now turned into a viable market offering that likely made the founding employees wealthy. The customers win in that they are getting advanced technology that enables them more fully to develop their internal business capabilities and competitiveness, obtaining this new technology from a company with Cisco's reputation instead of from a no-name start-up. Cisco's shareholders win because the acquired technology can be rapidly transformed into a product offering that, when run through the Cisco process, has the potential of becoming a real profit driver. Moreover, such technological advancements did not require a substantial outlay of R&D cash.

In sum, purchasing leading (or "bleeding" for the very advanced) edge technology from another company after it is already proven from both a design and a market perspective takes much of the financial risk out of the technology's introduction. Let the smaller company take the development risks while all the time knowing that this smaller company will likely never be able to exploit fully the market potential of the technology once proven. When Cisco purchases the company and "blows" its products through the Cisco operation, a substantial revenue opportunity is created that the smaller company could never have accomplished on its own.

Perform the lower-risk, incremental development activities using inside engineering resources. This has a much higher likelihood of success since the projects are not based on unproven technology but rather represent an extension of technology that already exists and has a proven market demand and predictable revenue opportunity.

CISCO'S ASSUMPTIONS

Fundamental to the Cisco approach is the intention to provide the best possible, proven solutions to Cisco's customers: to be the end-to-end supplier of the customer's network needs. This is a strongly market-driven focus that is secondarily technology driven.

Many technology organizations are driven to provide the best (aka "coolest") possible technology. They adopt an internally developed and funded R&D methodology that primarily promotes technology development, with proven marketability also being considered, but as a secondary issue. More than one new company has come into being from successful development efforts performed within a larger company that did not eventually turn into product of-ferings. The larger corporation, by not realizing the value of the technology or simply determining that the technology did not meet company strategic objectives, curtailed further development. The frustrated developers, who now totally believe in their newly founded ideas, often leave the company to start their own ventures. Much of the entrepreneurship present on the American technology scene can be traced to R&D projects inside companies like Fairchild, Motorola, Xerox, Texas Instruments, and IBM.

Cisco, in fact, exists because of an internal development effort sponsored by Stanford University as a way of improving their inter-nal networking capabilities. Not interested in commercializing the product itself, Stanford let Sandy and Leonard take their router idea with them when they started Cisco. From Stanford's perspective, commercializing the technology was simply not worth the effort and expense and/or not in alignment with its focus as an academic institution.

We see here that Cisco's overall corporate, customer-oriented goals and objectives drive the microscopic decisions that actually make a company run. It is seductive to want to develop the hottest technology out there. The allure of breaking new technology barriers is very attractive to engineers, and the interest in turning a new tech-nology into a thriving product that generates its own marketplace is addictive. Just ask any successful technology entrepreneurs, and they will most likely validate this statement. Keeping this urge in check by maintaining an intense customer-benefits focus is what helps Cisco stay on course with respect to its internally developed/externally purchased product decisions. Instead of becoming mired in a num-ber of advanced technology development projects that have limited potential for design and market success, Cisco keeps its fingers on the pulse of start-up entrepreneurial development efforts while leverag-ing its internal expertise in creating the best incremental technology products on the market. When the technology, product designs, and customer marketplace are ready, Cisco buys the start-up and fully in-tegrates its products and people into the Cisco operation. The next generation of products to come from this acquired group after acquisition will have a Cisco emphasis and will likely push the start-up's products into a dominant market position that could not have been achieved by the start-up alone.

Notice that this strategy again reflects Cisco's clear emphasis on an acquisition actually being the purchase of people and intellectual property, not the purchase of existing products or infrastructure.

PORTABILITY EVALUATION

If a company exists in a relatively mature industry where developments are incremental and not revolutionary in nature, then Cisco's type of acquired R&D approach may not have as much value. Networking technology is constantly being pushed into new, uncharted areas. Few could have predicted 10 years ago that network communications would look like the field does today, and few today will accurately predict the state of network communications 10 years into the future. This is an industry that has undergone and will undergo again a rapid expansion and change that has a tangential impact on many other businesses. These impacted industries will experience increased performance benefits but will likely not experience a complete obsolescence of their operations and offerings. A Cisco Systems, on the other hand, that does not stay on top of technology developments while simultaneously remaining reliable and profitable may find itself in serious revenue growth trouble, or worse.

Any company that has the opportunity to leverage a smaller company's products or services in such a way that, once proven, they can represent a large revenue opportunity may seriously consider adopting the Cisco R&D approach. It represents an excellent blend of new technology financial risk mitigation while ensuring that the company leverages its internal engineering talents to best advantage. Placing heavy emphasis on new technology acquisition when the marketplace is not open to its adoption may put the buying company in the position of having acquired technology in need of a solution.

Developing advanced technology and licensing it throughout an industry is also a viable approach, as was demonstrated by Qualcomm with its wireless technology. Luckily for Qualcomm, its developments were well received. Otherwise, it could have found itself with a lot of technology R&D investment expense and minimal revenue stream.

Cisco understands the dynamic nature of its market and the pitfalls associated with "bleeding edge" R&D and product design. It has adopted a technology acquisition strategy and approach that capitalizes on its industry's start-up tendencies, minimizes financial risk, and promotes its customer-oriented business objectives, while ensuring the acquisition of viable intellectual capital. Understanding your own industry and its salient attributes while maintaining a clear customer focus will instruct the reader in the proper usage of the Cisco approach for your particular situation.

SHORT-TERM WINS FOR EMPLOYEES AS WELL

Retaining acquired employees is a key success measure for a Cisco acquisition. It is one thing to provide longer-term stock options (over several years) that keep employees in place for the long run. It is another to provide short-term employee incentives that keep people with Cisco long enough to see if the merged relationship will work out. After all, you never get to the longer term if employees leave within days or weeks of the acquisition being finalized.

Chapter 12 provides a detailed examination of the various ways in which Cisco facilitates the integration of acquired employees into the Cisco fold. It covers both the short-term actions and the longer-term incentives provided not only to keep employees around, but to actually motivate them to work toward the common good of Cisco corporate and their fellow employees.

Suffice to say at this point that paying between $500,000 and $53 million per employee for an acquired company and then losing a substantial percentage of those employees in the immediate post-purchase time frame is a very poor investment situation. Special employee emphasis is placed on the days leading up to and immediately following the purchase to ensure that employees are integrated in the most straightforward, painless, yet welcoming way possible. Chapter 12 outlines many of the detailed steps taken by Cisco's Mimi Gigoux and her team to assimilate acquired employees quickly into the Cisco employee family.

THE FINAL ANALYSIS

As communication networks have become more mission-critical, their reliability has also become more important. A network outage can seriously hamper a company's operations and cost large sums of money. If Cisco offers the products that comprise that network, you can bet that a serious customer network outage will cause several ears at Cisco to burn as the customer attempts to make sure that the outage does not happen again. The larger networking companies and customers tend to err on the side of reliability and caution when implementing new technology. They typically implement only proven products or services in a production environment. There will always be some risk takers, but the majority of customers will not take new product risks since more than one career has been stalled or ended by a network decision that caused major corporate disruption or outage.

Customers rely on Cisco to verify that the technology and products offered are reliable. Customers assume that Cisco has done the bulk of the performance testing that verifies that the products and technologies perform as specified. The old adage that "nobody ever got fired for using IBM" when it came to mainframe computers now also applies to Cisco when it comes to Internetworking. Staying on the cutting edge while still maintaining high reliability and profitability is an excellent way to maintain market leadership, and Cisco has effectively maintained this balance through a blend of strategic investments, partnerships, internal developments, and acquisitions.

Investors have come to expect that Cisco will expand its revenues at a 40 percent or higher annual growth rate while maintaining high gross margins. Only by rapidly pursuing growing industries while providing reliable, cost-effective, yet contemporary technology can Cisco continue to fulfill investor expectations, although those investor expectations have been tempered by market realities in recent times. Acquiring companies and technologies that afford a ready, unique entrée into growing marketplaces enables Cisco to establish itself quickly as a market leader. This leadership generates large future revenue opportunities. Acquisition-based R&D provides a less risky approach than developing advanced technology using internal engineering resources.

Carefully choosing its target markets, selecting the right acquisition targets, and fully integrating the acquired company's personnel, technology, and products into the Cisco process enable Cisco to produce substantial short-term returns for its shareholders.

CHAPTER 6

GOOD VIBRATIONS

You have to avoid the temptation to say, "Well, our cultures are different, but I can still make it work." They normally don't.
— John Chambers, President and CEO, Cisco Systems

Cisco Rule #3

There must be a high degree of compatibility between the target's culture and Cisco's culture.

The merging of two companies into a single entity requires that each party make accommodations. Making these accommodations is easier if they are not too drastic or do not substantially rub against the core values of the party asked to make the changes. Adults understand that some level of compromise is required to make relationships work, whether personal such as a marriage or professional such as an alliance. But asking people to compromise on something that they see as a core value will likely meet with a high level of resistance at best, simple refusal to compromise, or even subversion of the intent of the relationship altogether.

Knowing the cultures of the two organizations is critical to making a valid judgment regarding the level of ease and success with which a postacquisition environment can and will be managed. Cisco Systems clearly understands that for its purposes the value associated with an acquisition is in the target's employees. People make up a culture, and the culture is inextricably linked to the value of the people involved. If the target's personnel cannot be expected to integrate reasonably into the Cisco culture, then the acquisition will not succeed since a large number of acquired employees will likely leave within a short period of time after the acquisition is finalized. Losing these people means that the acquisition was a failure, from Cisco's perspective, and should never have been pursued in the first place. By placing a heavy emphasis on culture evaluation as part of the initial transaction interactions and particularly during due diligence, Cisco personnel gain a personal sense and assessment of whether the cultural merge will work.

FROM INSIDE CISCO

You cannot overemphasize the importance of chemistry in determining the suitability of an acquisition.

—Beau Parnell, director of human resources, Cisco Systems

DEFINING A CULTURE

When you are part of a culture, you learn to play by its rules and naturally interact in a way that is appropriate for that culture. Things and actions that one is used to would seem completely foreign to someone from another culture. As a Westerner visiting Japan for my first time in the mid-1980s I was amazed by the low crime rate, while the Japanese tend to take that for granted. Theft, for example, was unusual in Japan. It was common practice in smaller Japanese towns for people to leave their shopping bags on the street as they browsed shops, not appearing concerned in the least that their bags might be stolen. I mentioned my amazement to a local Japanese man who remarked that stealing someone's bags was not something that any Japanese person would do. "Why would I want to steal that person's bags?" he asked. "They're not mine."

This same person coming to the United States may experience a sense of fright since that honesty security blanket with which he had been raised does not apply in the United States. Despite all of the wonderful things that they find in America, many foreigners choose to return to their home countries simply because the cultural things that they must give up to adjust to the American culture are simply too important to them. Perhaps they could not define their culture if asked to, but they can surely recognize when important cultural aspects are taken away.

This is the problem with the merging of cultures. Something is usually lost to one party that becomes another's gain. Those being acquired must feel that what they lose by integrating into the buyer's culture is offset by what is gained by the combined entities.

THE COMPONENTS OF CULTURE

Here are six ways of determining the culture of an organization.

1. Observe behavioral regularities such as organizational rituals, ceremonies, or specific internally generated jargon or slang.

2. What are the dominant values espoused by the organization, such as "high product quality," "no layoffs," or "family comes first"?

3. Is there a philosophy that guides the company's employees and management in their respective interactions?

4. What are the unspoken rules of the game by which any employee must play, such as never challenging the boss even though he or she asks for "honest feedback"?

5. What are the norms expressed within the organization, such as flying after normal business hours instead of on company time or "you had better be dying if you take sick time"?

6. What is the overall feeling you get from the organization? Is it a happy place to work, is everyone somber but efficient, or are people miserable and simply "going through the motions"?[1]

No one of these items by itself will present an accurate picture of the company's culture, but putting them together will present you with an enlightening view of what it is like to work for this particular company and what these people will expect from the buyer after acquisition. By the way, any manager new to a company should get a clear understanding of the culture of the company being managed, as unhappy surprises may lurk for those who make changes without first qualifying the impact on personnel.

Cultures are in a constant state of action generation, interpretation, and reinforcement or change.

The content of a culture involves important shared understandings, beliefs, and expectations. This content generates the manifestations of the culture, such as goods or services (shared things), verbal expressions (shared sayings), behaviors (shared activities), and emotions (shared feelings). Employees observe these cultural manifestations and interpret them, or infer meaning into them. If they agree with what they see, they go along with things; this reinforces the culture as it stands. If they do not like what they see, they will either try to change the culture or simply leave. More than one company, or society for that matter, has been disrupted or completely dismantled when employees or citizens decide that the culture needs to be changed and take actions to implement those changes. Those who do not like the culture and don't want to stay and work for change will simply leave and go somewhere else.

If the primary goal of an acquisition is the future successful performance of acquired personnel, and the culture into which they are being integrated has no intentions of changing, then the culture of the acquired company must be carefully assessed for compatibility. If this issue isn't given serious consideration, the buyer may experience a mass exodus upon purchase completion. This exodus would obviously undermine the value of the acquisition. The problem could have been avoided altogether if cultural animosity could have been predicted early in the acquisition process.

In my opinion (an opinion that is shared by many others), traditional acquisition methodology places too little emphasis on this cultural integration issue and too much emphasis on the acquired assets. It is difficult to imagine a way that complementary cultures between buyer and seller could ever be construed as a negative. It is easy, however, to see where cultural conflicts can lead to serious postpurchase problems. If the people are not important to the acquisition, then cultural compatibility is only a "nice-to-have" and may not be mandatory. But if postpurchase personnel retention and enthusiastic cooperation is important, then cultural compatibility must be given a very high level of due diligence.

CISCO'S CULTURE

Cisco uses a number of heavily reinforced statements to define the framework of its culture. First, Cisco's mission statement: "Be the supplier of choice by leading all competitors in customer satisfaction, product leadership, market share, and profitability."[2]

FROM INSIDE CISCO

We are going to change the way people work, live, play, and learn.

—*Printed on the ID badge of each Cisco employee*

91

Next, Cisco's business purpose: "To shape the future of global networking by creating unprecedented opportunities and value for our customers, employees, partners, and investors."

Five core values help Cisco in achieving its mission and business purpose:

1. A dedication to customer success.
2. Innovation and learning.
3. Partnerships.
4. Teamwork.
5. Doing more with less.

Cisco's Mission Statement

"Be the supplier of choice by leading all competitors in customer satisfaction, product leadership, market share, and profitability."

Cisco takes this statement seriously and, it can credibly be said, has structured the organization and its operational goals specifically around fulfilling this mission. Notice the first core value, "a dedication to customer success." If you are dedicated to your customer's success and deliver on that dedication, it is difficult to imagine a customer that would not be satisfied. These are good words, but Cisco implements programs tailored to drive employee performance toward this goal.

To start with, all managers have a compensation program that is in large part tied directly to customer satisfaction. The satisfaction level is ranked from 1 to 5, with the goal for the year 2000 set at 4.23. Employee bonuses are paid based on an annual customer survey that monitors 70 satisfaction items. Typical items measured include product quality, quality of the sales representative, ease with which customers can obtain Cisco-related information, and the level of fit between Cisco's products and the customer's networking needs, among others.

Cisco also has a "critical customer" list, which is a listing of customers that are currently experiencing serious difficulties with Cisco and/or its products. Anyone in the company can put a customer on this list, and the customer remains on the list until the problems are resolved. Chambers gets a nightly report of this list's status, and even gives customers his personal telephone number so that they can call him directly if they have a problem. He also spends as much as 50 percent of his time with customers helping with problems, if needed, while also learning more about the customers' needs and industry perceptions.

At the executive level, Cisco has a senior vice president of customer advocacy, whose purpose is to ensure that the customer's voice is heard with authority within the organization. This position was created in the mid-1980s, which gives you an idea of the level at which customer satisfaction is a permanent part of the Cisco culture.

Product leadership is achieved when you are the first to market with a new technology or product that addresses an important customer need. Cisco's blend of internal development and an aggressive acquisition strategy ensure that if Cisco cannot develop the product in time for early entry into a marketplace, it will purchase the company that can get it there.

Cisco's market share data in large part speaks for itself with respect to the success the company has when it enters a market. Remember that Cisco's goal is to be either number one or number two in the markets it serves. As of October 1999, according to Chambers, Cisco focused on 20 product areas; it was number one in 16 of those areas and was number two in the other four.[3]

And as for profitability, Cisco enjoyed at the end of its fiscal 2000 year $18.8 billion in net sales, up from $12.2 billion in fiscal 1999, a 54 percent increase. On these sales, Cisco generated a net income of $2.7 billion in fiscal 2000 (14.4 percent net profit), up from $2.0 billion in fiscal 1999, a 35 percent increase. It is really an amazing feat to grow a $12 billion company at a 54 percent annual rate, but here are the numbers that speak for themselves. And this performance was at the end of a number of years of comparable financial performance. Cisco was obviously doing something very right from a profitability perspective.

Finally, from a financial perspective, the company listed on its fiscal year 2000 period ending July 29, 2000, that it had over $4 billion in "cash and cash equivalents" and working capital of $5.9 billion. Its quick ratio was over 2.0 for the same period. I have looked at a lot of balance sheets in my time, and those that are growing at these types of rates are often very cash poor. Cisco seems to have avoided this pitfall: It has experienced extraordinary growth for a company its size while not depleting its cash position.

Cisco's Business Purpose

"To shape the future of global networking by creating unprecedented opportunities and value for our customers, employees, partners, and investors."[4]

Cisco doesn't simply want to work harder or smarter, although hard work and intelligent activity are important to getting things done. But Cisco recognizes that the Internet economy is not like anything that has ever happened before and has no models against which it can credibly be compared. Effective use of Internet-based technology can truly transform the way a company does business, and anyone who doubts this being true should look at Dell Computer Corporation's success or the way that the so-called old economy companies are ravenously consuming this new technology as a way of streamlining and upgrading their existing operations.

To paraphrase Jack Welch from General Electric (GE), as I saw him talking in a television interview in early 2000, "These smaller companies are getting the attention, but you will really see this industry take off when the big, established players such as GE start putting this technology to work in their own operations." Jack, if you read this, sorry if the words aren't exactly right, but they should be consistent with the intent of your comment.

And Cisco uses itself as its own test case. It actually uses the technology that it spends so much time convincing its customers they should be using. This in itself can be considered a high-technology novelty. Cisco has set up an electronic networking support and operations system that not only handles the bulk of customer questions but also trains new employees on Cisco's operations. New products are integrated into the Cisco manufacturing system so that newly acquired products are quickly Ciscoized and look to a customer just like any other Cisco product. A huge percentage of Cisco's customer orders are placed over the Internet.

Cisco espouses a partnership model where each member of the partnership gets to perform his duties in accordance with what that particular company does well. Cisco contends that the vertically integrated companies of the past simply do not apply to the Internet economy, and declined the tempting 1999 purchase of International Network Services (INS) substantially because it would have violated this fundamental belief that partnership, and not vertical integration, is the success model for the new economy. By the way, INS was later purchased by Lucent, a Cisco competitor.

FROM INSIDE CISCO

We don't just want to work harder, or smarter. We want to be asking, "How can I do it differently?"

—*John Chambers, commenting on the need to foster innovation at Cisco*

Unprecedented is a key word in this business purpose statement. Doing it differently is truly a definition for unprecedented.

Cisco's Dedication to Customer Success

Staying close to customers has been elevated to an almost obsessive level with Cisco,[5] starting the John Chambers and his "critical customer" list of troubled accounts. Perhaps this is a carryover from Chambers' Wang days, with the exception that at Wang the intent was there but the execution was lacking. I remember a personal meeting I had with Dr. Wang where we were discussing a fairly small Wang account in Texas that was having problems. He seemed truly interested in resolving the problem—more interested than other managers, and not just for business reasons or to save a program, which would have been reasonable motivations. I mentioned that his interest seemed very personal, to which he replied, "My name is on the machine. Every one is personal to me." And he meant it. This level of commitment from the top of an organization usually permeates the rest of the organization. Unfortunately this did not happen at Wang, but it does appear to be happening at Cisco, much to Chambers' credit.

There is an old marketing and sales saying, "When the customer succeeds, the companies that help them succeed also succeed along with them." I believe this to be true, and so does Cisco as a corporation and Chambers in particular.

Cisco's Commitment to Innovation and Learning

Cisco's entire acquisition strategy is designed to capture and commercialize innovation.[6] Throughout, this book is in one way or another discussing this point, so I won't go into it at any length here.

Learning, on the other hand, is a hidden trait of Cisco Systems that is worth noting. Learning from customers and the industry keeps Cisco informed regarding industry trends, companies, and technologies that warrant consideration as new Cisco additions. Making sure that this information is routed to the proper people is an integral part of the Cisco internal communication mechanisms, and the planning matrix provides a structured way for collating learned information for future planning purposes.

Cisco is also active in promoting learning within the general user community, which not only helps those learning but also helps Cisco.

Some estimates place the 2003 need for worldwide network engineering personnel at around 500,000. Network engineering is a complicated process that is akin to learning a new spoken language. There is not, as of this writing, a way to learn quickly the various acronyms, technologies, and methodologies that are needed to address the industry in general and Cisco's products in particular. It takes time and training.

Cisco has its own academies that train students to become Cisco certified. Partnerships have also been established with firms such as KPMG International for network design and training support. Estimates are that over 60 percent of installed network services are outsourced due to the complexity of the tasks and the difficulty in hiring and retaining highly demanded network engineering personnel. As networks expand in scope and complexity, the need for additional highly trained engineers will simply increase. Cisco is already taking proactive steps to address this growing need for trained, experienced talent.

Cisco and Partnerships

Cisco Systems makes a point of incorporating partnerships in its business model.[7] Once again, this is consistent with the overall vision of the Internet economy: Those companies that produce products and provide services that comply to standards while also maintaining a short time to market with new offerings will win in the marketplace. Every company has its area of expertise, and customers will likely require a broader range of expertise than the company itself can offer. At this point, the company is faced with a choice, assuming that it wants to meet as many of its customers' needs as possible in a one-stop or turnkey fashion. Either the company can vertically integrate by internally developing the expertise, it can vertically integrate by acquiring the expertise through a merger, or it can horizontally integrate through partnerships.

Vertically integrating requires that the company now maintain a high enough level of expertise in the new area to remain competitive. With this approach runs the danger of diffusing the buying company's focus from the core competency that fostered its initial success.

As an example, one of my clients publishes newsletters that are sold through a telemarketing procedure. He decided to integrate telemarketing into his operation and, within a short period of time, found that he had become first a telemarketing company that did publishing instead of keeping his focus on first being a publishing company. He has since outsourced the telemarketing while implementing tight controls over the methodologies used by the telemarketing company. Telemarketing companies do telemarketing. Publishing companies do publishing. A partnership in this regard makes far more sense than either company trying to do both.

In short, Cisco makes a point of partnering where possible and acquiring when the expertise acquired directly complements Cisco's core business objectives. Partnering can even be construed to extend to the outsourcing arrangements Cisco practices in its manufacturing operation. Cisco performs in-house manufacturing on those products or stages of product manufacture that require a higher level of expertise. It outsources the manufacture of products that are routine in nature and don't require a higher level of personnel to complete satisfactorily. In this way, Cisco personnel perform the tasks that best utilize their talents, and the outsourcing companies use their personnel to perform those tasks that would otherwise use Cisco's personnel in a nonoptimal way.

In short, Cisco looks to partner, when possible, and has integrated this partnership mentality into the cultural mentality of the organization.

Teamwork at Cisco

Internal operational teams are now accepted as an effective way of doing business, but effectively implementing teams can be difficult. I have worked at more than one company that has brought me in to foster a team attitude, only to find that the personnel have taken almost every team-building seminar on the market and factional infighting still exists. Further digging usually indicates that an unwritten yet very real corporate culture rule is that "Team building is fine for everyone else, but it doesn't apply to me." Usually this attitude permeates from the top of the organization downward, with the lower-level managers and personnel adopting the attitude of the top management.

Cisco takes the approach that teams and diversity are good and actually make the company stronger.[8] Instead of diversity confrontation being something to tolerate, Cisco treats diversity as a treasure of unique and different ideas. From this diversity come unique ways of looking at and solving problems.

FROM INSIDE CISCO

In our organization, if I've got a leader who can't be a team player, they're gone. That doesn't mean we don't want healthy disagreement, but regardless of how well they're performing, if they can't learn over time to be part of the team and to challenge when appropriate, they really aren't going to fit into our long-term culture.[9]

—*John Chambers' definition of teamwork at Cisco Systems*

In some ways I think that Cisco Systems mirrors something intrinsic to being an American. We are mostly a melting pot of many different cultures, religions, and ethnic backgrounds that come together to make us something unique. From this diversity comes a fresh perspective on life that causes the United States regularly to renew itself—although this process is often painful, as anyone who lived through the 1960s can attest. When the renewal process is over we are a stronger country than we were before the clashing. And we then work together as a people from whatever that next evolutionary level may be. A truly diverse company that embraces the diversity to capitalize on its benefits while still retaining the commitment to the overall good of the organization has a great formula for avoiding capture in its own dogma. Cisco seems to have found that balance between fostering creative conflict and at the same time ensuring that personnel eventually work together as a team to achieve agreed-upon goals.

John Chambers sums up his view of the culture in this way: "From the beginning we built a culture that wanted people from different environments and different backgrounds. There is no mold here. This is a culture that accepts outsiders with the realization that brainpower is what counts. . . . We have a culture that not only accepts new ideas and people, but also thrives on it."[10]

"How can I do it differently?" Remember? Disagreement is encouraged, but team play is a must. Diversity embeds different thinking as an integral part of the organization. Working in teams while fostering diversity is a Cisco strong point.

Doing More with Less

A number of examples exist where Cisco Systems shows its frugal side. Here are just a few.[11]

- All travel is compensated for up to coach class. No first-class tickets are compensated.
- Managers have work spaces that rarely exceed 150 square feet, and they are generally placed in interior locations without windows. Support staff get the window locations.

- Cisco's professional salaries are low compared to those paid by other companies in the area. Cisco compensates by providing longer-term stock option incentives instead of large salaries. In addition, 42 percent of Cisco's stock options are awarded to nonmanagers.[12]

- John Chambers' salary and benefits, excluding stock options, for fiscal year 2000 totaled approximately $1.3,[13] which doesn't seem like a small amount of money until compared with salaries of other CEOs running $20-billion-revenue companies. A large portion of his incentive program is tied up with stock options, which according to the September 29, 2000, annual shareholder announcement, as of July 29, 2000, total just over 25 million exercisable and unexercisable shares.

- The average 1998 management salary at Cisco was about 65 percent of the industry average. Unexercised stock options, on the other hand, for the average employee with over one year of employment represented over $125,000 in profit.

John Morgridge, current chairman of Cisco's board, while previously serving as CEO decided to cut overhead expenses by reducing the number of fruit juice varieties offered for free to Cisco employees through vending machines. When the reduction actions were taken, the Cisco e-mail system was tied up for days with people complaining about their "right to Snapple." The e-mail volume was so high that important e-mails from the Tokyo office were not getting answered. Within one week, the fruit juice variety was reinstated. Morgridge walked away from this experience with a strong respect for the power of cultural norms and learned never to offer something to employees in the form of a perks or a promise on a continuing basis, since taking it away might cause employee complaints and a loss of morale. This attitude also justifies his running a very frugal ship, which is critically important to the success of any company and mandatory for a start-up.

SCHEINMAN'S RULES

Here are Dan Scheinman's rules of thumb, as reported by *Fortune* magazine:

> Look for a bad deal. Any start-up should have one glaring mistake it's learned from. If the company hasn't done a bad deal, it's not daring enough. If it's done too many, it's, well, stupid.
>
> Role play. Go over the decisions that management made, and see if you'd come to the same conclusion. If so, the company's execs probably think the way you do and are likely to fit in fine.
>
> Move fast. There's no need to hang up on little issues that don't matter. . .
>
> Observe what's going on in the negotiations. "We've been involved in deals where people start negotiating for themselves," Scheinman says. "There was one deal where the engineering and business teams of a startup didn't show up at the same time, and each negotiated about how to screw the other guys."
>
> Don't be afraid to pull the plug at the last minute. The night before Cisco was going to buy Chipcom, a maker of Internet switching systems, Scheinman says, he couldn't sleep. "The board asked me if I thought we were doing the right thing, and I said no." Chipcom ended up being acquired by 3Com.[14]

CISCO'S ASSUMPTIONS

The basic assumption associated with Cisco's cultural compatibility requirement is that people who share the same values and purposes in life tend to work better together. Unfortunately, we tend to think that we can overcome any problems that might arise from cultural incompatibility, but often we find that these cultural differences reside at a deep level of our psyches.

Acquiring people who will not be compatible with the Cisco culture that will inevitably exist after the acquisition makes little

FROM INSIDE CISCO

The pain if you don't pick the winner is enormous, so we'll bet on the company that has momentum.[15]

—Dan Scheinman, senior vice president, Cisco Systems, commenting on the need for the target to have some level of success under its belt before Cisco acquires it

sense if one key ingredient of the acquisition is the retention of acquired personnel. Unhappy people will leave, or worse, make life miserable for the company that acquires them. Cisco chooses to avoid this issue by making cultural compatibility a qualification criterion.

PORTABILITY EVALUATION

This rule involves people, and people exist in all companies and industries. As a result, this rule is highly portable. Should the buyer have no intention of integrating the target into the buyer's cultural organization, then there may be some flexibility applied to this rule, knowing that any joint projects or meetings will likely have some sparks associated with them as the cultural differences raise their heads.

THE FINAL ANALYSIS

Is it possible to make a set of incompatible cultures cooperate to the point that an acquired company's personnel will be happy working as Cisco employees? Anything is possible, but few of us would take a bet on the side of a large number of incompatible acquired personnel remaining with Cisco any longer than is legally and minimally required. Why would anyone remain employed by a company offering a culture with which that person feels incompatible? They wouldn't, and will eventually leave.

Cisco takes a similar view: Why would Cisco want to acquire a company with a culture that conflicts with Cisco's? It wouldn't, and doesn't.

CHAPTER 7

MAKE IT A LONG-TERM WIN, TOO

I know it sounds corny, but it is true.
　　　　　　　—John Chambers, President and CEO, Cisco Systems

Cisco Rule #4

The acquisition must provide long-term benefits to Cisco's four major constituencies: employees, shareholders, customers, and business partners.

GOALS DETERMINE LONG-TERM WINS

All of us know of business decisions aimed at achieving a short-term business goal that have been to the longer-term detriment of the organization as a whole. MBA types refer to "goal congruence" as the intersection between company goals and employee motivations. When goal congruence exists, the company's employees are motivated to move their section of the corporation in the direction that meets the best overall goals of the organization. When a lack of goal congruence exists, employees do what benefits them personally the most while really not being concerned with the longer-term impact of their actions on the overall company.

　　　When goal congruence exists between a company and its shareholders, then the shareholders, are more willing to hold on to a stock as the company spends financial resources achieving its goals. When goal congruence exists between a company and its customers, the customers are more likely to work with the company to ensure that future products meet the customers' expectations to the highest possible degree. When goal congruence exists between a company and its partners, both parties take the steps needed to further the success of the partnership. Ensuring goal congruence is rarely a negative characteristic. Achieving and maintaining goal congruence is often a difficult process. And without goal congruence, longer-term strategic goals are more difficult to achieve.

Assume that a company has a goal of decreasing its inventory levels, which have been determined to be too high. A reward plan is provided to inventory control personnel that rewards them on the percentage reduction of inventory levels for a given accounting period without tying those inventory reductions to overall product shipments. The inventory levels may be reduced through decreased part purchases by procurement, thus achieving their short-term goal of reducing inventory and obtaining their bonuses. However, part shortages may result from the lower inventory levels; these shortages may interrupt finished product shipments and in turn cause overall company revenue to drop; and decreasing revenue is almost never a positive business sign.

The classic example of a lack of goal congruence occurs when an executive is rewarded based on the performance of the company's stock and not on some underlying operational criterion. Earnings can be increased in the short term by substantially cutting expenses while maintaining revenues, and this is a common way to cause a quick upturn in corporate earnings. But substantial cost cutting can undermine the underlying performance capabilities of the company as a whole. As a result, the short term looks more positive, but the longer-term prospects of the company have been diminished.

Balancing short-term interests against longer-term viability requires a blend of longer-term vision with shorter-term execution management, always remembering that the short-term actions of today eventually create the longer-term reality of tomorrow.

Cisco carefully considers the longer-term strategic impact of an acquisition on four groups that it calls the major constituencies: employees, shareholders, customers, and partners. Cisco will pass on an otherwise attractive acquisition if it deems the acquisition contrary to the strategic interests of any one of these constituencies. This statement makes common business sense, but amazingly company managers often overlook the strategic impact of their actions on these constituencies; their actions can only result in future tension if not viewed as beneficial by those constituencies.

This chapter takes a look at these four important areas of strategic consideration, outlining the Cisco approach to maintaining longer-term trust and goal congruence when considering a target acquisition.

BENEFITS TO EMPLOYEES

Cisco may pay over $20 million per acquired employee while already having a substantial investment in its own personnel. Cisco believes that the most valuable assets acquired with a company purchase are the personnel. Losing these people in the short term would seriously undermine the expected return on investment associated with the acquisition, as would the loss of these people in the longer term. Remember that the intention is not only to purchase the existing product lines but also to purchase the next generation or two of products that these people will develop after joining Cisco. These people must be kept around.

Cisco deals with the short-term issues immediately after the acquisition is finalized, and this portion of the integration process is covered in detail in Chapter 12. This section looks at Cisco's longer-term employee retention procedures.

There are a few attractive aspects to being an employee of a growing, dynamic company, especially if you live in Silicon Valley. For starters, longer-term employment is not considered a norm or a right in Silicon Valley. People tend to transfer between companies every few years, with some believing that remaining with a company for a longer period of time is the mark of someone who is stagnated from a career development perspective. With a new start-up frequently appearing around the corner, there is always some new temptation trying to lure solid professionals to take a chance at "making it big." And many people take that chance and do become wealthy within only a few years. Many other opportunities, however, turn out to be less profitable than initially expected; the "founder" stock may become worthless. Providing Silicon Valley personnel with a blend of job security and credible stock appreciation benefits is certain to attract solid personnel and keep those acquired around for a while to see how the merger works out. This is essentially the Cisco approach.

Cisco grows revenues at incredible rates. It is one thing to grow a $10-million-revenue company by 40 percent in a year. It is completely another to grow an $18-billion-revenue company by 40 percent. This growth creates a huge demand for management personnel, which, in turn, creates attractive professional advancement opportunities for existing personnel.

Professional advancement is simply more likely in a growing business environment than in one that is static. A large number of career advancement positions open up with growing companies that are more likely to be filled with internal personnel than with outsiders since the internal personnel are known entities who already understand the corporate culture. These internal personnel can typically come functionally up to speed more quickly than an outsider simply because they already understand the Cisco way.

Providing personnel with stock options creates an incentive for employees to consider not only the short-term impact of their decisions, but also the longer-term stock appreciation impact of those decisions. Employee stock ownership is often symbolic at companies where the likelihood of future stock appreciation is minimal. But even in these circumstances employees often refer to themselves as "shareholders" or "owners" and take a pride of ownership in being shareholders. I can't even count the number of times I have heard "the ownership motivation" speech in discussions with Home Depot or United Air Lines employees. I remember several times, in my production engineering days, when line personnel would hold my toes to the fire with respect to documentation updating deadlines. My delaying of documentation would occasionally hold up their production activities, thereby costing the company, and them as shareholders, money. Stock ownership, in my opinion, really helps to create a spirit of camaraderie along with peer pressure that is truly hard to duplicate with almost any other incentives.

Cisco provides stock options to most of its employees, with 40 percent of Cisco stock options held by people without managerial responsibility.[1] When a company is acquired, its existing stock options are converted to Cisco stock options, which usually provide a much higher future appreciation opportunity than those of the start-up on its own. These options vest over a period of between four and five years.

People at Cisco do take the stock ownership and appreciation opportunity seriously and personally. "If I do my job right it will support the stock. If I screw up and the stock goes down, people will come around and beat on me with hammers," says one employee.[2]

In fact, Cisco uses immediate vesting of options as a heavily weighted disqualification criterion when looking at an acquisition prospect. Should acquired personnel's stock options vest immediately upon the sale, then their incentive to remain with Cisco after the acquisition is reduced. They may leave for another start-up where they can obtain another option. After all, the options from their last company are now fully vested, they own the stock, and it is now in good hands (Cisco's). It will perform well with or without the acquired employees' involvement. If the intention is to keep the employees around after the acquisition for at least one new generation of product, then they should be motivated to remain with Cisco for at least two years.

"Golden handcuffs instead of golden parachutes" is a common saying from Cisco management when referring to acquired stock option plans. Key acquired personnel will also be asked to sign a two-year noncompete agreement. In essence, this keeps them from leaving Cisco for 24 months, which, oddly enough, is about the amount of time it takes to develop the next generation of product. Putting this into practical terms, Cisco sets vesting over a several-year period, which means acquired employees may not instantly become rich when the purchase finalizes. In addition, they sign a two-year noncompete that keeps them from earning a living elsewhere in their industry. With no income and no immediate vesting, the employees have a strong incentive to remain at Cisco and make it work for at least the two years of the noncompete agreement. At that point, they either will beCiscoized and like where they are or will know that it is a bad fit and move on. In fact, Cisco has a "mutual separation policy" that works like a no-fault divorce in that employees who are not happy or do not fit the Cisco cultural mold leave for other opportunities. Around 5 percent of employees leave on this basis annually.

FROM INSIDE CISCO

Employees who have just been acquired can be very uncomfortable. . . . They've got to see a future. They've got to see a culture they want to be a part of. They have got to see an opportunity to really do what they were doing before or even more.[3]

—*John Chambers, Cisco president and CEO*

So how successful is Cisco at retaining acquired personnel? In 1999, Cisco had experienced a voluntary attrition rate for acquired company personnel of 6 percent per year over the prior two-year period. Chambers claims that the industry norm within two years of an acquisition is 40 to 80 percent and feels that, based on these numbers, Cisco does a very good job of retaining acquired personnel.[4]

BENEFITS TO SHAREHOLDERS

Benefits to shareholders are fairly straightforward to understand, especially since Cisco does not pay a dividend. Shareholders ask this basic question: "Did the stock appreciate in value between the time when I purchased the stock and today?" This appreciation is compared to the other possible investment opportunities available to investors during the period in which they held the stock in question.

Anyone holding Cisco stock purchased in early 2000 is likely not to treat Cisco stock as a solid investment in early 2001. At the time of this writing the stock has hit a 52-week low of around $13 and people are predicting that it will go even lower. If you are someone who purchased the stock in early 2000 when it was in the $80 range you are undoubtedly wondering whether holding on to your Cisco stock was the right thing to do. But if you are someone who bought Cisco in early 1998 and watched your stock price climb 600 percent or so within a two-year period, you were absolutely thrilled with the way Cisco was being managed. By the way, Cisco frequently used to point out that $1,000 invested in 1990 in Cisco stock would have been worth $100,000 in 1997.

Keeping shareholders happy is an art form that presidents and CEOs must develop. In general, investors like to see increasing revenues, increasing earnings per share, and decreasing expenses as a historical starting point for determining a stock's performance to date. Watching CEOs during their quarterly earnings reporting periods clearly underlines the need for a president or CEO to be in large part a salesperson. Chambers is certainly that.

Investors will look at the expected future performance of the company to determine the possibility of future stock appreciation. If revenues are expected to decline over the next 12 months, then price-to-earnings multiples will likely drop since the forward-looking projections are not as rosy as they appeared in the past. A drop in the price-to-earnings ratio brings down the market price for a stock, which means that existing shareholders will lose some of their investments, whether real or paper losses. A drop in share price that extends over several quarters usually indicates a company under severe pressure to perform operationally in such a way that share prices increase.

How does this tie into a discussion about acquisitions? Remember that buying companies uses corporate (shareholder) assets to purchase the target company. Those assets may be any combination of cash, stock, or other financial consideration. Investors are wondering when they can expect to recoup the purchase price. If the buyer cannot make a solid case that the money committed as part of the purchase will provide a reasonable investment return to shareholders, then shareholders have every right to question the reasonableness of the purchase.

Chambers likes to refer to acquisition returns in a way that reflects the added products, revenues, and market capitalization that resulted from that purchase. And, if you think about it, this approach provides a fairly good basis for evaluating whether a purchase was justified. In 1997 Chambers was quoted as saying, "Our acquisitions in local area network switching cost us $500 million and now contribute more than $1 billion in revenues-or more than $8 billion to our market cap. So our strategy has worked out well."[5]

The $8 billion number is based on Cisco's market capitalization at the time being eight times its revenues. Thus, if a product area contributed $1 billion in revenue that is directly attributable to the company purchased then each dollar of incremental sales revenue adds $8 in market capitalization, using this multiplier. Dividing that total market capitalization increase by the number of outstanding shares provides the amount of increase that each share experienced as a result of this product line development.

According to the Cisco acquisition approach, companies are purchased partially for their existing products but mostly for the personnel and the technology products that they will create in the future. Cisco tries to have the purchase at least earn back the purchase price within a three-year period.

For example, Grand Junction Networks, Inc., a Fremont, California, company purchased by Cisco in September 1995 for around $400 million in Cisco stock (5 million shares)[6] manufactured switching systems. At the time of purchase, Grand Junction Networks had 85 employees and projected annual sales of $32 million. As of March 1997 (18 months later), sales of products directly derived from the Grand Junction Networks purchase had increased by 800 percent to

$256 million! According to Howard Charney, former CEO of Grand Junction, "There were 40-plus millionaires created [with the purchase]. . . . Cisco projected we'd do $119 million the first year. We did $124 million. We'd never have done that on our own."[7]

By the way, Cisco stock closed at $68 per share on September 27, 1995, and closed on March 3, 1997 at $54¼, with a 2:1 split along the way, making that closing price the equivalent of $108½. This represents an increase of $40½, or roughly 60 percent, over the 17-month period. Not a shabby return by almost any investment standard, especially when you realize that the Nasdaq, over the same time period, increased from 1,026.54 to 1,311.18 (+284.64) or 27.72 percent.[8]

"The way we measure the success of small-to-medium-size acquisitions is straightforward. Within three years, we would like to generate in revenue what we paid for the company. If we do that, then the acquisition was a good, solid base hit. If we do more than that—say we do it in two years or even in one year—then the acquisition was a home run or a grand slam. Crescendo was a grand slam," says John Chambers.[9]

BENEFITS TO CUSTOMERS

The entire motivation for Cisco to do what it does is to further foster its relationship to its customers. It would certainly make no sense at all to pursue an acquisition that did not benefit Cisco's customers in the long run, and Cisco makes a point of considering the impact of its acquisition decisions on its customer base. A lot of this book revolves, in one way or another, around Cisco's customer commitment philosophy, so I will not go into it in this section in great detail. But dynamic marketplaces apply pressures to customers and vendors that are typically not present in more static marketplaces.

Technology changes make obsolete not only products for vendors but also existing products installed by customers. Obvious as this may sound, it is the customer's side of the obsolescence situation that eventually drives the vendors. But vendors that change products quickly can put their customers in an awkward position. Any customer that has spent a great deal of money on a specific technology only to have it discontinued by its primary vendor will likely feel betrayed by that vendor.

A vendor that does not keep up with technology trends with products incorporating newer technologies and other value-enhancing features is also not doing its customers a favor. Cisco believes that networking customers would rather deal with a single vendor as an end-to-end supplier than deal with many suppliers. If Cisco does not evolve its products and technologies, then customers, driven by the need to remain competitive in their respective marketplaces, will look to other vendors for the products and support they need. This situation could force a predominantly single-supplier customer into diversifying its vendor mix, which inevitably complicates the customer's life.

Should a vendor find itself on shaky financial ground, it will also find it more difficult to close major business deals with customers since the customer may, rightfully, believe that the vendor can go out of business. Customers who have invested large sums of money into mission-critical systems must ensure the future financial viability of the vendor; otherwise networks, products, companies, and careers could later be compromised. Cisco makes a point of keeping financially healthy while also providing customers with a contemporary product mix. Even through its difficult early calendar 2001 period, Cisco has maintained nearly $5 billion in cash on its balance sheet.

Cisco makes sure, before any acquisition, that the acquired company shares Cisco's intense customer-driven focus. Long-term benefits to customers are obtained when Cisco can consistently, year after year, deliver at a high level in all critical areas. If personnel are acquired who do not share this intense customer commitment, then the customer focus may erode over time. It may not happen all at once, but may start first in pockets of problems that can eventually infect the rest of the organization. This lack of focus could well cost Cisco its customer relationships and subsequent orders—a losing situation for all constituencies involved.

BENEFITS TO BUSINESS PARTNERS

The Cisco business model makes extensive use of business partnerships. Partnership, in this context, should not to be assumed to have the same meaning as a legal partnership. It is more of an alliance between separate business entities. Cisco is motivated to create these partnerships as a way of ensuring that its customers get the services and products they need from credible providers, while also keeping Cisco focused on its core areas of expertise. This is the basic implementation of the Cisco horizontal instead of vertical business approach: Keep Cisco heavily focused on its core competencies (networking), and let others provide the ancillary services and products that, if provided by Cisco, could distract the company from its core business.

Cisco was faced with an acquisition decision in 1999 regarding International Network Services (INS), a Cisco partner. Cisco already had an 8 percent ownership of INS, which provided network design, planning, implementation, and maintenance services. In 1999, INS had more than 2,000 employees, 37 offices, and $300 million in annual revenues obtained with a $31 million net income. INS had 200 Cisco-certified engineers (out of a total of 1,200). INS referred its customers to Cisco's products, and Cisco referred its customers to INS for consulting services. The relationship was only a little over a year old but working well when word came down that Lucent Technologies Inc., one of Cisco's biggest competitors, intended to purchase INS. If Cisco did not act quickly and purchase INS it could lose INS to a competitor.

FROM INSIDE CISCO

If you are the leading arms maker, why would you want to buy an army?[10]

> —*Doug Alred, senior vice president at Cisco, commenting on the rationale not to purchase INS*

A major conflict issue related to the purchase was that buying INS could represent a shift for Cisco with respect to its horizontal business model. Purchasing INS would represent a step in the direction of vertical integration and put in doubt Cisco's commitment to the other horizontal partnership relationships it already had in place.

Much of successful business is based on trust. Partners in an agreement must believe that the other party intends, in good faith, to comply not only with the letter of an agreement but also with its intent. I believe that legal agreements spell out, in legalese, what the parties have already agreed to and that a contract should rarely be pulled out for review except with the intention of verifying agreed-upon conditions. No legal agreement can force someone to be enthusiastically motivated over an extended period of time. Only a shared understanding of the mutual benefits and a shared understanding of the intent of an agreement can make that happen. Cisco's horizontal business model was a tacit assumption in its partnership agreements existing at the time of this decision. Purchasing INS could put doubts into the minds of other business partners and cause a ripple effect of uncertainty that could affect not only other partners directly but indirectly customers as well.

Cisco determined that this particular purchase, although particularly tempting on a number of fronts, could jeopardize the partnership relationships that Cisco already had in place. It would run contrary to the fundamental rules of Cisco acquisition. Cisco passed on the purchase of INS, and Lucent did indeed make the purchase in September 1999 for $3.7 billion.

CISCO'S ASSUMPTIONS

Cisco's belief in the Internet ecosystem is intrinsic to its very operation. The belief that the Internet truly creates a new business model that is best addressed with a horizontal, not vertical, business model is a fundamental assumption to any discussion of Cisco's acquisition practices. Also fundamental is the belief that companies must want to cooperate with each other if any type of alliance/partnership is to succeed. Undermining that trust in any substantial way can jeopardize not only that particular partnership but set a questionable example for other partnerships, potentially undermining their trust as well.

Alliances and partnerships are relatively fragile relationships that must be cultivated and protected if they are to survive. It is a little like the difference between living together and getting married with children. A business alliance can be broken off with relative ease as compared to the steps involved with extracting a company that has already been fully integrated into the buyer's organization.

Notice also that this partnership emphasis, supported by Cisco's passing on the INS purchase, also implies that Cisco expects to continue the cultivation of additional partnership relationships. Steps must be taken, and consideration given, to ensure that the longer-term success of these partnerships is preserved and fostered. Losing these longer-term partnership arrangements might force Cisco into a vertical business model, which it does not believe to be the best way to address its particular customers' needs. In addition, Cisco is not managerially or culturally oriented toward a vertical business model. Team spirit, consensus building, and cooperation are intrinsic to the Cisco management philosophy. Heavily vertically integrated organizations can often create factions that do not foster, and often interfere with, team psychology.

Other fundamental assumptions are: (1) that providing a longer-term financial benefit to shareholders keeps the stock from being volatile, providing a more attractive investment opportunity; (2) that customers want to work with a company that has the customers' longer-term interests at heart, implying explicitly and tacitly that the vendor is in this relationship for the long run; (3) that providing a stable yet stimulating work environment with large employee income potential is an excellent way to retain employee talent and attract new talent.

These assumptions simply make sense to me, and most managers would agree that any business that adheres to them should benefit in the long run. Agreeing that these assumptions make sense is one thing. Actually creating an environment within which these assumptions become manifest is something completely different and heavily dependent on the people and industries involved.

PORTABILITY EVALUATION

Cisco has a unique problem in that it is a leader in a technology area that reinvents itself on "Internet time" while simultaneously decreasing time and space as experienced on a daily basis. A browser can click and view information from the other side of the globe simply because all the technology/networking links between the user's system and the Internet server are working properly. If some point in that connection has a problem, the user will want an almost instant solution to the problem. The network provider will expect its vendor to be there in the correction of the problem should the network provider not be able to correct the problem using internal resources.

Here is the key point: Asia may be only a click away on my browser screen, but it still takes almost a full day's plane ride to get there in person. This is an industry that, out of necessity, uses its own technology to maintain and fix its own technology. Sitting in California, a vendor's support person must be able to assess and correct a problem on another continent without ever leaving his or her chair. Support plans, backup, reliability, and redundancy plans are designed specifically to address the mission-critical needs of the users of Internetworking equipment. Partnerships work very well in this environment since they are predominantly based on international and de facto standards.

Several years ago I had the opportunity to train a group of Russians on a Microsoft Windows NT Server 4.0. The entire lecture portion of the class was translated from English into Russian. When we got to the labs, they understood everything even though the operating system was displayed in English. The layout and iconized display was all they needed to be able to effectively navigate and configure this operating system. They could not order lunch in English, but they could configure a local area network in English. I thought this profound and likely an indicator of the future we can all look forward to, if you are in high technology.

If, on the other hand, you are building large refinery plants in a foreign country with a depressed domestic economy, then a vertical business model may well be the more effective approach. Having control over the design, construction, and maintenance stages will likely speed up the implementation of the refinery while also ensuring a higher degree of compliance with expected design criteria. Having to depend on local companies for critical-stage items may or may not be the right approach; the determination must be made on a case-by-case basis. If the local economy companies do not exist so that a partnership can be feasibly implemented, then the vertical business model may be the best, and possibly only, approach.

Shareholder issues also vary between industries since certain industries have different investment time windows from that of high technology. Most investors do not expect an older economy stock such as a steel manufacturer to exhibit the same type of financial performance as a Cisco Systems or Microsoft. These older economy stocks are less volatile, as indicated by a beta that is often less than one or even negative in some cases. My latest check of Cisco's beta (June 23, 2001) as presented on a Standard & Poor's Stock Report put it in the range of 1.83. Highly volatile stocks make investors happy when times are good but also make investors miserable when times are bad since volatility works both ways. Maintaining an optimistic yet realistic future projection while growing revenue at 40 percent or more annually and maintaining a secure set of financial statements at the same time is a balancing act that Cisco has historically managed. But more is also expected of Cisco simply because it has the potential to deliver on those expectations.

Keeping employees around is also tricky with a volatile stock when employees view a large part of their financial compensation as being derived from their stock options. These options have a strike (purchase) price that is often based on the market value of the stock at the time that the option was issued. If the stock price drops substantially, as was seen with Cisco's stock in early 2001, then employees may find themselves the owners of a stock option plan that merely enables them to purchase Cisco stock for more than they can sell it for on the open market. These types of options are referred to as being "under water" and are really of little value to the employee, unless the employee is led to believe that the stock will recover within what the employee believes to be a reasonable time frame.

Alliances and partnerships only work effectively between parties that are willing to cooperate to achieve a mutually agreed upon and beneficial common goal. If one party has a "my way or the highway" or a serious "not invented here" temperament, then the likelihood of the partnership working out over the long run is small. This tightly controlled type of company may be forced into a vertical business model so that it can maintain the level of control that it believes it needs over each step of the customer value delivery process. In certain industries this may well be accepted. In fact, this used to be the norm for the high-technology arena up until the ubiquitous adoption of standards by customers as a fundamental criterion for product purchase acceptance.

Complying with industry standards enabled the customers to purchase products from any number of vendors as opposed to being locked into a specific, proprietary technology from a specific vendor, such as IBM, Honeywell, or Wang. The adoption of open standards released the lock that these vendors had on customers and forced vendors to cooperate with each other in servicing customers. Vendors began to specialize in specific product or service areas, developing a very deep yet narrow expertise in that area. Partnering with other companies enabled these smaller companies to provide a high level of expertise to customers without having to take the financial and managerial risks associated with merging everything into a single company. Customers win in that they get highly qualified people working on each stage of their required processes and likely have a central point of contact for overall project management.

Until late 2000 Cisco enjoyed the luxury of having a leading market share in growing markets during a booming economy. Cisco's historical stock and financial performance shows that Cisco employees and shareholders benefited from this success. Few companies and industries have experienced this type of fortuitous opportunity over an extended period of time. Companies cannot pattern their own business models after Cisco's if the external marketplace or industry-specific business models cannot support them.

With that said, it is difficult to imagine a time when considering the positive or negative strategic impact of an acquisition on a

120

buyer's or seller's employees, shareholders, customers, or partners would work to the detriment of the transaction.

THE FINAL ANALYSIS

Before making a purchase, Cisco evaluates the possible longer-term impact of the acquisition on its employees, shareholders, customers, and partners. If the purchase cannot be reasonably shown to provide a positive strategic return to each of these constituencies, then Cisco looks seriously at passing on the acquisition. After all, if the purchase does not provide any longer-term benefits, then it is really a short-term transaction. It may be okay to use a stopgap measure to quickly fill a hole in the product mix. But repeatedly using stopgap purchases with minimal likelihood of longer-term derived benefits runs the risk of diverting the company into managing a number of hot immediate projects that distract from the company's core operation.

Keeping customers happy over the long term is always excellent news in that the future becomes much more predictable when there is a stable customer base. A predictable future enables more accurate financial forecasting, which is always appreciated by shareholders. When those shareholders are employees holding stock options, a more stable stock performance expectation leads to lower turnover and higher motivation. And a combination of the previously listed three constituencies makes it easier to attract motivated, successful partners who want to work with another winner. Purchasing a company that provides a short-term fix while jeopardizing these longer-term strategic relationships just simply doesn't make business sense.

CHAPTER 8

CLOSER IS BETTER

If you are doing a large acquisition, the minute you get on an air-plane, you've got a problem.[1]
—John Chambers, President and CEO, Cisco Systems

Cisco Rule #5

Any large acquisition target must be geographically located close to a major Cisco facility.

In an age when technology makes time and distance of little relevance with respect to information retrieval, it is seductive to believe that human beings have adapted to the technology as fast as the technology itself has evolved.

Human beings function as a group through communication. And communication between human beings happens on many different levels. As much as 80 percent of our communication occurs nonverbally through mechanisms such as body language. Body language is simply not viewable through the telephone, e-mail, or other online communication means. Even videoconferencing, as effective as it has become in recent years, still does not provide the rich means of communication of a face-to-face meeting. If you think this is not true, think about the difference you would experience between dating someone in person or using videoconferencing. I know which I would prefer.

Chambers contends that a necessary rule for target selection is that, for large acquisitions, the target must be geographically colocated with a major Cisco facility. This chapter takes a look at Cisco's implementation of this rule, the assumptions that underlie it, a rationale for its validity, and how portable it is to other industries.

CISCO RULES

In a nutshell, this is Chambers' version of the geographic proximity rule.

"Geography is key. If you are doing a large acquisition, the minute you get on an airplane, you've got a problem. It is different if you are doing an engineering or technology acquisition, because those can be remote. But if you are combining two large companies and the center of manufacturing or marketing is in San Jose, California, and you are in Boston, what future do you have? It is very limited."[2]

Stated another way by Chambers: " If you're doing large acquisitions, you need to have geographic proximity to your current operations. Otherwise, you'll have the head of finance in one location, the CEO in another, the chairman in another, the head of sales in another, the head of marketing in another, and you'll actually create the politics forever, in terms of the two different cultures, and you never get the efficiencies."[3]

Cisco has its headquarters in San Jose, California (Silicon Valley), along with several manufacturing facilities. It also has major operations in Research Triangle, North Carolina (near Raleigh), and Chelmsford, Massachusetts (near Boston). Cisco has performed most of its acquisitions, larger or small, in the Silicon Valley area of California. From the latest to the earliest, these are the acquisitions to date at the time of this writing that were purchased for over $1 billion: ArrowPoint Communications ($5.7 billion, May 2000, Acton, Massachusetts, outside of Boston); Pirelli Optical Systems ($2.15 billion, December 1999, Milan, Italy); Cerent Corporation ($6.9 billion, August 1999, Petaluma, California, north of San Francisco); GeoTel Communications Corporation ($2 billion, April 1999, Lowell, Massachusetts, outside of Boston); and Strata-Com ($4.666 billion, April 1996, San Jose, California).

Notice that to date, with the exception of the Pirelli purchase, Cisco has remained true to its rule of acquiring only those companies that are close to a major Cisco facility. Some reports contend that the Pirelli acquisition hasn't met expectations. In particular, the market for Pirelli's products is reported to have doubled from 1999 to early 2000, while Pirelli's share of that market is reported to have dropped from 5 percent to 1 percent. Cisco is also reported to have started selling some of the Pirelli assets to help finance the acquisition, which does not appear to be going smoothly.[4]

ASSUMPTIONS SUMMARY

Different kinds of mergers required different approaches. Different company types add another level of variability with respect to how an acquisition is best handled.

There are really four different motivations for a merger: diversification, stronger market position, company turnaround, and technology acquisition. Cisco is primarily interested in the technology acquisition type and specifically avoids the diversification type, preferring to focus on its core competencies and to expand horizontally to meet customer requirements. Cisco does not acquire companies as a financial tool where the acquired company is treated as a stand-alone investment. Cisco could be construed as pursuing the market position enhancement acquisition since some of the companies it has acquired, such as Crescendo, enabled Cisco to enter a new market quickly and with considerable strength. Since most of the companies involved were young, thriving company they were not in need of a turnaround approach.

FROM INSIDE CISCO

Geographic proximity. That is always a tough one. If you look at some of the acquisitions that haven't worked out as well, geography plays a key role.[5]

—*Barry Eggers, former Cisco business development leader and now venture capitalist, commenting on the negative impact of geographic separation*

Once again, overall corporate direction drives the Cisco acquisition strategy and dictates the types of acquisitions that Cisco will pursue. Given the intense focus on technology acquisition, Cisco must place a strong emphasis on personnel integration since the people who designed the current version of technology products are required to design the next generation that will be offered under Cisco's label. Given this emphasis on personnel integration, cultural compatibility between Cisco and its targets is a requirement.

If, on the other hand, a company were acquiring another firm as a financial investment with the full intention of leaving it operating as a separate, stand-alone organization, then personnel integration becomes a low-priority requirement. It is very possible that acquired employees may never have direct exposure to the buyer's organization, and postacquisition may look very similar to preacquisition from the acquired employee perspective.

Integrating corporations requires the integration of people. People live where they live for a reason, and the integration of a company that is located substantially distant from a Cisco facility would require that the acquired facility either become a Cisco outpost, which complicates the Cisco operational model, or be closed down, resulting in the relocation or possible loss of many acquired personnel.

Summa Four, acquired in July 1998 for $118 million in stock, is an example of the difficulties associated with relocating acquired personnel. Summa Four was situated in Manchester, New Hampshire (just over the state border near Lowell, Massachusetts, which is northwest of Boston), and had around 200 employees at the time of purchase. Cisco has a research location in Chelmsford, Massachusetts, also near Lowell, that had around 1,000 employees at the time of the Summa Four acquisition. The Summa Four engineers (65 of them) were reluctant to relocate their work facility even the short distance from Manchester to Chelmsford, around 40 miles. Cisco let them remain in their Manchester facility with the understanding that their development efforts on the upcoming Project Alpha, a major reason for the acquisition, would continue in tight alignment with the work of the Cisco Chelmsford development personnel.[6]

Cisco ended the 1998 fiscal year with revenues of $8,459 billion and over 14,000 employees, meaning that the Summa Four acquisition was not large by either a financial or a personnel measure with respect to the overall Cisco organization. And even this small acquisition had its problems with respect to relocating the key personnel, the engineers, into a locally operated Cisco facility. Assuming, for analysis purposes, that Cisco intended primarily to acquire the 65 engineering personnel, with the others coming along for the ride. Then Cisco paid $590,000 per employee if all 200 employees are considered, and over $1.8 million per engineer if only the 65 engineers are considered. Losing even a few engineers by mandating a relocation would have been an expensive way for Cisco to force its way on acquired personnel, especially at $1.8 million per lost employee. And losing engineers also means that their expertise is lost when designing the next generation of products, which is why Summa Four was acquired in the first place.

The Summa Four example shows that acquiring even a small number of employees will come with its own set of complexities. When a StrataCom with 1,200+ employees is acquired for $4.67 billion (around $389,000 per employee) it is clear that retaining employees while also obtaining the highest possible level of acquired employee productivity in the postmerger environment is important. Without this retention and ensuing productivity a successful return on investment becomes more difficult at best. Clashing of large corporate cultures that can result from a merger of equals or leaving a large, established entity as a remote outpost can engender an "us versus them" attitude toward the buyer (Cisco). Having large acquisitions geographically located close to a Cisco facility enables acquired personnel to be personally brought into the Cisco fold. They can be welcomed with personalized training packages, mentors, and other human touches that remove uncertainty from the process and provide a more individual touch. When the acquired company is far away from a Cisco facility, it is simply more difficult to drop by and see how things are going. And it is more difficult to have acquired personnel drop by Cisco to get a personal sense of the buying organization.

COMMUNICATION LEVELS

Communication theory provides some basis for understanding this relationship between proximity and communication effectiveness.

Communication media range in their characteristics from a lean medium, such as a mailed letter, to a rich one, such as face-to-face interaction. Notice that a lean media mode (a letter) does not allow for modification of what is communicated based on the reaction of the recipient of the message. A rich media mode, such as face-to-face, does provide the party with a way of modifying the message and/or its presentation based on the other party's reaction.

Communication theory states that the more risk associated with a message by the recipient of the message, the greater the need for a rich communication medium. If the message is a simple one with little implied risk, such as the changing of a telephone extension number, then the level of perceived risk on the part of the message recipient is low. A memo or e-mail covering this fact will likely serve nicely for communicating the information with minimal complication. If, on the other hand, the message is one related to the closure of a production facility of the relocation of corporate headquarters, then there is little doubt that the recipients of this message will see extensive risk to them and their livelihood embedded in this message. A rich communication medium such as a face-to-face meeting is called for when delivering this type of message. Closing a plant with an e-mail would almost universally be perceived as a heartless move, and this version of communication theory provides a construct within which to understand this reaction.

Highly structured, highly routine activities are associated with low-risk activities in that the outcome of the activity is fairly well defined and anticipated. For this reason it is possible to place a manufacturing plant in a remote geographic location with acceptable results. The manufacturing process, the outcome of the process, and the criteria for acceptance are well-defined and repeatable. But try to produce a new product that is still in the late stages of development at a remote production facility, and anxiety levels will increase along with a likely decrease in project success. The product is still not finalized, there is variability in the manufacturing process, and the risks associated with shipping a product that does not meet design specifications are substantial. Using this rationale, many companies perform their initial product runs using in-house facilities, defining the manufacturing processes with in-house personnel and a more rich communication mechanism. Once the process is defined and repeatable (low risk), then it can more reliably be shipped off to a remote manufacturing facility.

Geographic proximity plays a role in the prior example in that the manufacturing process changes can be worked out on the floor by simply calling the proper engineers, managers, or other involved personnel as issues arise. Working out this level of rich contact between, for example, an Asian manufacturing facility and an American engineering team is simply not possible, no matter how much time people spend on planes.

Acquiring a company creates a risk situation in the minds of the acquired personnel in that their fates, once in their own control, are now in the hands of another company, the buyer (Cisco). They will have questions about their jobs, their products, their daily work routines, their customers, their fellow employees, and any number of other areas that are specifically related to the acquired company and its prior cultural norms. If the target is a smaller company with only a few years of history, its culture may not be rigidly defined and acquired personnel may well be open to integrating into a larger, more established, and, historically, potentially more lucrative Cisco environment. It will likely be more open to assimilating into the Cisco culture with minimal disruption.

And even this relatively simple situation can be complicated by a lack of believable information on the part of the target's personnel. Cisco, with the best of intentions, could be working in what it feels is the best interest of the acquired personnel. But if Cisco communicates its intentions using a lean medium, such as e-mail, and not in person, the message may be completely misinterpreted by acquired personnel, causing perceived risk levels to rise, fear to manifest, and distrust to enter the transaction. By having Cisco people on-site at the target's facility, not only is there a more rich and familiar communication mechanism back to Cisco's facility, but also the target's personnel get firsthand experience with Cisco personnel. Brainstorming can happen at the watercooler. Personalities can be assessed over lunch, dinner, or drinks. The possibility of a miscommunication causing major disruption of the integration process decreases when a richer communication medium is used.

Cultural assimilation becomes mandatory when looking at a large acquisition, for without the assimilation the company will likely remain divided along historical company lines. The more geographically remote the buyer and seller are to each other, the less rich interaction can occur and the more likely it is that the acquired company's culture will remain intact. If the intent of the acquisition is to keep the acquired culture intact, then distance may work to the merger's benefit. But if cultural assimilation is desired, then the distance will likely be counterproductive to that assimilation.

The value of rich, interpersonal contact when assimilating an acquired company's personnel cannot be overestimated. The buyer must place personnel at the target's site during the period of assimilation. The target must place some of its key personnel at the buyer's (Cisco's) site during the period of assimilation. A small acquisition will require a small number of people to smooth this transition. A large acquisition will require a much larger group of people from both sides of the merger, and this personnel interaction is more easily and reliably accomplished when buyer and seller are geographically close to each other. It is easy to hop in a car and drive 45 minutes to the other site. This type of trip can be done at the drop of a hat. Flying from California to Miami to deal with a problem is not only expensive but time-consuming and simply cannot be done at the drop of a hat.

Alan Warms, an executive with Participate.com, provides his perspective on geographic proximity in a *Chicago Tribune* article. He is talking about proximity as it pertains to a start-up situation, and I contend that acquiring a company creates a mini-start-up situation in which a lot of the rules outlined by Warms still apply.

> An executive team—or any team for that matter—really shines when the players can almost read each other's minds. They begin to anticipate each other's moves. They don't always agree, but they know how to disagree. . . . A CEO will want proximity with his team. In that way, he can call an impromptu meeting to seek advice or stop by someone's office to brainstorm. . . . That type if interaction is difficult when the team is divided by geography. Telecommuting still requires a person to maintain a heavy travel schedule to stay on top of developments such as personnel issues, new business initiatives, client wins and proposals. . . . As time progresses, telecommuting might work, but only after he [the CEO] has established some chemistry between his company's key players.[7]

Or as Chambers is quoted as saying early on in this chapter, "If you are doing a large acquisition, the minute you get on an airplane, you've got a problem." Making a large acquisition work requires a high level of communication. Geographic proximity simply makes that process easier to accomplish.

▬▬ LIMITATIONS DISCUSSION

An obvious limitation of this geographic proximity rule is that life is not always accommodating enough as to place our desired target companies within driving distance of the buyer's facilities. Abiding by this rule means that a buyer may have to pass on an acquisition that would otherwise appear attractive.

Another limitation is implied by the assimilation assumption that underlies the Cisco approach. A buyer with a highly structured culture may want to acquire another company of comparable size that is more entrepreneurially oriented, with the express intent of not integrating the two cultures. Under these circumstances, close geographic proximity could work to the detriment of the intent of the acquisition in that the structured culture of the buyer could "infect" the free spirit of the target and undermine the very value initially purchased. Buyer and seller must, for this example, ensure that the best practices of each company are exploited and cooperation at the corporate levels maintained. At some level, effective and rich communication will be required to make this type of situation work or the target and buyer could find themselves working at cross-purposes, or simply not working together at all.

▬▬ PORTABILITY EVALUATION

This geographic proximity selection criterion is highly portable between industries and companies. It is most heavily based on human nature and not so much based on the technologies or specific corporate cultures involved. The geographic proximity requirement is also heavily based on the motivations for the merger, which are again fairly standardized by acquisition type and not specific to Cisco's methodology.

For example, if the intent of an acquisition is to hold the target for a while and then resell it, fully integrating the acquired company with the buyer's does not make sense. The upheaval and expense associated with the acquisition's integration will simply be repeated when the integrated entity is again resold in the near future. Cisco does not perform acquisitions with the intention of reselling the companies. It performs an acquisition with the intention of acquiring the target's technology, people, and products. Those acquired assets are then offered as if they came directly from Cisco, making full integration a high priority. Notice that Cisco's ultimate objective with respect to the acquisition drives everything else surrounding its acquisition approach.

The geographic proximity criterion stems from Cisco's expressed intention of fully integrating the target. If full integration is not required by another company working within another industry, then geographic proximity may not be as important a target selection criterion. But if full integration of the target is a desired result from the acquisition, then geographic proximity should be considered an important selection criterion by all buyers.

Remember that ultimately you are always dealing with people when buying a company. People work best together when they share a common culture, set of values, and overall company vision. If melding of buyer and seller cultures is a requirement of the acquisition, then more "face time" with each other will foster that melding. It is simply easier to get more face time when the buyer and seller are geographically close to each other. The larger the acquisition, the greater the challenges involved with melding the organizations and the greater the need for more face time, a need that increases the desire to be geographically close to each other. Notice that this requirement is based simply on the particular needs of the acquisition and not necessarily on anything specific to Cisco or its industry.

THE FINAL ANALYSIS

Any time that interpersonal relationships are required and there is a level of perceived risk by either party, a richer mode of communication is desirable. There is no question that an acquisition creates uncertainty and fear on the part of acquired personnel, and anxiety may arise on the part of buyer personnel as well. If integration of the two companies of any size is desired, then a higher level of interaction is strongly recommended. If the company being acquired is large in any respect, particularly with respect to the number of employees being acquired, then the buyer should allocate a great deal of time for personal contact with the acquired company's employees. If the acquired company is geographically located close to one of the buyer's main operational centers, then facilitating this higher level of personal interaction is accomplished relatively easily. But if the two companies are geographically distant from each other, then the sheer logistics of travel may preclude extensive visits by the buyer to the target and vice versa. The more limited the amount of personal interaction, the less likely it is that the acquisition integration will be successfully accomplished.

For all of these reasons, Cisco contends that large acquisitions must be geographically located near a major Cisco operational center. The fundamental assumptions with this contention are that full integration is best accomplished with a lot of human interaction and this interaction is simply more difficult when the buyer and seller are geographically separated by a long distance. If full integration of the two companies is not a purchase requirement, then this stipulation can be relaxed somewhat; but the importance of executive-level personal contact should not be minimized, or the acquisition may foster fractionalizing that undermines any anticipated acquisition benefits.

CHAPTER *9*

NO MERGER
OF EQUALS

I don't believe mergers of equals work.[1]
— John Chambers, President and CEO, Cisco Systems

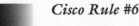

Cisco Rule #6
No merger between companies of equal stature within the
same industry is viable.

The Cisco methodology ideally targets privately held companies with fewer than 100 employees that have a product near market introduction. This target type is not, by most standards, considered a large company. There is a preconceived rationale for this type of approach to target selection in that Chambers believes that a merger of equals increases the likelihood that the acquisition will not meet with success. To date, most of Cisco's targets have been acquired for under $200 million. The StrataCom acquisition (April 1996) for $4.67 billion, GeoTel Communications Corporation (April 1999) for $2 billion, Cerent Corporation (August 1999) for $6.9 billion, Pirelli Optical Systems (December 1999) for $2.15 billion, and ArrowPoint Communications (May 2000) for $5.7 billion have been the largest-valued acquisitions up to the time of this writing.

The fact that these are certainly large acquisitions from a strict dollar-spent perspective tends to imply that in Chambers' view a

135

large acquisition is not the same as a merger of equals. This chapter takes a detailed look at this important contention and its impact on Cisco specifically and acquisitions in general.

THE CISCO RATIONALE NOT TO MERGE IN 1993

Synoptics and Cabletron were around the same size as Cisco in mid-1993. At this time, talk started about whether Cisco should consider merging with either of these companies, certainly producing a networking powerhouse for that time frame. A primary issue arose as to whether it would be better to merge with one of these companies or whether Cisco would be better served going it alone and acquiring other companies. As we now know, Cisco chose not to merge with either of them and instead acquired Crescendo in September 1993. We also know that Synoptics merged with Wellfleet Communications to form Bay Networks, a company that directly competed with Cisco. Bay Networks was eventually purchased by Nortel Networks in 1998 for $6.9 billion.

FROM INSIDE CISCO

There's no better example than the deal between network equipment makers Synoptics and Wellfleet. Our two toughest competitors combined and took themselves out of business.[2]

—*John Chambers, Cisco president and CEO*

Although a merger of equals has benefits, Cisco management at the time determined a few important aspects about the potential merger that swayed them away from merging and sent them in the direction of acquisitions instead. Cisco had worked with both Synoptics and Wellfleet before on smaller projects and understood much of what comprised the cultures of the two companies. This helped a lot in understanding the vision and culture of these two potential merger partners.

According to Chambers, five items directly impacted the decision not to merge: (1) statistics showed that 50 percent of large-scale acquisitions fail; (2) merging two rapidly growing companies slows the growth and momentum of both as they work out the inevitable details associated with the merger; (3) Cabletron was perceived as being technology driven where Cisco is strongly customer focused, and this strong vision difference was considered a problem; (4) Cisco estimated that as much as 60 percent of its existing channel partners would go to other vendors if the merger occurred; and (5) future alliances would be more complicated or difficult if Cisco merged with another major networking products provider. For all of these reasons, Cisco chose not to pursue this particular merger in 1993.[3]

Some people also contend that Chambers, then second in command at Cisco, was looking for a political lever that he could use to establish himself inside Cisco as his own management person. Merging with Synoptics or Cabletron would have presented a whole new level of management personnel and issues that could have eroded his position as opposed to enhancing it. By taking Cisco in the direction of acquisitions, specifically with the Crescendo acquisition, he had that chance to sink or swim on his own. With the incredible success of Crescendo, Chambers and his acquisition strategy were validated and, as it is said, the rest is history. In retrospect, Chambers and Cisco made the right decision not to merge and instead to develop acquisition as an intrinsic strategic weapon.

It is not uncommon for things to evolve because of a specific need at the time that later on is evaluated as part of a longer-term plan. Quite often, the opportunity presents itself simply because you were in the game and necessity dictated the actions that were taken. We now know that mergers of equals present huge problems that are simply not an issue with smaller acquisitions. Whether Cisco management in general, and Chambers in particular, knew in 1993 that a merger of equals was a recipe for trouble may never be answered definitively. But Cisco made the right choice in 1993, and that is likely what differentiates Cisco from other companies like Synoptics or Wellfleet that made different choices and did not meet with the same levels of success.

A professor friend of mine summed the situation up this way when we were discussing an important decision related to my own company. He said, "Ed, you know everything you can about this decision at this point in time. Your job is to make the decision today. My job is to take a look at the decision several years into the future and evaluate whether you made the right one or not." Successful entrepreneurs tend to assess the facts presented to them at the time of decision making and then make the more effective choice more often than those who are not successful. In some ways, it is just that simple.

What is important about the Cisco approach to decision making is that it tends to encourage involvement by different personnel and groups who can provide differing perspectives and opinions on the decision topic in question. Distilling the input down to the most important points and then assessing them so that the best possible decision for the circumstances is made is the art of good management and managers.

CISCO'S ASSUMPTIONS

A few assumptions underlie the contention that a merger of equals is not a good starting point for a successful acquisition.

An important initial assumption is that the merging of two companies is not a trivial process no matter the size of the companies involved. Even as Cisco acquires smaller companies with the intention of integrating the acquired personnel into the Cisco corporation, there is still a lot of effort spent on making the acquired personnel feel a part of Cisco as quickly as possible. And these acquisitions involve typically under 100 people. This process simply becomes highly critical and substantially more complicated as the number of personnel increases to many thousands.

Secondarily, a large organization will have its own set of ingrained cultural ideas, standards, and rituals, which will likely differ from those of Cisco. If the merged organization is to appear as one after the merger, then it is important that the cultures somehow blend into a hybrid; otherwise one culture will survive with the other becoming subordinate. If this blending does not work out smoothly, the infighting, squabbles, and daily distractions associated with a poor cultural merging can make the combined entity far less valuable than the total of the two separate companies. In essence, the merged cultural issues not only can create a poor postacquisition value, but can also erode the values of the two previously healthy companies. This is particularly true with respect to the interactions between managers of the two merged companies.

In 1987, 3Com was a leading local area network (LAN) equipment supplier, and Bridge Communications had created a large company providing access between terminals and mainframe computers. Bridge had gone public in 1985; 3Com had gone public in 1984. The two companies merged in 1987, but all was not happy after the merger was completed.

Bob Metcalfe, founder of 3Com, expressed his dissatisfaction with some of the choices associated with the merger. "3Com was two or three times bigger than Bridge at that time, but we treated it as a merger of equals, which was stupid. We ended up with two heads of sales, two heads of France, two heads of Germany, two heads of marketing, two heads of engineering, and they spent the next couple of years trying to kill each other." William Carrico was made president of the merged companies. As time passed it was realized that he was not really suited for management of a large organization since he could not effectively manage "managers of managers of managers." Carrico left the company soon after the acquisition was finalized. His wife, Judy Estrin, left with him and went on to become Cisco's chief technology officer and senior vice president. Good for Cisco. Bad for 3Com.

Two large companies from within the same industry will also have substantial overlap with respect to vendors, customers, and distribution channels. Salespeople from the seller will likely call on the same accounts and personnel as the salespeople of the buying company. Distributors that carry the buyer's products will also likely carry the seller's. Vendors that supply the buyer will also likely supply the seller, and likely with many of the same parts. Engineers in the buyer's company will have a similar expertise as many of the engineers of the seller. As these overlaps and redundancies are uncovered during due diligence and in a postacquisition environment, conflicts will arise as to how these overlaps will be resolved. The personnel redundancies will likely be dealt with by eliminating redundant employees unless they can be cross trained to another more needed skill.

As people start to get laid off, the acquired employees may begin to view the buyer with disfavor as they watch their fellow colleagues leave the merged entity. If this dissension leads to a decrease in morale and intercompany cooperation, the future health of the merged entity is substantially brought into question.

In addition, large companies from the same industry will have developed their own way of functioning within that industry. After all, both companies were successful enough to become equals within the industry. This means that they did something right, which reinforces the belief that the companys particular way of doing things is the best way to get things done. When two equally powerful companies merge, both have a strong cultural history of success. If the cultures are complementary, the merger is starting out on a positive note. If the cultures differ substantially, then problems will inevitably appear. These problems won't appear on a balance sheet as they are more cultural than financial in nature, but these problems can effectively derail any future benefits that can be derived from the merger.

According to Barry Eggers, who acted as lead on several early Cisco acquisitions when formerly with Cisco business development, a merger of equals involves a large acquisition and thus typically involves a number of problems not present with a smaller acquisition.

"Cisco really doesn't need to acquire companies with sales forces, finance groups, or manufacturing capabilities, either. A bigger company will have all of those. That's a problem. A lot of redundancy exists [with a merger of equals], and you always end up compromising when you have all of that redundancy. People are always unhappy when you have that redundancy. There is always someone on one side that is unhappy."[4]

In looking at the StrataCom acquisition, Eggers contends that problems arose in large part because of the size of the company.

"The problem with large acquisitions is that you have overlapping jobs. You have two sales forces, and I think that Cisco made some mistakes in integrating the StrataCom sales force. We lost some good people because of that—people who are now competing with Cisco, by the way."[5]

Notice that there is an implicit threat associated with not handling an acquisition within the same industry properly. Acquired people who are not happy with being acquired will leave to work for other companies, typically within the buyer's industry. These people now become competitors, when a well-done acquisition could have kept them in the buyer's organization, working for the buyer, not against it. Unfortunately, my experience also has shown that the most qualified people are often the first to leave since they have the easiest time obtaining new employment. So not only does the buyer lose the most qualified, key acquired people, but most likely the buyer also loses them to a competitor. This is a double injury to the buyer.

There is a caveat present with respect to a merger of equals. This caveat says that a strategic merger between equals can work if the redundancies are minimal and cultures associated with the two organizations are compatible. A look at the AOL–Time Warner merger presents an example of a merger between equals that was strategic in nature and, as a result, avoids many of the problems listed here.

America Online (AOL) is an Internet service provider (ISP) and provides a direct connection to its subscribers but does not produce much of the content provided to those customers. Time Warner, on the other hand, has a high level of expertise and asset valuation tied up in content that can be provided to customers, and is always looking for new avenues through which its content can be delivered to customers. Notice that the two companies have different expertise and even though the two organizations are large from both a revenue and an employee count perspective, the amount of overlap (redundancy) between them is relatively low. As a result, the problems outlined by Barry Eggers are less likely to derail the acquisition than in the case of a merger between two companies within the same industry, as would have been the situation with a Cisco–Synoptics merger.

Keeping key people around after an acquisition is a key Cisco success criterion. Keeping those people around becomes much more complicated and difficult with a larger acquisition. When you are a company of Cisco's size, any merger of equals will involve a large acquisition and consequently should be avoided.

PORTABILITY EVALUATION

This integration of personnel is a common problem to almost any acquisition that involves the acquisition of people along with tangible assets. Few of the assumptions associated with Cisco's avoidance of a merger of equals are restricted to Cisco specifically or technology industries in general. When people are involved, and they always are, serious respect must be given to the cultural and redundancy issues outlined in this chapter. And those issues exist in every business and industry situation, making a merger of equals a potential problem for almost any industry.

When Cisco, a much larger company with many thousands of employees, acquires a small company with an employee base of under 100, it is an almost foregone conclusion that the smaller company will wind up adopting Cisco's culture. And the percentage change in employee population is not substantial enough to present much of a challenge to the existing Cisco culture. But have Cisco merge with a company with an equal number of employees and comparable revenue stream, and things are now very different from the smaller acquisition. Even with the best of intentions at the executive levels to have the other company assimilate into Cisco, completely adopting its culture, it will not happen. People simply don't change that quickly, and the cultural inertia behind the target's prior culture is simply too strong to be overwhelmed by Cisco's. The likely result of a merger of equals will be a blending of the two merged cultures into a single culture that reflects, hopefully, the best attributes of each, making the blended entity much stronger than either culture was on its own.

Perhaps the best single statement of the expected results from a merger of equals is presented in the book *Winning at Mergers and Acquisitions: The Guide to Market-Focused Planning and Integration:* "In any merger or major acquisition, the combining companies—in my view—are really starting all over from scratch. After the deal closes, you have a whole new group of people and, most times, a whole new lineup of products. Consequently, it's a chance to forge entirely new ways of doing business in a way that brings all these diverse yet complementary elements together and moves them toward a common goal."[6] This quote is attributed to a "corporate development officer, Fortune 1000 electronics manufacturing company."

Making this process of integration work takes time, effort, and focus. All this energy being spent on making the integration work is energy that cannot be spent on moving the buyer forward at a fast clip with respect to sales and product development. There will be an inevitable stall that results from the merging of the two companies, and, in a dynamic market, it may take years to recover from that stalled period. The Synoptics–Wellfleet merger is an example of what can happen when the merger of two equal companies detracts from the basic business of performing in a dynamic marketplace. Managers start having meetings to resolve management differences instead of to discuss new product or market development. Money is spent on special, company-wide integration issues that could have gone to R&D or market development. And if the two merged entities come from the same industry, there are also likely many heated discussions regarding which will have to lose personnel as a result of the inevitable redundancies. In short, a merger of equals comes with a whole set of challenges that are simply not associated with a smaller acquisition. And these challenges exist independent of the industry involved.

Cisco was able to assimilate smaller companies and continue performing and adapting to dynamic market changes while Synoptics and Wellfleet were working out the daily issues related to their merger into Bay Networks.

▬ A CLOSER LOOK AT THE COMPANIES IN 1984

Cisco management is not bashful about referring to the merger in October 1994 of Synoptics and Wellfleet to form Bay Networks when highlighting a merger of equals that did not work out as planned. Both Synoptics and Wellfleet referred to the transaction as a "merger of equals." It was contended in the press at the time that this merger resulted from Cisco's acquisition of Crescendo, which provided Cisco with both routing and switching product lines. In theory, the combined Synoptics–Wellfleet entity would be a company with comparable revenues to Cisco that also would provide routing and switching hardware. Table 9.1 presents data pertaining to the two companies in 1994, when the merger was finalized.

Notice that the two companies provided networking products to the same industry. Notice also that even though Wellfleet had revenues that were less than half those of Synoptics, it had almost four-fifths the number of employees. Notice also that the two companies were on opposite sides of the country, making geographic proximity

Table 9.1 1994 Synoptics, Wellfleet Communications, Cisco

Company	Location	Employees	Revenues	Net Income	Comments
Synoptics	Santa Clara, California	1,707	$720 million	$73 million	Network hubs, switches, and software
Wellfleet Communications	Billerica, Massachusetts	1,350	$340 million	$60 million	Routers
Cisco Systems	San Jose, California	2,262	$1,243 million	$315 million	Routers and switches
Crescendo Communications	Sunnyvale, California	65	$10 million	Not profitable	Purchased by Cisco in September 1993 for $95 million; switching systems

problems a likely consideration. Cisco had considered merging with Synoptics at roughly the same time and had chosen not to merge; instead it acquired Crescendo. Synoptics and Wellfleet at the time were the third and fifth largest companies in the networking hardware industry, and when combined expected total annual revenues of just over $1 billion, which rivaled Cisco's size at that time of $1.2 billion in revenues.

A Dataquest networking analyst, Tam Dell'Oro, was quoted in a Mercury News article dated July 6, 1994, commenting on this merger and its viability. "In general, high technology company mergers have a troubled history, and a bicoastal match may create more problems than usual. . . . And, this is the first time that a major hub vendor and a major router vendor—each with a huge installed base of customers—are joining forces. Customers concerned about protecting their existing investments may decide one is more important than the other. . . . This merger has to work or both these companies are sunk."[7]

John Morgridge, Cisco president and CEO at the time, is quoted in the article as saying, "To make the merger work, these companies will have to exert a lot of energy. That instability creates opportunities for us [Cisco]."[8]

So how did the merger fare? At first announcement, the stock prices of both companies dropped by over 20 percent. Eventually the stock price came back so that by November 1995 the market valuation of Bay Networks had increased over fourfold to $9 billion. Unfortunately, from that point forward, Bay Networks' valuation declined until in May 1997 the valuation had dropped to $3 billion. How did this compare to Cisco for the same period? A Robertson, Stephens & Company report from December 1996 presents the relative company performance based on a comparison of return on invested capital (ROIC) and net operating profit after paying cash taxes (NOPAT), figures that it contends more accurately reflect the investment return of an organization.

Bay's business is substantially less profitable than Cisco's. Furthermore, its business has been declining in profitability for the past six quarters. . . . Essentially, during this period [calendar Q2 1995 to Q3 1996] Bay has been unable to generate significant and sustainable returns from a huge increase in invested capital deployed in its business. . . . While Cisco more than tripled its NOPAT from calendar Q1 1994 to Q3 1996, Bay managed to increase its NOPAT [by] only 49%. With the networking industry's growth surging, Bay's stagnating returns on invested capital have resulted in a decline in its share of the industry's total profits to 6% in Q3 1996 from 11% in Q2 1995 and 13% in Q1 1994.[9]

Bay Networks went on to acquire a number of other companies over the years and eventually merged with Nortel (Northern Telecom) in June 1998 at a valuation worth around $9 billion. At the time of the merger with Nortel, Bay Networks had over 7,000 employees and revenues of over $2 billion. Cisco closed out fiscal 1998 at around $8.4 billion in revenues and over 14,000 employees.

Certainly from this assessment, Bay Networks' strategy of combining Synoptics and Wellfleet forces to beat Cisco did not work when viewed from an ROIC perspective. It can be seen from Table 9.1 that Cisco's acquisition of Crescendo Communications added switching capabilities to Cisco's product line with minimal additional employees or debt. In essence it was a lower-risk option compared to the complete merging of two large organizations. In addition, Crescendo was located in Silicon Valley, making interaction between the two organizations far simpler than working across the distance and time zone differences that separate Silicon Valley and Boston.

THE FINAL ANALYSIS

If redundancy is minimal, the cultures are compatible, the companies come from different industries, and the merger makes strategic sense with respect to providing incremental value to shareholders and customers of both companies, then a merger of equals may well work out. But if any of these areas present the problems outlined earlier in this chapter, then passing on the merger may better serve both buyer and seller.

"No merger of equals" is simply a fundamental target selection rule that Cisco used to practice when it was smaller from the revenue, market capitalization, and employee perspective. Now that its revenues are over $20 billion, its market capitalization is one of the highest in the world, and it has over 30,000 employees, the number of companies that could be considered an equal is reduced to very few.

This premise of not merging with a company that is your equal is highly portable between companies and industries and one that should be carefully considered by executives. Two companies with radically different cultures will likely have a difficult time merging, regardless of their relative sizes. But if the merger goes poorly and the target is small, then the negative impact on the buyer (Cisco) would be unfortunate but minimal. If the acquired company is large compared to Cisco, then a whole different problem presents itself in that the poor merger can now have a materially detrimental impact on Cisco's personnel morale, operations, customer relations, shareholder relations, and finally on Cisco itself. Add to this mix the redundancies associated with acquiring a large company in the same field as the buyer, which will likely create the turf battles and infighting that will divide the two companies along intercompany lines.

If, on the other hand, a large company (an equal) can be found with a different market presence, customer base, operational model, and core competency—such as is seen with the AOL–Time Warner merger—then a merger of equals might be exactly the right move. Each partner in the merger gets an added capability that simply was not there prior to the merger. The level of operational redundancy is very different between the two companies, implying that substantial layoffs may not be required and each party gets a clear benefit from the success of the merged entity. Only time will tell if this was a good move for the two companies, but this type of example indicates that a merger of equals being a bad idea may really be applicable only to equals within the same industry.

CHAPTER 10

TARGET
PRACTICE

We have a saying here: "Early if not elegant." If you are a year late, that market might not exist anymore. We'd rather learn from our mistakes. If we are not making mistakes, we aren't moving fast enough.[1]

—Charles Giancarlo, Senior Vice President, Cisco Systems

It stands to reason that starting with more qualified acquisition targets makes the acquisition process much simpler and more efficient. After all, if the target is already prequalified before Cisco even begins discussions, the entire acquisition process will simply go more smoothly and likely with fewer surprises. And a more qualified prospect is also one that can be contacted, evaluated, and purchased much faster and with more confidence than one that is unfamiliar.

Think about the Cisco acquisition machine: Assuming that the company acquires only 1 out of every 10 targets it considers, and performs 15 or more acquisitions a year, then it follows that Cisco must consider at least 150 targets each year as possible acquisition candidates. That is a lot of prospecting. Honing the target acquisition process is an integral part of making the Cisco A&D methodology work as well as it does.

HARVESTING A CO-OP GARDEN— SILICON VALLEY

The best part of being a Cisco is that you are the 800-pound gorilla that everyone already knows about, wants to work with, wants to get a piece of, or wants to avoid. But if you are in networking in Silicon Valley, Boston, or Research Triangle you must also consider Cisco as part of your business planning process. It is even highly likely that these networking start-ups have ex-Cisco personnel in key employee positions. Such is the case with SS8 Networks (with former Combinet/Cisco employees) and Longboard (former Cisco executives as officers). When a company is as large as Cisco and has the track record of Cisco, it leaves its mark all over the Valley specifically and the industry in general.

My point from all this is to say that someone somewhere at Cisco is probably aware of someone somewhere in the industry—probably working at a start-up—who is developing exactly the type of technology that could be used by Cisco to round out its product matrix. These start-ups then become possible and often probable acquisition targets, since by the time the start-up is ready to be acquired the personnel and technologies involved are familiar to Cisco, and Cisco is certainly familiar to the start-up personnel.

Just as a co-op garden has people planting and tending their own crops while staying aware of what co-op neighbors are doing, so does Silicon Valley foster a cross-pollination between companies such that people know what others are doing.

Most venture capital (VC) firms in Silicon Valley have fairly ready access to Cisco's acquisition team. If they have funded a start-up that has a technology that would round out Cisco's product offering, these VCs will likely talk to Cisco about the possibility of a purchase. In fact, many of them are wealthy ex-Cisco employees who are using their Cisco-acquired wealth to fund start-ups. These people still have access to key Cisco personnel and can at least get their start-ups considered as possible acquisition targets. And, let's face it, they know what Cisco is looking for from the inside out.

Inside the Valley

Being with Cisco has a double edge to it. I spoke with several ex-Cisco people on my last trip to the Valley who have little interest in once again becoming a part of Cisco. They left there once and do not want to go back, preferring a smaller company environment instead. Several of these people are independently wealthy as a direct result of their Cisco days, and still they have no interest in going back. When asked whether they would want Cisco to purchase their companies, several answered that "it is always a possibility, but not one that I would hold out for or really want to pursue." Just as most divorced people do not turn around and remarry their ex-spouses, ex-Cisco employees feel no desire to once again be assimilated back into the Cisco collective.

Dev Gupta seems to understand the Cisco acquisition algorithm well. Cisco acquired the New Jersey firm Dagaz, an xDSL (digital subscriber line) high-speed access products company, in June 1997 for $126 million. Gupta was an executive with Dagaz at the time of the acquisition. Now turn your sights to Cisco's August 1999 purchase of high-speed IP telephony products firm MaxComm Technologies of Chelmsford, Massachusetts for $143 million. Gupta left Cisco in 1998 to found MaxComm. Do you notice a pattern forming here? Mr. Gupta certainly seems to have found one that has been successful for Mr. Gupta and obviously also for Cisco Systems.

In summary, when you are well known, as Cisco is, and recognized for having an active acquisition program, which Cisco has, and industry insiders have a solid feeling of what Cisco is likely looking for, which ex-Ciscoites will, there is a ready source of acquisition prospects regularly coming Cisco's way.

If you buy them, they will come. Or something like that.

151

HAPPY CUSTOMERS HAPPILY GIVE REFERRALS

Any good salesperson knows that the best possible referral you can receive is one from your already satisfied existing customer. That customer who refers another to you has already done much of the prospecting legwork for you. She certainly knows your company and its offerings, since she is already a customer. She likely knows the prospective customer whom she referred to you and understands his needs. Additionally, she also has some reason to believe that your company's offerings can help her colleague in some way, or you would not have received the referral (unless, of course, she thinks of this colleague as an enemy and wants to create an annoyance for him, which is highly unlikely and certainly not neighborly). Finally, when you call that referred potential customer using the name of the referring customer, you will likely get a friendly reception since that customer also must believe that the referring customer has some excellent reason for making the referral, all mischief aside. Referrals are the best possible leads. Period. Chambers, being the salesguy that he is, understands this very well and solicits acquisition referral candidates from his existing customer base. And what better combination can you have, from Cisco's perspective?

Assume that this particular customer knows of a start-up's offering and wants to give it a try but does not want to rely on the start-up for support. Likely, the customer has concerns about the financial staying power of the start-up and is reticent to make a substantial purchase out of fear of being left with products and no manufacturer. If that product, on the other hand, could be offered by Cisco, this customer may just be willing to place a large order out of faith that Cisco will have evaluated the product and will support the product if sold as a Cisco offering. The customer wins in that she gets the cutting-edge start-up product she wants. Cisco wins in that it has a guaranteed order upon its purchase of the start-up. The start-up wins in that it becomes liquid quickly and sees its products take a market prominence that would not have been possible without the Cisco operation. It is a win-win situation for all parties.

In short, referrals are not only good—they're grrrreat!

Cisco Fact Sheet

Cisco bought TransMedia Communications, Inc. of San Jose, California, in June 1999 for $407 million. The company made asynchronous transfer mode (ATM) switches and voice products. The referral supposedly came from James Crowe, the CEO of Level 3 Communications, Inc.[2]

Cisco bought NetSpeed, Inc., a high-speed xDSL Internet access product aimed at the home marketplace, in March 1998. The CEO of US West, a regional Bell operating company (RBOC), Solomon D. Trujillo, was interested in NetSpeed's products but did not want to take a chance on the start-up. According to Mike Volpi, a customer with a purchase order in hand is a strong motivator for Chambers. "Chambers said our customer is willing to write a purchase order," recalled Mike Volpi. "You have to do it." And he did, for $265 million.[3]

Chambers actually credits one of Cisco's customers with setting Cisco soundly on the acquisition path when Boeing recommended that Cisco work with a small company also in Silicon Valley (Sunnyvale, California) that made switches. These switches were much less expensive than the routers that Cisco currently sold and appeared to customers as an easier network product to manage. Boeing got the attention of Chambers, the consummate salesguy, by saying that unless Cisco worked out some type of arrangement with this smaller company, called Crescendo, Cisco would not get a piece of the large contract Boeing was looking to issue. To add spice to the equation, Ford Motor Company, more than halfway across the country, told Cisco that it was seriously considering making a major investment in local area network (LAN) switching equipment. In short, Cisco had solid nudges from two major customers that switching was a hot technology that Cisco should be offering and didn't. Crescendo, all of a sudden, looked very attractive.

153

FROM INSIDE CISCO

The tough part is figuring out whom you trust and whom you don't. If you can't trust them the first time around, you quit sharing information.[4]

—Mike Volpi, Cisco Senior vice president,
referring to his ongoing conversations with
Silicon Valley venture capitalists

Cisco did purchase Crescendo in September 1993 for $95 million. Cisco's switching business unit started with the Crescendo purchase and has since added other acquisitions. It generated $7.5 billion in switching revenue during fiscal 2000, accounting for 40 percent of Cisco's revenue. Not bad for a customer recommendation, don't you think?

HARVESTING YOUR OWN GARDEN

As great as Silicon Valley and the other start-up hotbeds are for creating the next great technology offerings, there is often nothing like simply growing your own. Cisco attempts to assist the creation of start-ups that will meet its ultimate product matrix strategic requirements through a number of ways including conventional early investment programs and a new method called a "spin-in."

Cisco has had an aggressive investment program in place for many years. In fact, it made its first external investment in 1993 with a minority equity investment in Cascade Communications. Take a look at Table 10.1 to see the relationship between the number of minority investments Cisco has made and the number of total acquisitions.

In the fall of 1997, Cisco made a minority investment of 10 percent in Monterey Networks, an optical Internetworking products company located in Richardson, Texas. The press was hounding Cisco at the time for not having a viable offering in the optical Inter-

Table 10.1 Comparing Cisco's Acquisitions against Its Investments

Fiscal Year	Acquisitions	Investments
1993	0	1
1994	2	0
1995	2	4
1996	7	6
1997	9	6
1998	6	2
1999	10	38
2000	26	23
2001	8	Not available

networking arena, and this was Cisco's way of testing the water. The 10 percent gave Cisco additional access that it would not have had were it not a minority investor. A company the size of Cisco needs very large markets into which to grow, and the $20 billion a year optical Internetworking marketplace is just the kind of market that gets Cisco's attention. Monterey Networks, a company of 132 employees, looked so good, by the way, that Cisco purchased the entire company in August 1999 for $500 million.

Along these same lines, in 1998 Cisco had also made a minority (9 percent) investment in another optical technology company, Cerent Corporation of Petaluma, California. The objective of the investment was, once again, for Cisco not only to get a closer look at the technology of a company but also to get a sense of its culture and the other intangibles that are critical to a Cisco acquisition. It must have worked out, because Cisco bought Cerent in August 1999 for a whopping $6.9 billion in stock! Cerent had around 287 employees and a *lifetime* sales figure of only $10 million. Chambers must have definitely felt that the chemistry was right on this one!

These areas of investment involvement on Cisco's part have been going on for a while but are likely to accelerate in coming years with the erosion of the capital markets and the resulting hesitancy on the part of investors to take on more risk.

About Cisco

There is some talk around the Valley that Cisco's track record for successful acquisitions is nowhere near 100 percent. Some claim that only four or five acquisitions have provided stellar returns, with the balance either barely breaking even or being dismal failures. Others say that Cisco's results approach more of a standard venture capital model—30 percent providing excellent returns, 40 percent breaking even, and the balance being failures, with the returns from the 30 percent successful acquisitions more than offsetting the losses from the failures. Cisco's incredible revenue growth over the 1993 to 2000 period certainly indicates that whatever its internal success results, the leverage of these acquired technologies through the Cisco operation is as close to a money printing machine as you can get.

Cisco has even entered the venture capital business as of January 2001 with a $1.05 billion initial funding of a venture fund run by Softbank Corporation in Asia. Cisco's acquisition engine is dependent on a large number of potential candidates from which it can choose the right set of criteria from chemistry, vision, and other deal stoppers. It is imperative that this start-up pipeline not dry up, so Cisco is using its financial strength to make sure that the pipeline remains full of new technologies. "The [capital] markets are not being efficient right now," says Mike Volpi, prior business development vice president and now senior VP and chief strategy officer for Cisco. "Some good ideas are not getting funded."[5]

Barry Eggers, former Cisco executive who is now general partner with Lightspeed Venture Partners, a venture capital firm in Menlo Park, California, has a little different view of the venture capital situation. "I think that we have slowed down our funding and there are going to be fewer companies to pick from. But there were probably too many companies to pick from. We had overfunded. So, I think that there are still going to be high-quality companies," says Eggers.[6]

Making a minority investment in a start-up with the expressed intention of getting a specific product and technology out of it may sound like a good idea at first, but then a few realities start to move in. Start-ups are relatively freewheeling and tend to push the envelope of convention, which is why they come up with great technology before larger companies do so. Predictable creativity is in some ways an oxymoron, and comments made by Mike Volpi indicate that Cisco might have found this out the hard way.

Cisco made a minority investment in Ardent Communications Corporation of San Jose, California, a company that produced integrated voice, video, and data equipment that Cisco thought had a future place in its product offering. In return for the investment, Cisco got two seats on Ardent's board and ready access to its engineering staff. All this did not work out as planned, and Volpi feels that they might have tried to micromanage the company too much.

"It's a tricky balance between telling them what you want and letting them act as a start-up. We tried to keep it too tight and the product doesn't have the spark of a typical start-up," claims Volpi.[7]

Something must have worked out okay, though, because Cisco did purchase Ardent Communications in June 1997 for $156 million.

Perhaps these experiences with minority investments were what prompted Cisco to look for an alternate method of fostering entrepreneurial creativity while also ensuring that the company and product would ultimately meet Cisco's product and business objectives. That alternate approach is called a "spin-in."

Spin-In Explained

If you want to control the culture of start-up and get great technology products in the process, why not fund the start-up with your own money and put your own people in charge of it? When the idea is proven viable, simply bring the company back into the Cisco mother ship and assimilate the Cisco-like culture and employees back into the fold. In the Valley, this process is being called a "spin-in." It is being treated like some type of secret, but many people seem to know about it, so go figure! I'm happy to report that when I was a nuclear weapons repairman we did not handle secrets with the same level of casual secrecy.

A spin-in works something like this. Assume that Cisco finds a particular technology or company that it is interested in cultivating, but the company is not at the stage where an acquisition is appropriate. Cisco places some key Cisco employees inside this external company. These people have the charter to cultivate the desired technology and build it into a marketable product that meets Cisco's future expected product requirements. Cisco offers stock in the fledgling company to the Cisco employees who participate in this venture along with an agreement that, once the product is operational, the company and its personnel will be brought back into Cisco. The products will then be sold just like any other Cisco product. And Cisco then acquires the new venture for a multiple of its sales at some predefined future time. The Cisco personnel who participated with the spin-in get a new infusion of Cisco stock in exchange for their spin-in company stock and feasibly can become wealthy in the process. Cisco is peppering the target with its own people and design processes, just as if it were an internal department, and then bringing the company back into Cisco, or spinning it in instead of spinning it out. I thought the term was cool.

With a spin-in, the technology and products get funded to marketability with a strong, proven Cisco-selected management team at the helm. The participating Cisco personnel get a chance to create a start-up that has an outstanding chance of being acquired by Cisco if the start-up meets its objectives. These same Cisco personnel then come back to Cisco with more entrepreneurial experience under their belts, which benefits Cisco. Cisco gets to acquire a company that has an almost guaranteed cultural fit since its leaders all come from Cisco. Finally, Cisco will have a strong say in the design of the products, which means that they will more seamlessly integrate within the Cisco engineering and manufacturing operations. In short, this spin-in process seems to have a lot of good stuff going for it, which is likely why Cisco is pursuing it in the first place.

SETTING UP TO BE BOUGHT BY CISCO— A ONE-TRICK PONY

There is some talk around the Valley about starting up a company specifically to be purchased by Cisco. Dev Gupta appears to have had some success in this regard with his selling of two companies, Dagaz and MaxComm, to Cisco within a few years. Have others been successful with this approach? Very possibly, but the question remains, how many tried to do this and failed, leaving themselves with no other outlet for their company to become liquid?

Barry Eggers contends that setting up to be bought by Cisco may actually undermine the value of a company. Although Eggers admits that several people have had success with this developing-for-Cisco approach, it is not one he would recommend.

"In general, you build a company to go public, and those are your strongest companies. And if they get acquired, they get acquired for the most money," contends Eggers.[8]

Dave Newkirk, controller with Combinet when it was acquired by Cisco in 1995, echoes some of Barry Eggers' sentiments.

"If you are going to [set up to be bought by Cisco] I think it's gotta be part of the plan from the get-go. This means that your Sand Hill Road investors have to have the right connections to be able to help to pull something like that off," contends Newkirk. "If your business plan is to get acquired by Cisco and it doesn't happen, you're left holding the bag. That's one of the pitfalls of doing the 'Let's get acquired' strategy. It might limit your value to everybody else. But if that is a valid plan from the get-go I am sure it has already happened a number of times."[9]

If, after these comments, you are still interested in setting up your company to be acquired by Cisco, here are a few things to consider:

- Cisco typically targets start-up companies that have under 100 employees.
- The company must have a great technology product that will be ready for customer release within the next 6 to 12 months.

- The company should ideally still be held privately.

- Most of Cisco's acquisitions have been companies located in Silicon Valley near Cisco's headquarters, along Route 128 near Boston, and in the Research Triangle in North Carolina.

- Stock options that accelerate upon acquisition provide a golden parachute for key employees and may be looked upon as a disincentive to purchase from Cisco's perspective.

- Products should be based on open standards.

- Products should already have been through customer trials, and customers should be ready to place additional product orders.

- The engineers and key management personnel must be willing to stick around after the acquisition and become part of the Cisco operation for at least a two-year period.

- The culture, chemistry, product, and industry visions of key personnel must be in sync with Cisco's.

This is by no means an exhaustive list, but it will get you started. And, by the way, creating your company with these goals in mind will likely make your company more successful and valuable if you are lucky enough later on to sell it or successfully go public. But beware that you do not make your product so Cisco-like or Cisco-compatible that it is difficult for another possible buyer to adapt the technology or products to its needs. Although being purchased by Cisco is certainly an attractive possibility, Cisco is not the only company out there with money or an acquisition strategy. It is okay to present yourself to Cisco in the most favorable light, but take care not to close off any other possible sale avenues by focusing exclusively on the possible Cisco sale.

Once again, Dave Newkirk has what I feel are great words of wisdom with respect to this particular topic.

"I think that you try to deliver what the market wants and build a successful company. Good things are going to happen to that company," says Newkirk. "You might get some offers to get acquired along the way. If your investors stick with you, you might make it all the way to a public offering. . . . If the company is doing the right stuff, good things will happen."[10]

CISCO'S ASSUMPTIONS

As with everything else Cisco does regarding its acquisitions, there are some very clear underlying assumptions that guide its actions and decisions.

- Cisco knows what it expects from the acquisition and limits its target searches to companies providing the best chance of meeting those expectations.
- Cisco sticks with its selection criteria regarding culture, proximity, and other considerations that it has learned need to be present for the acquisition to work.
- Cisco listens to its customers and, rightfully, contends that those products that its customers are the most willing to buy are the ones it should be acquiring. Why not let the people who will eventually pay you tell you what they are willing to pay for? It really seems too obvious, doesn't it?
- Cisco believes that making a minority investment in several advanced technology companies, prior to when that technology is actually needed, provides an opportunity for Cisco personnel and the targets' personnel to test the water with respect to working together on a regular basis. It's a little like living together before getting married.
- Cisco knows that whatever it is selling today may likely be obsolete in a few years. Mario Mazzola, senior vice president at Cisco, sometimes comments that these technologies and products are "perishable" and have shelf lives of around 18 months.
- There will always be another potential target company out there, and this large number of targets allows Cisco to be se-

lective in its purchases. If the venture capital markets become inefficient, as Mike Volpi contends they might, then Cisco will step in and fund the development activities itself.

- Cisco also aggressively pursues its target selection and acquisition activities in the belief that delay simply permits new market opportunities to be exploited by someone else. In essence, Cisco operates with the assumption that whoever gets into the marketplace first wins and everyone else will always play catch-up, if they can remain in the game at all.

- It is better to take a few chances and have them not work out than to play it very conservatively and miss huge market opportunities that could have created vast new revenue streams. Just expect that you will hit the right opportunities more often than you will select the wrong ones. And the revenues generated from the right acquisitions in the right markets will more than offset any mistakes made on unsuccessful acquisitions.

PORTABILITY EVALUATION

The general aspects of the Cisco approach are highly portable in that a focused acquisition effort that screens candidates based on a refined set of criteria weeds out those prospects that simply do not stand a chance of becoming successful in a postmerger environment.

Investing in a company as a way of becoming better acquainted with its management, culture, products, and technologies is not a new approach and is certainly portable to other industries.

The Cisco obsession with being first is also not a new approach, but the need to continually reinvent yourself on an Internet year's time frame is unique to high-technology fields and may not apply to more established industrial types of environments.

Spinning in technology and products is also a portable approach and provides more established companies with a way of introducing entrepreneurial thinking into the organization. It also provides employees with a financial incentive to stay with the company when start-ups may be wooing them on a daily basis. This approach is highly portable and should be strongly considered by established companies.

IBM did a type of spin-in when it set up the PC team in the early 1980s. It put a group of IBM engineers in a set of buildings in Boca Raton, Florida, where they were segregated from the standard IBM environment. Although this group was part of IBM, you would never have known it if you were to walk around the halls, other than from the high level of security present. And this group became incredibly entrepreneurial, taking chances that the standard IBM way would never have allowed. I even heard people at the established "towers" IBM complex comment that this group of renegades would at some point have to be gotten under control-they were simply not acting like IBM. And I say, "Thank goodness!" By the way, the spin-in that happened later with the AT and other products did what IBM corporate wanted and reined in those mavericks, stifling the very entrepreneurial spirit that caused the immense success of the initial IBM PC and then IBM XT computers. The moral of this story is that you can always take a spin-in approach, but make sure that you don't spin the value out of the venture when you bring it in-house.

THE FINAL ANALYSIS

Cisco makes a point of ensuring that its prospect pipeline is always full. In this way it can maintain its highly selective method of finalizing its acquisition choices. As a way of testing the culture of the prospect on a practical basis, Cisco may make a minor investment in a company to learn more about its products, technologies, culture, modes of operation, and management styles. If that experiment shows a high level of concordance, Cisco may purchase the rest of the company and fully assimilate it into the Cisco operation.

Cisco doesn't assume that every acquisition will be a whopping success but does make every possible effort to ensure that the cultures of the target and Cisco align. In this way, should the products themselves not meet with huge market success, Cisco wins by obtaining the engineers and management personnel it needs to move successfully into the future. Always conscious that technology changes in Internet years, Cisco wastes no time in cultivating and acquiring a company should it appear to be a viable acquisition target.

Focused goals and clear objectives are key to the Cisco target uncovering and selection process. Listening to customers in conjunction with feedback from internal business units adds prospective targets to the Cisco "acquisition" list. Should the venture community become too conservative, or inefficient as referred to by Mike Volpi, then Cisco will generate viable acquisition candidates through a combination of venture funding or its own start-ups, ongoing minority investments, or spin-ins that capitalize on the experience of Cisco personnel in making start-ups successful enough to be purchased by Cisco.

CHAPTER *11*

THE CISCO DUE DILIGENCE "SNIFF TEST"

If you are selecting a partner for life, your ability to select the partner after one date isn't very good. If you don't spend a fair amount of time on the evaluation of what are the key ingredients for that, your probability of having a successful marriage after one date is pretty small. We spend a long time on the up-front.
—John Chambers, President and CEO, Cisco Systems

Due diligence at Cisco is more than just verifying the financial, legal, and asset value status of a target company. It is a test—a test of the ethics, honesty, team spirit, professionalism, and customer commitment of the target. Notice that these items don't appear on a balance sheet, an income statement, or a statement of cash flows. These are due diligence items that require one human being facing another while working on a common project—the acquisition and integration of the target company.

Sure, Cisco does the standard due diligence checks to verify all of the things that must be verified. But underlying the due diligence process is the search for the answer to an overriding question: "Will these people, their products, and their culture merge

165

well with Cisco's so that they will be seamless with Cisco within a few months?"

That is the essence of Cisco due diligence.

FOCUS ON WHAT'S IMPORTANT

Due diligence can be a self-expanding process in that the more you learn, the more you want to learn. At some point, the due diligence team must call it quits and decide if the acquisition meets Cisco's acquisition objectives. So, it is critical that the team know, going in, what the major items of value are that require the most intensive due diligence effort. Once again we see that focus on a clearly defined set of objectives is a key to success.

"You really need to do good, solid due diligence," says Kim Niederman, former Cisco executive and current CEO of LongBoard, a Silicon Valley start-up, verifying the need to perform due diligence. "A lot of companies didn't do enough due diligence—they got burned. They spent a hundred million dollars on a company that never got its products off to market."[1]

Niederman then drives home the need not to lose sight of the ultimate goals of the acquisition.

"There are a number of reasons why companies make acquisitions, with several being more prominent than others, such as the potential to grab market share, increase revenue, round out a product line, and/or acquire a great engineering team," he says. "Once the decision to acquire is made, the buyer must develop an extreme focus on evaluating the top-priority items. Cisco developed a well-defined 'prioritized focus system' to accomplish the due diligence phase expeditiously. A primary objective of the investigation was to determine whether or not the target company was mature enough to get 'out of the box' and actually bring a commercialized product to market."

Focus enables Cisco to determine relatively quickly whether the value that it intends to purchase is present. This speed has enabled Cisco to acquire some companies with minimal competition since the other suitors are busy doing due diligence in areas that are simply not vital to the value items of interest.

FROM INSIDE CISCO

We had interest from other companies, but they didn't move as fast as Cisco. They were still considering us when the announcement came out that Cisco had bought us.

—Joe Bass, former CEO of Monterey
Networks, acquired by Cisco in 1999

When Cisco was buying Kalpana, Inc., in 1994, it beat out IBM by not getting bogged down in details that seemed superfluous to Cisco's value objectives with respect to the acquisition. IBM delayed its purchase decision because it wanted to run some groundwater tests at the Kalpana corporate headquarters in Sunnyvale, California, to ensure that the site was up to code. Cisco came in, saw what it wanted, checked out the report that Kalpana gave them regarding groundwater code compliance, made an offer, and closed the deal in a weekend. Dan Scheinman, senior vice president at Cisco, remembers the events in this way: "I guess in that one we took some groundwater risk—or maybe we didn't. We had the report."

By the way, the Kalpana acquisition brought Mimi Gigoux to Cisco along with others who are now the masterminds behind the well-oiled acquired personnel assimilation process. Kalpana not only brought its technology and engineers to Cisco, but also brought motivated professionals, many of whom are still with Cisco.

TEAMWORK AGAIN MAKES IT WORK!

Due diligence starts when the initial Cisco executives meet with the target's executives. At this time, these two groups of people on opposite sides of the transaction are sizing each other up for various traits. Cisco's and the target's executives know that the company has some type of product or technology to offer that is important to Cisco's customers. Otherwise, Cisco would not be interested in talking with the target in the first place.

During these discussions, the important areas of management vision, management style, overall desires from an acquisition, and other salient points from the Cisco must-have list are evaluated. If the initial qualification criteria are found and a purchase price is agreed to, then the due diligence teams themselves kick into action. Naturally, any agreements signed at this point are contingent on the successful completion of due diligence.

At this time, a Cisco project team takes over to perform the due diligence evaluation itself. The team consists of a team leader from the business development group who then coordinates the activities of the other team members who come from the various functional areas of Cisco. There are representatives from marketing, engineering, and manufacturing, with manufacturing's emphasis placed squarely on evaluating the level of compatibility between the target's manufacturing processes and Cisco's.

The manufacturing intention is always to integrate the acquired products into Cisco's manufacturing operation, so the level of work involved to make that happen is carefully evaluated. (See Chapter 13 for a detailed discussion of manufacturing's overall integration processes.) Either products are assimilated into the Cisco manufacturing operation or the target continues to produce the product after the purchase but using Cisco's testing and manufacturing scheduling systems. In either case, the final outcome of the manufacturing due diligence is to determine the level of transferability of the acquired products and to make recommendations as to which products are to be assimilated and which are to be left with the target. A lot of the manufacturing due diligence is done over a several-day site visit whereby the processes are investigated by the Cisco team. A listing of questions and areas of interest is provided to the target a few days before the Cisco team arrives so that the target can be prepared to address Cisco's concerns.

Marketing evaluates the level of sales expertise present with the client. The skill set of the sales team is evaluated along with important sales-related items such as close rates, primary marketing strengths, customer base, methods of distribution, compensation schemes, training, and other related sales and marketing issues. Notice that Cisco is primarily interested in the technology and products and minimally interested in the sales force, so this evaluation is likely to focus heavily on the top-performing salespersons with the emphasis being to determine how adaptable they would be to the Cisco way. Cisco often uses the acquired salespeople initially as internal Cisco salespeople training the existing Cisco sales organization on the application and sale of the acquired product lines. Once the existing Cisco sales force is up to speed on the products, the acquired salespeople likely will be offered homes in the Cisco sales organization.

In the case of the StrataCom (1996) integration, the sales integration was not handled well, and many of the acquired salespeople left for competitors. In the case of the Cerent (1999) acquisition the salespeople were left initially independent, calling on their same accounts, even if that account was called on by an existing Cisco salesperson. In this case, the salespeople remained after the acquisition.

A CLOSE LOOK AT THE TECHNOLOGY

Engineering also steps in as part of this due diligence effort. Engineering's primary interests are in making sure that the target's products actually perform up to specification and in determining the level of adaptability of the designs. This adaptability has become more important as Cisco has grown larger, according to Mario Mazzola, senior vice president of new business at Cisco and founder/CEO of Crescendo (1993). Mazzola contends that acquisitions get more difficult as Cisco's installed base of products and customer applications expands.[2]

"[Cisco wants] to make acquisitions which are more in the

technology space, such that you have a technology which is sufficiently advanced obviously in technology. But it is a technology that you have to mold into an architecture [Cisco's]," says Mazzola, expressing his personal opinion that this matching of acquired products with Cisco's architecture presents unique challenges that should not be underestimated. "Especially if you acquire something that is already there, good or bad, it is very difficult or impossible to change. You know, you [may] miss something," possibly requiring a reengineering effort. "Also, it is difficult for the team that you acquired. Because if you acquire a company with their product and you ask them to change completely everything . . . we start not to fit."

Mazzola sums up the importance of this consideration for a larger, more established Cisco in this way: "You need to recognize that there is innovation. There is technology installed. But you need to understand if all that can be molded [to meet the] expectations of your customers and your global architecture."

Cisco takes great care to determine this level of engineering compatibility during the due diligence stages, with special emphasis and sensitivity placed on understanding if the chemistry of the target is a match with Cisco's.

"You need to feel that you can establish a good working relationship. That the chemistry is there. That the vision is there," says Mazzola, reinforcing many of the standard Cisco acquisition requirements. "If they feel that what they have been doing is perfect, and . . . cannot accept any change or modifications, or so on, then it will be more difficult to achieve the type of integration that is very important."

Teamwork and the ability to work together in the future is once again a critical underlying measure of success.

Obtaining the current product set without the cooperation of key engineering personnel is shortsighted. This type of acquisition situation would likely be pursued only if the current product is intensely needed by Cisco to meet a market demand and as designed the product integrates well with the current Cisco architecture. The loss of the original design engineers places additional learning requirements on the Cisco engineering team with respect to creating the next generation of that product, but the fact that the existing product will work for a while buys some time for Cisco engineering to come up to speed on the product so that it can be modified as needed for the next generation. This situation is undesirable and would likely be passed on if Cisco had another company with a comparable technology that provided a better personnel fit, independent of the cost of acquisition.

Obtaining the current product family knowing that it has operational and integration problems while also believing that there will be future personnel conflicts between design personnel would be a recipe for disappointment for all parties concerned. Cisco would likely pass on this type of situation.

Should the product not exactly meet specifications and present a few integration difficulties but have an enthusiastic engineering staff, willing to do what it takes to make it work for Cisco, then Cisco would likely pursue this purchase. Remember, the next generation of product is really what Cisco is looking for, combined with the retention of technical and management personnel. This type of situation is workable with regard to Cisco's desired value acquisition areas.

VERIFYING THE HUMAN RESOURCES SITUATION

The human resources (HR) members of the due diligence team are the primary culture monitors of the team. They are going to investigate the target's practices in the way of management styles, organizational structure, and other cultural issues. Interesting enough, the very process of undergoing an acquisition brings out the underlying cultural fabric in a way that would not necessarily be possible in normal circumstances.

People being acquired are concerned about what the future will hold. They are worried about their jobs, benefits, pensions, options, and work assignments. They want to know about the bosses they will have inside Cisco. The are primarily concerned with whether they will have jobs after the deal is finalized.

FROM INSIDE CISCO

What I really love about this place is the contest of ideas. Because we have people from different companies, there are different approaches to solving problems. That creates an atmosphere of excitement that even the best small company can't duplicate.[3]

—Howard Charney, former CEO of Grand Junction Networks, acquired in 1995, commenting on Cisco's culture

Part of the HR due diligence involves an evaluation of the target's benefits policies and how they compare to Cisco's. (Chapter 12 takes a detailed look at the postpurchase personnel integration process.) This evaluation is needed not only to make sure that there is not some major mismatch between what Cisco offers and what the target's personnel already enjoy, but also to put together the welcome and orientation packets that are handed out to employees when the acquisition is announced. It takes time and knowledge to put together these packets, and due diligence provides the information needed to make them happen.

Due diligence does pay off. In one instance, the HR due diligence turned up over $60 million in existing pension liabilities that had not been discussed at that point in the negotiations. This $60 million was more money than was being discussed as a purchase price. Other evaluations have revealed details about the target's stock option plan that would have made it difficult to keep key technical people around after the acquisition. A few changes were made to make staying more attractive to the intended personnel, and they remained on after the purchase was finalized.

HR's read on the culture and management styles is important to the go-ahead with the acquisition. Should HR find that there is a discontinuity between what management presented as reality in early discussions and what HR determines to actually be the case, then credibility becomes a concern, opening up a whole new level of attention and discussion with management. If these problems cannot be worked out before the acquisition, Cisco will likely pass. Due diligence in these types of circumstances certainly is an excellent ounce of prevention avoiding years of painful cure.

HOW MUCH TO REVEAL IN DUE DILIGENCE?

Knowing where to draw the line with respect to revealing confidential company information is always a tricky process for targets. How this process is handled with respect to Cisco is important since the target must walk that line between providing Cisco with enough information not only to fulfill the due diligence need but also to not appear uncooperative. On the other hand, the target does not want to reveal information that, should the deal not go through, could be highly advantageous to Cisco and detrimental to the target's future prospects.

Kim Niederman has some guidance in this regard. He sees the due diligence process happening in a series of layers, each one more detailed than the previous one.

"The first discussions may involve 'standard released' information. After these initial discussions, the parties need to determine a (serious or not) level of interest. The second 'layer' is a little more precarious—involving information under NDA [nondisclosure agreement] . . . and even under NDA it's difficult to know how much to disclose. For example, should you discuss future direction beyond the next 12 months? However, if the acquiring company has done its homework with regard to the technology, they will already understand the 'framework' surrounding future direction and market implications."

You can see from his comments that even Kim has trouble setting a well-defined list of rules that can be followed in all circumstances. In reality, each set of circumstances is different and requires a different approach. Whatever that right blend of openness and self-protection may be for a target will likely be heavily dependent on the people and technologies involved. But keeping an open demeanor while protecting your proprietary future turf is probably a good idea—especially in the Valley where things have a way of circulating quickly.

DUE DILIGENCE AS A TEST OF THE CULTURE

People can date for years and get along perfectly but, upon deciding to get married, fight fiercely when it comes to planning a wedding. The first projects are always the toughest, and due diligence is really the first project that Cisco and the target are pursuing as a joint venture, unless the two companies have worked together previously on an alliance basis.

At this point, not only is Cisco checking out the target for compatibility but the target should be checking out Cisco as its future employer. Cisco is determining if it wants these people for employees, and the employees should be determining if they want to work for Cisco.

Cisco has no interest in taking over a company that does not want to be acquired. A hostile takeover defeats many of the basic objectives of an acquisition and is best avoided. Targets going through due diligence can feel as though every aspect of their lives is being combed through—a fairly nerve-wracking experience. It is common under these circumstances for tension to occur between the due diligence team and the target's personnel. Target personnel need to walk that line between disclosure and secrecy while also realizing that they are not just trying to close the deal. They are also evaluating Cisco as a future employer and will likely have to work with the very people who are doing the due diligence. Cisco, on the other hand, needs to be sensitive to the charged nature of the due diligence process and not alienate the target's employees before they even become Cisco employees. In many ways, the target and Cisco are in the acquisition boat together, since they both want it to work out, cooperation being the best possible method for achieving that outcome.

CISCO'S ASSUMPTIONS

The general assumptions associated with Cisco's due diligence apply to any acquisition. Those assumptions are summed up best by the Latin saying that anyone who has ever purchased a lemon product knows: caveat emptor—let the buyer beware. Vendors and salespeople always try to present their offerings in the most positive light and may be wrong in what they are presenting, even if no deceit is involved. They may simply not be aware that they are wrong. For example, a lawyer friend of mine who specializes in M&A transactions reported to me that one recent deal in which she was involved fell apart during the due diligence evaluation stage of an established corporation. What due diligence found out, much to the surprise and chagrin of the seller, was that the corporation was not a registered corporation with the state in which it operated. The charter had lapsed. How that can happen I am not sure, but it did.

Due diligence is simply the right thing to do and is an incredibly valuable tool for verifying that what the sellers say is true is actually true. In this way, the buyer can minimize the surprises associated with the purchase. Cisco due diligence adds another assumption in that Cisco believes that the best way to test the viability of a longer-term relationship is by trying a smaller project first,

175

and due diligence is an excellent way to test the cultural water. If you cannot work together at smoothly handling due diligence without a lot of personality conflict or squabble, then the likelihood of a longer-term relationship working smoothly is pretty slim. Let's face it. When a purchase gets to the due diligence stage, the seller really wants to sell and the buyer really wants to buy. They are simply making sure that nothing is in the way of the transaction working out as planned. If two groups can't get along when they are strongly motivated to do so, then the relationship will likely be worse when that strong motivation goes away in the postpurchase environment.

A culture that blends during due diligence is likely to blend after the purchase. One that does not blend during due diligence should likely be avoided, making the due diligence effort more than worth the investment.

Cisco also has a technical assumption that becomes increasingly important as Cisco grows along with its installed base of products and customer base. Whatever Cisco purchases must have the ability to be cutting-edge while, at the same time, being supportable within the Cisco architecture. Cisco's customers expect its products to be compatible with each other within the bounds of the technology involved. If the acquired products must be substantially reengineered by Cisco to functionally work within a Cisco network, then the cost and time of reengineering may substantially decrease the attractiveness of an acquisition. Time must be spent on this technology due diligence aspect to ensure that Cisco does not buy a product line that

---

About Cisco

Cisco occasionally takes a minority investment in a company as a way of testing the cultural water. Alliances are another way of getting to know a company better without having to commit to a purchase. These two approaches can be thought of as an initial project and a mild form of due diligence.

---

will not work well enough after purchase to be put into production as a Cisco-offered product.

Speed to market is another major underlying assumption with the Cisco due diligence process. Getting bogged down in details only to lose the opportunity to acquire the major items of value is simply not the Cisco way. First, ascertain the status of those few items that are absolutely critical to the future success of the target after assimilation. Then look for the other deal stoppers that could cause the acquisition to become a nightmare. But don't take so long or become so burdened with the details that the big value picture gets lost. Always remember this overall assumption for all Cisco acquisitions: It is not the current value of the company that is being purchased; it is the company's much larger value when run through the Cisco processes that is of interest. The immense expected future gains will likely offset anything that might be missed from a less than perfect due diligence effort. Remember also that most of the acquired companies are very small compared to Cisco, and anything that is missed during due diligence will likely not be very substantial to Cisco when it might have been huge to the much smaller company.

Being perfect and losing the game is not the Cisco way. "Play hard, play fast, take a few chances, and win the game. We'll deal with the other stuff when and if it comes up. And, by the way, I like working with you while we are winning." That is the Cisco way.

PORTABILITY EVALUATION

The Cisco approach to due diligence is highly portable in that it does not depend on anything that is Cisco-specific; instead it is situation-specific. If the assumptions associated with the overall Cisco strategy in general and the due diligence procedures in particular are applicable to an acquisition, then applying the Cisco rules would be appropriate. If, on the other hand, the target being acquired is comparably sized, or even larger than the buyer, and a missed due diligence item (such as the groundwater example used in this chapter) could have a seriously detrimental impact on the merged entity, then a more extensive, time-consuming due diligence process is warranted.

The essence of what is portable from the Cisco due diligence process is the heavy emphasis on verifying that which is of the utmost value and importance to the buyer and, subsequently, the merged entity. Making sure that the items of value are indeed what they were presented as being is primary. Taking time to review exhaustively the other items that are of a likely inconsequential nature at the possible loss of the target to another suitor, as happened with IBM and Kalpana, undermines the intent of the acquisition in the first place.

The due diligence team should take its lead from the acquisition team. The acquisition team must ensure that the team members understand the areas of critical importance to the acquisition transaction itself and the resulting merged entity. Then the due diligence process should be systemized as much as possible, with openness and professionalism driving the person-to-person interactions, all the time looking to ensure that the cultures and personalities involved will blend in the postpurchase environment. When all these items are performed like clockwork, you will have a portable due diligence process that will likely meet with the well-honed success of Cisco.

THE FINAL ANALYSIS

There is no easy way to do due diligence. The level of detail that can arise from an extensive due diligence process can take on a life of its own, sometimes bogging down the acquisition process to the point that the deal itself is compromised. But not doing due diligence is just plain irresponsible. Finding the balance between deeply verifying those target aspects that are important to the transaction while ensuring that no other unseen major obstacles are lurking in the shadows requires discipline along with a little luck.

The due diligence team members must keep their processes focused so that due diligence does not take on a life of its own, which it sometimes can. Due diligence is an excellent project for determining if the buyer and seller personnel can work together toward a common goal; in this way it has a completely new and important significance more substantial than simply verifying that the seller's assertions are true. Indeed, due diligence can also be a proving ground for the merging of personnel and cultures. Cisco keeps the due diligence stage focused on critical items while always, in the background, looking to answer the questions related to whether the acquired personnel will assimilate well into the Cisco environment.

Learning from prior due diligence projects helps to make later processes more reliable and efficient. Adapting due diligence to each acquisition situation is a must since what is of primary value from one acquisition may not be of primary value in another.

Do due diligence, but don't sacrifice what would otherwise be an excellent acquisition for the sake of compulsive completeness.

CHAPTER *12*

PERSONNEL INTEGRATION À LA CISCO—BAM!

Employees who have just been acquired can be very uncomfortable. . . .
They've got to see a future. They've got to see a culture they want to be a
part of. . . . That's what many people fail to grasp. . . . You're only ac-
quiring the employees.[1]

—John Chambers, President and CEO, Cisco Systems

This chapter takes a look at Cisco's personnel integration practices that entice people to stay after the acquisition is finalized. Some of this is common sense to which you will say, "Sure. That is obvious." It is one thing to think that something is a great idea or makes sense. It is another actually to implement policies, procedures, and personnel teams that functionally effect personnel integration. In other words, walk with respect to doing those things that will keep people around. Cisco is one of those companies that delivers on its promise to make acquired people at home as Cisco employees in the most expeditious way possible.

Cisco keeps its technical people. In an industry and geographic area with a high turnover on the order of 40+ percent per year, Cisco has maintained a turnover rate of between 4 percent and 6 percent per year. That is pretty amazing when you consider the temptations present in Silicon Valley, where everybody and their brother is either

181

involved with a start-up or knows someone who is. Where people in other parts of the country talk about their vacation plans over dinner, Silicon Valley people talk about when their options vest and what they will do in their retirements. (A little facetious perhaps, but not totally outside of the realm of reality.)

When Cisco acquires a company, it may pay as much as $15 million per employee! That is a lot of money by any standard. If it buys a 100-person firm such as Combinet (1995) for $132 million, Cisco is paying over $1 million per employee. If 40 percent of the employees leave in the first year, that means that around $50 million worth of purchased investment leaves with them. The people are the value, and if they leave you lose. Period.

FROM INSIDE CISCO

Cisco gives me the chance to build breakthrough products that can change the world overnight.[2]

> —Charles Giancarlo, senior vice president,
> Cisco Systems, and former cofounder of
> Kalpana, acquired by Cisco in 1994

Put into John Chambers' words, "If you pay $500,000 to $2 million per person for the people you acquired, and you lose 30 to 40 percent of those people in the first two years, you've made a terrible decision for your investors. If you go back and look at how many companies in this kind of acquisition deal lose 30 to 40 percent of their people in that period, it will shock you. That is why acquisitions in our industry fail."[3] And that is why Cisco has done so well. Period.

ASSIMILATE IN STAGES

Cisco is a huge company with extraordinary expertise and resources in sales, manufacturing, and finance, and it makes no bones about its desire to retain key technology personnel, managers, and executives who can productively make the transition from the target into Cisco. Integrating the sales teams is usually one of the most challenging since salespeople tend to be territorial in nature, or as John Morgridge said when asked about the merging of the StrataCom sales team with Cisco's, "Sales organizations have a zero-sum game mentality."[4]

Cisco typically integrates human resources, manufacturing, distribution, customer service, and finance into the overall Cisco infrastructure. However, engineering, marketing, and sales are often integrated into the Cisco business unit that is sponsoring the acquisition. Each acquisition has a business unit that becomes its inside-Cisco sponsor to ensure that the acquired company does not get lost in, or become overwhelmed with, Cisco and the integration process. Unfortunately, the sales force may still become a casualty in this integration process.

Dave Newkirk, controller for Combinet during its time of acquisition, felt that the acquisition integration was handled very well but adds that there were some problems integrating the sales teams.

"I think the only people that had a little bit of a tough time were some of the sales folks . . . who weren't as ambitiously recruited as the rest of the team. In my experience that's always been the toughest part of the integration-the sales force," says Newkirk.[5]

Cisco creates an integration team for each new acquisition that has responsibility for making their particular integration work as smoothly as possible while ensuring that acquisition business objectives are met as outlined in the acquisition business case. Think of the integration process as being divided into two stages: the structural integration stage and the cultural integration stage. Structural integration deals with the administrative and operational aspects of the integration. Items dealt with during this stage are the integration of payroll information, employee information, information systems, voice mail, telephone extensions, and other daily operational activities that are needed to make things run. It covers items such as getting a Cisco badge, obtaining and ordering office supplies, making travel arrangements, completing an expense report, and other mundane aspects of corporate life.

FROM INSIDE CISCO

The most important thing that you always have to remember with acquisitions is that the most important side is the personal side. . . . That's part of the measurement of a success. Not just the products that are developed by the initial engineers and how much revenue they have developed, but it is the team and what they have done in contributing to Cisco.[6]

—*Barry Eggers, former Cisco business development leader and current general partner with Lightspeed Venture Partners*

Cultural integration takes a little longer and is best accomplished face-to-face. For this reason integration teams are set up containing both Cisco and target personnel. This team's efforts are augmented by a buddy system wherein a member of the Cisco team is paired with a member of equal stature within the target. The objective of this pairing is to mentor the acquired manager in the Cisco way, having an experienced Cisco veteran working alongside, coaching as the process unfolds. Notice that this approach not only provides informational input to the acquired employee, but also, invisibly, transfers information about Cisco's culture.

The frustration associated with handling the mundane aspects of organizational change are often overlooked by senior-level managers when making their integration decisions. Changing the phone systems sounds simple on paper but will create immense angst within a company when employees cannot perform simple tasks like forward-

---

About Cisco

The Cisco integration team sets and tracks 30-, 60-, 90-, and 120-day milestones for determining the effectiveness of the integration process and to ensure that target productivity is not lost in the process.

---

ing calls, transferring calls, or putting a caller on hold. Making sure that training is part of that transition makes everyone happier with the new technology; otherwise they may simply resent this necessary change and those who forced it on them. Cisco goes overboard in making sure not only that acquired employees are welcomed properly, but also that they have someone they can go to during the important early days of the integration.

Orientation sessions are held on a regular basis so that acquired employees can ask questions and get answers from Cisco employees who were often themselves acquired at an earlier date. Sometimes change management training sessions are offered to help acquired employees deal with the changes associated with assimilating into Cisco.

"Face time" makes cultural integration happen. Face time happens only when people are working with other people.

PROTECTING TARGET EMPLOYEES FROM CISCO'S "HELPERS"

One key duty of the integration team is to provide a buffer between the target's employees and Cisco employees who want to "help" with the employee orientation. According to Barry Eggers, business development leader for the Newport Systems Solutions, LightStream Corporation, and Kalpana acquisitions, Cisco decided to formalize the integration process with its second acquisition. The intent of this process was to create a Cisco team that would stay on with the acquisition once the deal was finalized. Their responsibly is to make sure that the newly acquired company can be successful within Cisco.

Cisco takes key in-house personnel from between 10 and 15 functional areas and puts them on the integration team. According to Eggers, Cisco tries to allow the company to grow a little bit on its own within Cisco and then slowly assimilates the target into Cisco. During this critical transition period, Cisco requires that all Cisco-personnel-initiated requests of the target's personnel be directed to the integration team person responsible for that particular area. In this way, the level of communication between Cisco and the target is controlled. You don't have the target's personnel, especially their engineers, being instructed by dozens of well-meaning Cisco personnel who may only tend to confuse the situation even more than it already is simply by the acquisition process itself. If someone in Cisco manufacturing, for example, wanted to say something to the acquired company, that Cisco employee would first need to call the integration team lead from manufacturing to get an answer. Once the company is over its initial hurdles and starting to understand the Cisco way, these communication restrictions are relaxed.

FROM INSIDE CISCO

We focus on maintaining two major groups—the management teams and the engineers.[7]

—*John Chambers, president and CEO, Cisco Systems*

KEEPING THE GEEKS HAPPY

Engineers are a hot commodity in technology fields in general and in Silicon Valley in particular. Demand for their services is always high. But what basically motivates geeks is more complicated than only money, although money is an important part of the motivation equation; don't get me wrong. All personnel are driven by the desire to be part of a winning organization. Nontechnical personnel are driven not only by the opportunity to make a decent salary but also by the likely prospect of selling a vested stock option in a few years that will make them financially independent. And that has happened at Cisco a lot. You wander around Cisco—or any successful start-up for that matter—and you may find that the secretary, production supervisor, or maintenance personnel are truly wealthy from their stock options and a successful initial public offering (IPO). However, many of these people remain as employees long after their options have vested and they have become wealthy. Engineers, in particular, have a tough time leaving their industry. I have met engineers who were worth many millions of dollars who still worked 60+ hours per week. Why? Let's take a closer look at what makes a geek tick.

Technology and Product Vision—Have Some Fun, Grow Rich

Contrary to how it may appear on the outside or may be presented in the popular press, engineers are highly creative people. Think about it. They sit around an office or living room somewhere and come up with product or service ideas. They then take the steps to make those ideas a tangible, physical, viable reality. Out of nothing comes a product that solves a problem that was previously unsolved. That is the essence of creation that is common to the creative process of artists, authors, and architects. Being an engineer, especially one with a start-up, can be exciting in ways that have nothing directly to do with the money to be made.

Now add to this creative need the ability to work with other like-driven people who share your passion for technology, and you have not only a personal but a collegial experience that is highly re-

---

Inside the Valley

I used to travel a lot with an excellent engineer who helped found a highly successful company that went public, making him a multimillionaire. He worked hard, long hours designing products and bringing them into full mass production. I asked him what it was like having succeeded in doing what others of us had only dreamed about. He replied, "You obviously don't have a clue. I don't do it for the money, although it is nice to have the money. I would do this even if I didn't get paid a lot of money." This encounter happened over 20 years ago, and the situation hasn't changed much since then. Creative people are creative people. Period. Underestimating the intensity of this creative need is to underestimate the value of a creative professional in any creative field.

---

warding. Take a look around the Valley and you will find that many of the same engineers who started one company will get together and start another one. Just as you will find entertainers who work together on projects simply for the fun or working together, so will you find technical people reassembling to create a new technology or a new set of products.

Having watched this industry grow up over the last 25+ years, I can still safely say that I think it miraculous that this technology works at all. We take it for granted that clicking on a mouse in Chicago should provide instant access to a server in Australia. But truly understanding all of the various linkages that must work flawlessly for that simple and almost instantaneous connection to occur only inspires me with a sense of awe that it works at all. And even better, it works in a way that is so reliable that we take it for granted. And it becomes cheaper every year to make that connection. In what industry can you get more capability, more easily provided, in a smaller package for less money? Looked at in this light, there is something technologically miraculous about what has happened, and continues to happen, with technology. Being part of that technological evolution is a powerful motivator for any technical person—and those nontechnical people who support the design and production efforts enjoy being part of the process, too.

Anyone working for Cisco has had the experience of providing a product or service that truly changed the lives of the people who used it. The initial router products enabled the provision of networking capabilities to more people than was previously possible. Implementing switching provided this networking capability on a much lower cost-of-ownership basis, which once again extended the provision of network communication to more people. Extending the product line to high-speed, 100 Mbps, local networks and then to Synchronous Optical Network (SONET) and other high-speed wide area network (WAN) technologies enabled the transfer of multimedia information in ways that we take for granted today. Cisco's commitment to its customers requires that it remain on the cutting edge of technologically viable products and services. Being an engineer for a company like Cisco with its breadth of offering provides a variety of design opportunities that would simply not be available from a smaller company with its more restrictive offering. Being an engineer with Cisco is good. And you get to make money, too!

Cisco Sets New Industry Standards

Cisco is the big guy. It doesn't have to compete to be the big guy on the block. It *is* the big guy. However, it had best be worried about the next little guy who is around the corner with the technology that will knock Cisco on its rear. A decent paranoia regarding the arrival of that next "Cisco" is what keeps leaders in the lead. Taking a leading position for granted is one of the telling signs of a company about to be knocked out of a leadership position. In high tech, there is always someone in the wings with a newer, faster, more reliable, and cheaper way of doing what the other industry members are doing. Leaders are in the unique position of having a large amount of say as to what the existing and ensuing industry standards will be. As the industry leaders, they have a large installed customer base that will be impacted by any substantial changes from the leader's existing standards. This installed base gives leaders a lot of clout while also protecting their existing customer-installed equipment. For this reason, you will always find industry leaders sitting on or even chairing technology standards committees.

Talk to engineers who have sat on or worked on standards committees, and they will invariably let you know at some point that they have been on that committee. It is a point of pride to be able to define a standard to which the rest of the industry will comply.

A company like Cisco has the ability to define a standard simply by saying that it is adopting an approach as that standard. Cisco's Internetwork Operating System (IOS) is an example of a product that belonged to Cisco but, due to its preponderance in the marketplace, really defined a standard with which other vendors had to relate. IOS is the software that enables a network manager to keep tabs on network operation in general and individual products in particular. If something were to happen within the network, the network manager could use IOS to verify network or component status and then take actions to deal with the situation at hand. IOS is a Cisco-specific product, and non-Cisco products may likely not communicate with IOS, meaning that the network manager would have to use another set of tools to manage that product. The network manager would likely choose the Cisco option, all other things being equal, since IOS compatibility makes his or her life much simpler. IOS was and still is in many ways a de facto standard within the networking industry.

Remember, if you are on the IOS engineering team, you are defining the way that a huge number of customers, and even your competitors, will operate. Defining a standard is just, simply stated, cool. Working for a company like Cisco in engineering provides standardization opportunities that are not available from less prominent companies.

Get Better Tools and More Support for Development

Smaller companies, and particularly start-up companies, are usually strapped for money. They make do with the products they can afford as opposed to the ones they would like to have. And this is the right approach for a smaller company in that it should focus its use of capital exclusively on what is needed to make its narrow product range more successful. Working for a Cisco, on the other hand, opens up new worlds for technological evolution. There is a larger engineering community from which to draw technical guidance and support. In essence, the range of toys used by engineers to do what they do, along with the people with whom engineers get to interact, is wider and often more stimulating, as long as the entrepreneurial spirit of the organization is maintained.

Cisco does a solid job of providing engineers with challenging development projects that keep them pushing not only their own design skills but also the technology edge of the company.

Cisco Impacts the Industry

There is also no question that working for a company the size of Cisco provides opportunities to shape the direction of an industry. It is not possible to do so from a smaller company. By working with Cisco, people get industry recognition that is a direct result of their association with an industry leader. Watching the way the media treats John Chambers with respect to business issues is a sure indication of the high regard offered to Cisco-related personnel. If you are an engineer on a standards committee, your Cisco affiliation adds weight to your comments, just as occurs with the other major players such as IBM, Nortel, and Lucent, to name a few.

Many a person has left a large company expecting to receive the same treatment as a representative of their own company as they received as a larger company executive. Most have been shocked and disappointed as to how quickly they were forgotten once they no longer represented their former large employer.

Being a honcho with Cisco is valuable and will open doors within the industry that would not open for the individual not representing Cisco. This high level of access affords an opportunity for technical personnel to steer the direction of the industry, whether formally through standards or informally through speeches, articles, or white papers. A "best practices" paper will be better received from a Cisco engineer than from an engineer associated with a little-known smaller company.

Be One of the Big Guys

There is prestige associated with being one of the "big guys" of an industry. Being with Cisco definitely makes you a member of the "big guys" club, even if you are not one of the Cisco honchos.

HANDLING STOCK OPTION ISSUES

The invisible hand of greed is present throughout the American economy, and nowhere is it more prevalent than in Silicon Valley. Let's face it. You have to be fiscally oriented when you work in an area where a standard three-bedroom, two-bath house within commuting distance costs, on average, $500,000. And this same house, if located in the middle of Silicon Valley, may well cost you $2 million! And people can afford to pay for these houses for any number of reasons, a major one of them being that they have made tons of money from their stock options obtained by working for a start-up or other Valley company. Options are a way of life in the Valley, and Cisco provides a long-term incentive for its people to stay by offering options tied to Cisco's stock, which, until the 2000–2001 time frame, was as sure an investment vehicle as you could purchase.

FROM INSIDE CISCO

I have one friend who started with Cisco in the late 1980s, pre-IPO, and left the company in the late 1990s. She had a stock option plan associated with her employment that made her wealthy. Her final words on the subject of stock options and her Cisco employment were, "Pretty good move, huh?" I sure think so. She still makes me buy her coffee. Go figure!

Golden Handcuffs, Not Golden Parachutes

Retaining talented people requires providing them with a motivation to stay. Making people millionaires on the day of the acquisition without providing additional stock options tied to future Cisco stock performance is an almost surefire way to lose key acquired personnel. And, unfortunately, you will likely lose the most qualified and marketable of the bunch.

FROM INSIDE CISCO

We don't do a deal if the target has accelerated vesting [of stock options]. The minute you buy the company they all get rich. We prefer golden handcuffs.[8]

—*Charles Giancarlo, senior vice president, Cisco Systems*

For this reason, Cisco evaluates the way stock options will vest in the event of a purchase as part of the initial evaluation and due

---

Inside the Valley

It's easier to integrate engineers who are rich and happy than ones looking for a way out.[9]

—Paul Sagawa, analyst, Sanford C. Bernstein

---

diligence process. Some option contracts provide for accelerated vesting in that the entire employee option fully vests at the time the company is sold. Notice that this removes any future incentive for the employees to remain with the company, especially if they feel that they will be playing a minor role with the new company and will have little material impact on the future stock's performance.

When an acquisition is finalized, acquired employees' stock options vest at the rate they were at with their old company, but now they are vesting Cisco stock instead of their prior company's stock.[10] This has traditionally been a good thing in that the stock continued to increase in value up until late 2000. Some people I spoke with think that the lower Cisco stock price might actually bode well for those companies being acquired at the lower stock price in that getting Cisco shares at a lower price means that the stock has upside potential, whereas getting options at a much higher price meant that the stock had more downside than upside, as was experienced by many of these people when Cisco's stock slid. So, oddly enough, the lower Cisco stock price and subdued market conditions present in 2001 may actually work to Cisco's favor with respect to holding employees. And holding the employees is a key measure of the acquisition's success.

"When we acquire a company, we aren't simply acquiring its current products; we're acquiring the next generation of products through its people. . . . [If] all you are doing is buying the current research and the current market share, you're making a terrible investment," says John Chambers.[11]

So, how does a company deal with a situation where the options of employees may be "under water" from the perspective that the strike (purchase) price for the employee's stock option might be at a higher price than the current market price of Cisco's stock? Here is the Chambers' approach, as of June, 2000:

"We've been very open with employees in particular that we want them to view the opportunity for the long run. That's why we extended [the vesting period of our] options from four to five years and why we pass out options every year. It's why we wouldn't reprice options."[12]

REMOVING THE UNCERTAINTY

Getting people over the initial shock of being acquired is critical to their having a positive taste in their mouths about becoming assimilated into the Cisco culture. Where many buyers would let the acquired employees fumble around trying to figure out the systems and various other mechanisms of their new buyer's culture, Cisco takes a strongly proactive approach, which kicks in the moment the acquisition is finalized.

FROM INSIDE CISCO

The Mario Rule: Before any employee of a newly acquired company is terminated, both CEOs [Cisco's and the target's] must give their consent. The Mario Rule (named after Mario Mazzola, former CEO of Crescendo and still senior vice president with Cisco) was formally agreed to with the 1993 Crescendo purchase and is still followed to this day with current acquisitions.

The Mario Rule helps to get acquired employees over the initial uncertainty regarding their jobs. In the words of Carl Russo, former CEO of Cerent, "When they hear merger, it basically means layoffs." When Cerent was acquired, Chambers and Russo agreed that no Cerent employees could be fired or significantly reassigned without Russo's approval. Cisco usually goes along with this policy for around a one-year period after the acquisition, but in Cerent's case Russo got permanent veto authority.[13]

Cisco believes in being up-front with the target with respect to the people it wants to keep and those it feels are not desired as part of the acquisition. In this way, employees know that their jobs are either protected or not. If these people feel uncertainty about their futures, they will lose their primary focus, which Cisco absolutely wants kept on their jobs.

"We've learned that to make it [the acquisition] successful, you have to tell employees up front what you are going to do, because trust is everything in this business. You have got to tell them early so you don't betray their trust later," says John Chambers.[14]

This works in personal relationships, and it makes sense that it should work with acquisitions as well, since, after all, you are acquiring a personal/business relationship with the acquired employees that will extend into the future. Having that future based on honesty instead of distrust certainly seems like a solid foundation.

▬▬ DO IT NOW!

Cisco moves right into the acquired organization and begins the assimilation process as soon as possible, often within hours of the announcement. The objective is to integrate the acquired people just as quickly as possible.

Cisco recognizes that this transition is usually painful for the acquired company employees, since they are the ones having to adapt to Cisco as opposed to the other way around. Mimi Gigoux, Cisco director, was brought into Cisco with the 1994 acquisition of Kalpana. She manages a team of people whose job it is to help acquired employees make the transition to Cisco as seamlessly as possible. The good news at this point is that a large number of Cisco employees joined Cisco when acquired and therefore have a firsthand perspective on the process and what acquired employees can expect.

FROM INSIDE CISCO

The more flexible and positive you are, the better it will be for you.[15]

—*Mimi Gigoux, Cisco acquisition integration director, advising acquired employees preparing for integration into Cisco*

Cisco purchased Monterey Networks, of Richardson, Texas, in August 1999 for $500 million. Monterey Networks' optical Internetworking products allowed Cisco a rapid entry into the optical marketplace. Monterey Networks had 132 people at the time of the acquisition, all of whom remained at the Texas headquarters, with Joe Bass, Monterey's former CEO continuing to lead his prior team but now as a Cisco vice president in charge of the new Monterey-generated business unit. Cisco already had a 10 percent investment in Monterey Networks and decided that it wanted to own the rest, so made a purchase offer that Monterey Networks couldn't refuse.

"We had interest from other companies, but they didn't move as fast as Cisco. There were still considering us when the announcement came out that Cisco had bought us," recalls Joe Bass about the speed of purchase.[16]

But the purchase wasn't all that Cisco did quickly on the Monterey Networks acquisition. According to Lori Smith, Monterey Networks' former director of human resources, the Cisco integration team wasted no time in starting the assimilation process.

"We closed the deal at 11 P.M. on a Wednesday," recalls Smith. "When I walked in Thursday morning, we all had Cisco tags on our doors and a banner on the front of our building. And they had this huge Cisco art thing on the wall in the lobby. I saw someone in here putting bottled water in the fridge to replace our coolers. They really don't mess around."[17]

FROM INSIDE CISCO

All 95 employees were guaranteed a starting position in Cisco. . . . It was understood that they would have to perform at that point and everyone was going to get a stake in it. . . . It was almost as if they really made everybody feel like "we love you guys and we want you guys." . . . You got the impression that they were really going overboard to make you feel welcome [with] all the work that they put into it by dedicated and terrific folks.[18]

—Dave Newkirk, former controller for Cisco's fifth acquisition, Combinet (acquired in 1995)

WHO GOES WHERE?

I have found that the "sticky note" has helped me in any number of business activities. Cisco has found a use for the sticky note when performing its acquisitions. The name of each acquired employee is put onto a sticky note. These sticky notes are then put on a wall of a room in which will sit personnel from both Cisco and the acquired company. The intention of this meeting is to attach a subsequent Cisco job to the name of each person being acquired. This mapping of names to positions takes place even before the company is formally acquired, occurring during that period of time between the announcement of the acquisition and when the deal is finalized. For the Cerent acquisition, this mapping meeting took place at the Cerent offices on the second day after the announcement.

Barry Eggers, Cisco manager of the StrataCom acquisition (1996), says that a highly personalize approach was taken with respect to this acquisition to ensure that the best people went to the best jobs.

"I did the integration for StrataCom, which was the largest people-wise acquisition that Cisco had ever done. . . . We went through a process where we had the StrataCom lead, who was Sanjay Subhedar [former chief financial officer (CFO) with StrataCom, who became Cisco's vice president of WAN business], and myself in a room. We had everyone's name on a sticky note. We wanted to make sure that everyone had a good job," says Eggers.[19] This integration involved over 1,200 people, 200 of whom were salespeople.

Cisco also tries to put high-level acquired personnel into key leadership positions as well. This is an indicator to the acquired personnel that their people will have a say in their collective fate. In StrataCom's case, Dick Moley, StrataCom's CEO, became Cisco's senior vice president and general manager of the new wide area network (WAN) business unit that formed as a direct result of the StrataCom purchase. Given StrataCom's size, it was not needed that it fully integrate into the Cisco organization as it already had substantial facilities and personnel and a vibrant customer base. Adding StrataCom's technology to Cisco's enabled Cisco to provide both intranet and Internet product and support from a single source, over public, private, and hybrid networks. This capability was simply not available from any other single competitive vendor.

But even Cisco is not infallible, and problems arose from the StrataCom integration with respect to the sales and marketing force. First, Cisco underestimated the level of resistance that the existing Cisco sales force would exhibit with respect to adopting and promoting the

StrataCom product line. Some publications report that the StrataCom salespeople left as a result of Cisco's trying to speed up the sales cycle, but according to Eggers the problems arose when, at the request of the Cisco sales executives, the StrataCom salespeople were put on a "different" (i.e., lower) compensation plan than the Cisco sales reps. Within a few months of the deal closing, about a third of StrataCom's sales force quit as they saw their sales commission plans being changed.

"We made some mistakes in integrating the StrataCom sales force," admits Eggers. "We lost some good people because of that—people who are now competing with [Cisco], by the way."[20]

Chambers is reported to have echoed Eggers' sentiments in a meeting with Cerent employees where the StrataCom situation came up in discussion. "We didn't do that well," said Chambers, referring to the StrataCom sales force integration.[21]

The good news is that Cisco is always learning from its mistakes. When integrating the Cerent sales force, it chose to let the Cerent sales force remain independent, keeping their own accounts, even if those accounts were already visited by a Cisco salesperson. The sales team also received an average pay boost of between 15 percent and 20 percent to bring their income more in line with that of the existing Cisco sales personnel.

Most Cerent personnel kept their same jobs and kept their same bosses. Around 30 people were reassigned because Cisco already had people doing their jobs. Eight people relocated to Cisco's headquarters, which was around 90 miles away.

WHAT'S IN A MUG? OR, GETTING EMPLOYEES ORIENTED

Acquired personnel get a Cisco mug when the acquisition is announced. On the mug is the inscription, "Welcome to the team." At the initial employee announcement meeting we find the integration team is there handing out folders containing basic Cisco information such as phone numbers, e-mail addresses of a number of Cisco executives, and a benefits comparison chart that shows how Cisco's benefits compare with those that they had previously, including medical, vacation, retirement, and other standard benefits. General background information about Cisco Systems is also included in the packet. Over the next few days, people are invited to attend subsequent orientation sessions mug in hand, so that additional questions that come up can be addressed.

Mimi Gigoux, Cisco acquisition integration director, came to Cisco with the Kalpana acquisition. After the deal was finalized, she spent almost nine months looking inside Cisco for employment homes for her 127 fellow Kalpana acquired employees. This level of uncertainty took much of the steam out of the integration, and Gigoux is convinced that it was unnecessary. That is why she and her team now so quickly initiate the integration process. Peter Ruh, who was part of Kalpana during its acquisition and now works with Cisco on its integration team, laments that Kalpana's poor integration process substantially hurt the effectiveness of that acquisition. "We had momentum, and we just stopped," he says. Not any more. Cisco integrated all of StrataCom's 1,200+ personnel (acquisition #10) within 90 days; Kalpana's 127 people (acquisition #4) had taken nine months to integrate.

CISCOIZING THE ENVIRONMENT

Communication is key to a successful integration, and networking technology is a primary communication medium of high-tech firms in general and Cisco Systems in particular.

Cisco not only sells Internet-related equipment, it uses its own technology within is own organization. In the Valley this is referred to as "eating your own dog food" in that you not only sell dog food but you actually give the food you sell to your own dog. Unfortunately, in high-tech firms there is often a belief that customers should do as the vendor says, not as the vendor does, since the vendor may not practice its own recommendations within its own organization. Sad, but true nonetheless.

As for Cisco, it uses the Internet as a cohesion point for its customers, employees, vendors, and the general public. There is a tremendous amount of information contained on the Cisco web site (www.cisco.com), and readers are referred to this site for information ranging from the financial to the products.

Cisco employees get access to the Cisco Employee Connection (CEC), from which employees can, for themselves, find most anything they need to know about functioning within Cisco. Typical information would include health benefits registration, company event tracking, personnel expense report reimbursement tracking, or even making travel arrangements online. In late 2000, estimates had it that over 1.7 million pages of information were available from the CEC, and the CEC was accessed thousands of times per day by Cisco employees.

FROM INSIDE CISCO

We've held only one or two closing dinners. It's not the closing we celebrate—it's the integration.[22]

> —Dan Scheinman, Cisco senior vice
> president, commenting on Cisco's heavy
> integration emphasis

New employees have a strong need for the information provided by the CEC. Getting them online as quickly as possible is a major objective of the integration process since, once online, the employees begin to feel a part of the organization and start to get access to information for themselves, thus becoming more self-sufficient. Developing a sense of autonomy within a new organization is a solid first step for acquired employees who are working hard to feel more at home with their new employer. Cisco even presents employee meetings on the internal network so that the meeting can be viewed, in real time, by all Cisco employees instead of only those geographically located at the meeting's location. Communication lets people feel they are an important part of the organization. If you can't be physically face-to-face, at least you can be netted there over the internal company network.

There is also the Executive Information System (EIS), which

provides executive-level managers with real-time sales information such as bookings, billings, backlog, or other salient sales-oriented information. This information can be broken down by region, product, or any number of other ways such as customers or specific market area. Acquired company executives, trained on the operation of the EIS systems, then have access to information just as the already existing Cisco managers do. Once again, this helps tie together the acquired employees with those already working for Cisco.

Cisco's information systems (IS) department has a group of dedicated people who are chartered with bringing the IS infrastructure of the acquired target in alignment with Cisco's IS infrastructure. There are no multiple standards at Cisco. There is the Cisco approved standard. Period. Nonstandard technology is eliminated as quickly as possible, as long as its elimination does not materially affect the target's ability to deliver on the intrinsic value that it provides Cisco by its acquisition. Desktop systems may very well be changed along with applications. Training is provided to acquired employees to get them over the IS transitional hurdles, and the process is implemented as quickly as possible. Most acquisitions are technologically implemented within 60 to 100 days.

"Once the deal had been penned it started the clock ticking on the closing items," recalls Dave Newkirk, controller at Combinet when it was acquired by Cisco in 1995. "The place was crawling with Cisco people. IT guys getting us set up [to work] behind the Cisco fire wall. Telecom guys getting us cut over under the Cisco telecom system. They had people from all the functional areas—HR, MIS, telecom, facilities folks, accounting, and finance. As I say, the place was crawling [with Cisco people]."[23]

KEEPING THE EXECUTIVE TEAM AROUND— OR NOT

Cisco internal executive-level support for an acquisition is important. In essence, Cisco looks for an internal organization into which the acquisition can be integrated. In this way, managers and other employees have

Cisco people who can help them with the assimilation. According to Charles Giancarlo, now an officer at Cisco and previously vice president of business development, involvement during the negotiations from one of Cisco's business units is mandatory since the acquired company must be embraced by an internal "or it will flounder and die."[24]

FROM INSIDE CISCO

If you don't retain executive management, you don't retain the rank and file.[25]

> —*Charles Giancarlo, senior vice president, Cisco Systems, referring to the importance of retaining the acquired management team if possible*

Finding a way for the acquired executive to continue playing a major role within Cisco in the postacquisition environment is critical to motivating this person as a Cisco executive. Remember that as CEOs of their own firms they had to deal with shareholders, venture capitalists, board members, and other high-level partners who are needed to make a start-up company successful. In truth, a lot of these guys love the entrepreneurial aspects of a start-up and perform the business aspects because they have to. Joining Cisco enables them to have the best of both worlds.

It is not unusual for acquired executives to miss the freedom they once held as CEOs of their own firms. But not having to worry about many of the riskier business aspects of CEO-level management frees up entrepreneurs to do what they like to do most: create and produce products.

No matter how hard you try, it is likely that some of the acquired executive team will simply not like being acquired. Yet, if they are smart, which most of them are, they will recognize that the Cisco acquisition will likely be beneficial to them as well as their employees who had a stake in the prior company. Disgruntled executives who stay on after the acquisition, holding stock as payment for their shares in the target, have incentive for the acquisition to succeed once finalized. If they realize that they don't fit with the Cisco culture in a productive way, then it is best that they leave. And it is best not only for Cisco but also for the executives themselves and their former employees. How those exits are handled is critical. If the executives leave disgruntled, then they have left a bad taste in the mouths of their employees who stay behind and also with the Cisco people with whom they worked.

FROM INSIDE CISCO

"What they've given me instead is the chance to kick our products through the roof. I'm still running an operation whose mission is managing lives and technology, but I don't worry about cash flow. I don't worry about having enough R&D money to keep up with the big boys. We are the big boys."[26]

—Howard Charney, cofounder of Grand Junction Networks (acquired 1995) and now senior vice president with Cisco Systems.

For this reason, Cisco works with the acquired executive team during the negotiation and due diligence phases to ensure that there is goal congruence with respect to what Cisco and the acquired executives expect from the acquisition. If that congruence is not there and a reasonable accord cannot be reached, then Cisco will likely walk away from the deal since the likely future personnel clashes will undermine the future success prospects of the acquisition. The savvy selling executives, on the other hand, will likely see that their ego or personality issues should not undermine an acquisition by Cisco if selling to Cisco is good for their employees, customers, vendors, and shareholders while also making them a lot of money. Once again,

---

About Cisco

At the conclusion of each target integration process, the integration team has a "lessons learned" meeting at which the integration is discussed and process improvements are recommended and implemented. For Cisco, target integration is a continually evolving and improving process that is adapted, as needed, to accommodate the peculiarities of the specific target being acquired with an eye always on maintaining the unique value items of interest for this particular acquisition.

---

candor up front is better for all involved parties. Chambers understands this point clearly, and simply does not want to have a disgruntled employee on his executive staff, especially one who has the ability to corrupt what would otherwise be a healthy acquisition.

"We still retain the majority of the top managers of our acquired companies," says John Chambers. "Not all of them, but the majority. Most of those who leave we've already decided prior to the acquisition will leave. So you need to understand what's important to them—as basic as it sounds."[27]

Keeping those managers motivated once on board with Cisco is accomplished by Chambers by getting to know his people and providing the environment that most likely will motivate them to future success.

"If you take my top 100 managers in Cisco, I know what motivates most all of them and I know what's important to them. And it's a shame for the company to succeed and yet have members of the company not achieving their personal goals. So we try to align the goals of the company with the goals of the individual and make that work all the way through the organization. I've practiced it up at the top so that is should cascade all the way through the company." (This is Chambers' technique for ensuring managerial goal congruence as discussed in Chapter 6.)[28]

Once again, Cisco makes a point of determining both Cisco's and the target's key personnel's expectations with respect to the acquisition and subsequent integration. This approach makes sure that concordance exists up front and minimizes the later discord that will surely erupt if powerful people in key positions decide that they were wronged. These ill feelings are the foundation on which many an internal political turf battle has been waged that almost always turns out badly for the executives, employees, customers, and shareholders involved.

THE FINAL ANALYSIS

Keeping the acquired personnel is key to any successful Cisco acquisition. Believing that uncertainty is the worst enemy to personnel retention, Cisco does everything it can to remove the uncertainty from the acquisition and integration process.

During the transaction phase, Cisco personnel are candid about Cisco's intentions with respect to personnel, products, management, and other important areas of concern. Cisco also prepares for personnel integration during due diligence so that acquired personnel assimilation starts the moment that the acquisition is announced to target employees. In this way acquired people immediately start to experience being a part of the Cisco organization. They are made to feel wanted and welcome at Cisco in a way that usually works pretty well with most people I know. Now add to that the ability to enjoy the financial rewards of owning Cisco stock instead of the stock of a recently IPO'd start-up, and you have a pretty powerful personnel transition and integration package.

Whatever Cisco does, it appears to work. The personnel turnover rate is incredibly low given that its headquarters are in Silicon Valley, where people have been known to be recruited from one company to another during the Friday beer bust.

CHAPTER *13*

INTEGRATING PRODUCTS AND PRODUCTION

The integration of preproduction companies tends to be less difficult than integrating companies that are already shipping product, since we can have more influence and add more value on the manufacturing side. . . . We can integrate the company into our operations and set them up on our systems right from the start.[1]
—David Keller, Vice President of Manufacturing, Cisco Systems

Integrating merged personnel and cultures is difficult and requires expertise in the softer side of business management. Integrating the buyer's products and acquired products is also an art form that deals with the more tangible, and often overwhelming, details of product design and manufacture.

Anyone who has worked in engineering knows that designing and consistently manufacturing a product to a tightly designed set of specifications is difficult business, even when it is completely accomplished with in-house personnel. Start incorporating outside designers, manufacturing, testing, and distant geography, and the process is fraught with possibilities for error.

Cisco's customer credo mandates that the customer be unaffected by any internal Cisco operations, and that customers should feel that they are, at all times, dealing with Cisco as a single-point supplier. A natural extension of this overriding objective is that all acquired products, whether in development or in full production, should be transferred into the Cisco operational model. The Cisco acquisition team's manufacturing group sets specific time lines within which the integration strategy is defined, part differentiation is assessed, and eventual full Cisco integration is obtained. There are those rare instances where a product is manufactured by the target after acquisition as the equivalent of an outsourced product, but even in these instances, customers can order the product as though it were any other Cisco product.

Seamless customer interaction remains a fundamental objective of any Cisco Systems program, and acquired company products are no exception. When you acquire a large number of companies annually, a well-defined product design and manufacturing integration process is a requirement. Cisco has created just that. Manufacturing is one of several operational areas that are centralized at the corporate level and managed corporate-wide, where product development engineering and associated marketing departments are still managed on a decentralized basis. The intention of this management structure is to foster entrepreneurship at the development level while still obtaining economy of scale at the production level. This chapter introduces Cisco manufacturing's well-honed product integration methodology.

CISCO ON MANUFACTURING

Cisco heavily emphasizes outsourcing as an integral part of its manufacturing operation. This is not to say that Cisco does none of its own manufacturing internally. There are two manufacturing plants in San Jose, the Tasman and the Walsh plants, which were the initial manufacturing plants used to produce the initial router and LAN switch products. A third plant, the Silver Creek plant, located in South San Jose, came to Cisco through the 1996 StrataCom acquisition and is used to manufacture the higher-end Internet service provider (ISP) backbone products.

Cisco uses outsourcing particularly when dealing with the less variable aspects of the production process. For example, many of the more mundane production activities, which I refer to as the more routine aspects of manufacturing, such as stuffing parts into printed circuit boards and component board functionality testing, are outsourced to third-party manufacturers. This outsourcing does come with a Cisco twist. These companies must use Cisco's information and test systems as a way of ensuring that the outsourced products still meet Cisco's quality standards.

The less routine the activity, the higher the level of required personnel involvement. Cisco chooses to have more control over these nonroutine activities. The higher-end router products, for example, often require custom configuration to meet the customer's functional objectives. Producing the physical subassembly modules is a fixed, repeatable process that can be outsourced with a higher degree of confidence. Notice that for routine processes, the actual manufacturing process itself is highly repeatable and the final outcome of the process must meet a consistent set of technical specifications. Routine activities have, by definition, highly repeatable processes and a low risk of improper completion.

The final component integration, software configuration, and test, on the other hand, is a nonroutine process in that customer-mandated requirements will likely differ between customers. Each finished product may well have its own unique set of customer acceptance criteria. From the customer's perspective, if the entire product does not perform in accordance with the agreed-upon specifications, then the product is unsatisfactory and may well be returned, causing a larger, longer-term credibility problem between that customer and Cisco. For this reason, final product integration, configuration, and test for the higher-end products is usually performed within one of the Cisco facilities by Cisco personnel.

In the words of Carl Redfield, Cisco's senior vice president of manufacturing and logistics, "I want my people focusing on the intellectual portion, establishing the supply base, qualifying new suppliers, and developing better processes, not managing direct labor. We supply the intellect; they supply the labor."[2]

In essence, if Cisco can make it more cheaply than an outsource vendor can, then Cisco will likely manufacture the product internally. Cisco will continue to look for a supplier that can reliably manufacture the product at Cisco's costs, and if found, will outsource the manufacturing. Cisco has made a strategic commitment to outsourcing whenever possible.

The higher-volume, less complicated products may be completely outsourced, with the final product never seeing the inside of a Cisco-owned facility. These types of products also tend to be more commodity-like in nature with a low level of interproduct variation. They provide lower revenue per shipped product and ship in very high volume. Approximately 25 percent of Cisco's overall revenue and 50 percent of its unit volume are manufactured by and shipped by outsourced manufacturing partners.

Remember Cisco's overall value statements, as defined in Chapter 5. One of the core values is to foster and promote partnerships within the Internet ecosystem while also developing a horizontal, not vertical, business model. Notice that Cisco's manufacturing organization is designed and operates in accordance with this goal. As is seen in almost every area of Cisco's operation, all strategic and tactical decisions lead in the direction of fostering this partnership approach.

CISCO PRODUCT INTEGRATION METHODOLOGY

See Chapter 11 for details regarding manufacturing due diligence. This section deals with the postacquisition integration steps.

The acquired company must from the beginning come to accept that its method of production will eventually be converted into the Cisco way of doing things. This required integration mandate makes a lot of business sense from Cisco's managerial perspective since the alternative is to inherit the management of many disparate manufacturing processes, cultures, quality maintenance procedures, and testing standards. This is usually not an effective way to manufacture highly technical products reliably in high volume while obtaining normal economy-of-scale cost reductions.

Cisco takes an integrative approach and works hard, up front, to transfer the acquired products into the standardized Cisco manufacturing system. Ideally, at the end of the integration program the acquired products will look just like any other Cisco products, and unless someone knows the history of the products, a customer would never know that they were acquired from a third-party company. Stating this as a goal is one thing. Actually making this goal a reality is something else altogether, and, as stated previously, Cisco has this integration process honed to a fine edge.

How this integration is accomplished may vary between acquisitions, but the overall intent of the acquisition integration process should never be called into question. The target company's management should know that, to paraphrase the Borg on *Star Trek*, "Resistance is futile. You will be assimilated."

Ciscoizing Part Numbers

Cisco wants customers and employees to feel as though the acquired company is a part of Cisco from the moment the purchase is finalized. Numerous steps are taken to welcome acquired employees into the Cisco culture. These steps are covered in Chapter 12. This section covers the manufacturing integration in detail.

To start with, all acquired company products are given a Cisco-based manufacturing resource planning (MRP) database part number. The product itself has not changed at this point, but salespeople and customers now have the ability to order the target company's products, from day one of the merger, using a Cisco part number. This critical step is also a lean communication step in that it reflects information about the product in the MRP system, such as a Cisco part number and minimal additional product information. However, a customer order for this product cannot at this point be electronically processed within the Cisco MRP system, and the order will likely be manually transferred by phone, fax, or e-mail from Cisco to the acquired company's order desk for fulfillment. Products are built and shipped from the acquired company at this point; Cisco is essentially acting as an order taker.

The new Cisco part numbers are mapped internally within the acquired company and by the integration team against the historical part numbers used by the acquired company. At this point the products are themselves initially built by the acquired company, just as before the purchase. The difference, from a customer's perspective, is that the customer is now dealing with Cisco and not the target. The Cisco business objective of presenting an end-to-end uniform solution to the customers is once again put into practice.

Determining Products to Transfer

An important early step in the integration process is the determination of those finished products and ongoing projects that will be integrated. The integration of a product is not a trivial process and may not be feasible if the product either has a limited expected life span or has some specific technical characteristic, the transfer of which would potentially undermine the finished performance quality of the product.

Within 30 days of the acquisition date the Cisco manufacturing team makes its initial determination regarding the acquired products that will transfer completely to Cisco for manufacture and those that will continue being built by the acquired company. This team makes its determination by working in conjunction with the Cisco acquisition team and key personnel from the acquired company who have now become Cisco employees. The intent, from a personnel perspective, is to have the acquired company's personnel believe that they are part of this transition process. Once again, see Chapter 12 for additional details.

Remembering that Cisco's manufacturing model is to outsource the manufacture of as many of its products as possible, it is completely consistent to have acquired products still be manufactured by the acquired company's operation. The MRP system is designed to naturally accommodate this reality. Determining which products should transfer requires a blending of manufacturing expertise with the acquisition's business objectives.

Assume that the target was acquired for its current product family and that this particular generation of the product family has a long expected market life. In this case, it would make sense to expend the effort to transfer the products to Cisco's manufacturing processes so that economies of scale can be applied to the product costs.

If, on the other hand, the current generation of products is expected to be obsolete within a short period of time, as determined by the acquisition business case and the team members involved, then the full integration of the products into Cisco's manufacturing processes may not make sense. This may well be the case when Cisco acquires a company for its technology and not necessarily its product designs. In this type of situation it is likely that Cisco would want the acquired technology incorporated into a more Cisco-oriented design than the company previously had in place. The existing products would be offered to customers until a newer generation of Cisco-oriented product is available, at which time customers will likely be weaned from the older products and encouraged to purchase the newly designed ones. Once the older-product order volume decreases, its manufacture at the acquired company's facility is no longer needed and will likely be phased out. More about what happens to personnel at this point is covered later in this chapter.

If an acquired product has a very complicated, specific set of test parameters requiring specialized verification equipment that is difficult to transfer to Cisco, then this particular product's manufacture may also stay at the acquired company's facility until the transfer can be reliably accomplished.

The bottom line of this decision is that the primary emphasis is placed on transferring all products into the Cisco manufacturing processes so that they can later be treated just like any other Cisco products from component parts all the way up to final assembly, test, and shipment. The only reason not to Ciscoize a product is if it is a product with a short expected future market life and it simply makes more sense not to invest the extensive time and money performing the transfer.

Time Lines

Specific time frames are established for the various stages associated with manufacturing integration or products. Table 13.1 presents a summary of the stages and their respective times for completion.

Notice from the table that signs of company integration starts from the day of acquisition which means that much preparatory work has already been done before the deal is actually signed. Within 30 days of the purchase, people at both Cisco and the target know the direction that product manufacturing integration will take, and people from both companies are involved with the integration process decisions. The products chosen for Ciscoized integration are determined from the acquisition business case that outlines the major assets of interest to Cisco and time frames within which Cisco intends to capitalize on those assets.

Ciscoizing the Bill of Materials

Once the decision is made regarding the product integration objectives, the tedious task begins of converting the bill of materials (BOM) for each of the acquired products into a Cisco MRP-compliant BOM. A bill of materials is a complete listing of all parts used in the manufacture of a product, from components such as resistors to integrated circuits or printed circuit cards. A complete BOM lists all parts required to manufacture the assembly in question, with the combination of all assemblies comprising the finished product.

Components have detailed technical specifications that must be met for a particular part to perform as required in the finished product. A component failure can take a complete network assembly out of service, and deviation from a technical specification can cause the component, and as a consequence the assembly, to perform errati-

Table 13.1 Stages of Manufacturing Integration and Time Frames

Step	Time Frame in Days after Purchase	Comments
Define manufacturing integration team members	Upon deal closure	Contains personnel from both Cisco and acquired company
Assign Cisco part numbers to acquired products	Upon deal closure	Presents a common order front to customers
		Products still built and shipped from acquired company
Determine products that will transfer	Within 30 days	End-of-life products will likely stay with acquired company
		Others scheduled for transfer to Cisco MRP
Ciscoize acquired products' bills of materials	Within 90 days	Minimizes redundant parts and number of vendors
		Provides purchasing economy of scale
Ciscoize acquired company's MRP system	Within 90 days	Makes acquired operation look like an integral part of Cisco
Implement Cisco's Autotest system for acquired products	Within 90 days	Provides uniform final assembly testing methodology
Apply Cisco's outsourcing model to the manufacture of acquired products	Within 90 days	Modularize manufacturing so that outsourcing potential is maximized
Make final acquired vendor transfer determinations	Within 30 days	Minimize the number of suppliers and avoid redundancy
Acquired company adopts Cisco's forecasting procedures	Within 30 days	Ensures that manufacturing, sales, and marketing of both companies are in sync
Implement Cisco's new product introduction (NPI) procedures	Within 90 days	Ensures that future products meet Cisco's requirements for salability, reliability, cost reduction, functionality, and manufacture
Integrate acquired manufacturing facilities	As required by the specifics of the acquisition (no specific time limit)	May be sold off, closed down, or used by Cisco as was done with StrataCom
Integrate acquired manufacturing personnel	As required by the specifics of the acquisition (no specific time limit)	May be used at acquired plant, moved to Cisco plant, or let go

cally or simply fail altogether. Maintaining tight control of component specifications while ensuring that purchased parts comply with required specifications is an important part of a well-maintained quality control system.

It is quite possible that Cisco will already be using a component part that is identical to the one required by the acquired product's BOM. In this case the Cisco existing MRP part number is assigned to that component during the BOM conversion process. If no existing Cisco part matches the required specifications, then a new Cisco MRP part number is assigned to this component. Slight deviations on specifications can have a seriously detrimental impact on product performance, so attention to detail at this stage is critical. I have personally seen an instance where someone in purchasing decided to change a specification on a "small" part like a capacitor, and that change later caused product failures. In this particular case, a product recall was required along with rework to ensure that the product would reliably perform in accordance with published specifications. Seemingly small component part changes can have far-reaching negative impacts if not evaluated carefully.

This component-part comparison and conversion process is time-consuming and tedious but important to achieving full MRP integration. When finished with this process, Cisco obtains a higher level of quality control and some future economy-of-scale cost-reduction benefits.

Ciscoizing Vendors

Cisco has a group dedicated to working with and evaluating existing or potential vendors. This supply operations (supply ops) group evaluates not only Cisco's own vendors but also those of any acquired company. Supply ops are divided into three commodity groups, which are themselves divided into smaller subgroups:

1. Electromechanical commodities include items such as enclosures, fans, power supplies, connectors, and power supplies.

2. Semiconductors include products such as memory chips, microprocessors, and other solid state components.

3. The logistics and transformation group evaluates the contract manufacturers used for Cisco's outsourcing.

Vendors are evaluated by supply ops against a set of acceptance criteria. The vendors of any acquired company are evaluated against this same set of criteria. The vendor must be financially solid. Cisco's business cannot represent more than 20 percent of the vendor's revenues; otherwise a decrease in Cisco's business could have a seriously detrimental impact on that vendor and possibly jeopardize future part availability. The vendor must maintain a satisfactory rating on its quarterly scorecard. This scorecard is issued by Cisco as a summary of the vendor's ability to deliver quality products or services, deliver on time, provide customer support, provide acceptable lead times, and maintain its costs.

If a component is sole-sourced, meaning that it can be acquired from only one particular vendor, then Cisco will work with that vendor to ensure that part shortages do not become a future problem. In addition, Cisco will likely look for ways to alleviate the sole-sourced products as a longer-term objective. Ensuring component availability continuity, preserving solid vendor relationships, and simultaneously working to minimize the number of suppliers is a tricky balancing act that requires continual monitoring and a touch of finesse. Cisco tries not to negatively impact the business of the acquired company's vendors while, at the same time, continually working toward getting the acquired products and their manufacture completely Ciscoized. The ultimate goal is always to maintain consistency as seen from the acquired company's customers' view now that they are Cisco's customers.

"We don't want to impact the acquired company's business in a negative way," says Mark Beckman, Cisco's senior manager of global supply management for electronic components. "If we can switch to an existing Cisco supplier without having an adverse impact on their business, then we do. If we think it will have a real adverse impact, then we don't make the switch; we'll approve the vendor, but only for that particular product."[3]

Ciscoizing MRP Systems

Cisco intends that all acquired companies adopt Cisco's MRP system, with the desired time frame for adoption set to within 90 days. Should the target maintain its own internal manufacturing operation for products that were not converted to the Cisco MRP, then the target is allowed to run its old MRP system in tandem with the Cisco MRP. The focus is always there to work in the Cisco way, not as the company did before the acquisition. Once the legacy products reach their end of life or are completely transferred to Cisco's MRP, the target's prior MRP system is usually decommissioned. Notice that two MRP systems may be in use during the period of time that the target is building legacy (preacquisition) systems and its eventual integration as part of the Cisco organization.

Ciscoizing Acquired Products Themselves

Products are most easily outsourced when they are designed specifically with outsourcing in mind. Typical steps taken to enable outsourcing include dividing the product design into manageable subassemblies, defining specific functional and other quality test procedures associated with these subassemblies, and developing manufacturing procedures that accommodate easy transfer between organizations. If a product is designed for internal manufacture, which may well be the case with the acquired products, then engineering must modify the manufacturing procedures to accommodate outsourcing. Or engineering must make a determination that this particular product cannot be effectively outsourced (hopefully the Cisco acquisition team would have uncovered this during due diligence).

Outsourcing is done on several different levels: assembly of piece parts to form subassemblies, testing of board-level subassemblies, and final product assembly and test. Outsourcing of the first and second levels is usually possible without much liability, but outsourcing the third may not be possible due to product-or customer-application-specific complexities. Determining an outsourcing procedure for acquired products within 90 days of target purchase is an important part of the manufacturing integration process.

Ciscoizing Final Product Testing

Technology products, no matter how sophisticated they may be, must functionally perform in accordance with the overall product's specifications. This sounds obvious, but a great deal of time and effort goes into ensuring that these specifications are met and the listing of these specifications can be, and usually is, lengthy. Now add to the standardized specification list a set of customer-specific requirements, and a complicated situation can quickly become a nightmare.

Cisco developed its own Autotest system not only as a way of managing the standardized specification compliance testing, but also as a way of testing for customer-specific requirements. Cisco MRP is integrated with the Autotest system so that a final product's functionality can be tested by Autotest to the customer-specific requirements stored in the Cisco MRP system. One huge benefit of implementing Autotest is that the final product testing validity is not based on the advance skill set of the person performing the final test. The product itself is tested in a standardized way to a specific set of standards. Much of the human-based variability associated with testing is removed when Autotest is properly implemented.

Outsourced vendors are also tied into the Autotest system so that their particular tests are downloaded from the Cisco MRP as applicable. Acquired companies that continue to manufacture at their own facilities must implement Autotest just like any outsourced vendor. To make Autotest work properly, a set of Autotest-compliant diagnostic and test specifications must be developed, usually by the target's engineering staff, if not already a part of the target's manufacturing process.

Tracking Production Quality Levels

Quality is not simply a *goal* for the mission-critical communications systems of today's business environment. It is a *requirement*, and all efforts must be made to ensure that quality is both designed and built into a communication product. In conjunction with quality maintenance, companies must continually push for cost reductions. One area where quality can be improved while also decreasing costs is in optimizing the production process itself.

Cisco uses its own in-process quality monitoring procedures, which are keyed around Autotest results, but it requires that acquired companies design and adopt their own in-process quality control procedures. These procedures can then be adapted to the Cisco methodology. It is much easier to convert procedures that already exist than it is to create the procedures from scratch, especially when the creation requires that a high degree of product expertise first be developed. The target's engineering personnel already know their products and likely already have some type of quality control procedure in place. Having the target's engineers create a set of in-process quality procedures, based on their in-depth product knowledge, applies knowledge for maximum effect.

It makes sense that the target should do this development work since its personnel are very familiar with their company's products and procedures. Once these are defined, they can be more easily modified to comply with the Cisco quality procedures. This is exactly what happens.

Forecasting à la Cisco

Someone once said, "Forecasting is like driving a car while looking in the rearview mirror." I add to this that the only time you can feel confident about the accuracy of your forecast is when it becomes history.

When a company is first acquired, those who have the best sense of a realistic forecast for the acquired products are the acquired people who were historically responsible for creating acquired company forecasts. And, after acquisition, these same people become Cisco employees and must integrate their forecasting estimates with the Cisco forecasting methodology.

The acquired company forecast is provided to the Cisco business-level marketing group to which the acquired company became attached. This Cisco marketing group provides feedback to the new personnel and eventually arrives at a consensus forecast to which future products will be manufactured. The Cisco people know the Cisco side of the forecast equation, and the acquired personnel know their customers' side. The final consensus numbers are entered into the Cisco MRP system, which then dictates manufacturing requirements. The Cisco forecasting methodology is adopted by the target within 30 days of purchase.

Situation-Specific Considerations

The decisions related to integrating the company's manufacturing facility is heavily dependent on the manufacturing requirements determined early in the integration process. If products will continue to be manufactured at the acquired facility, then it must remain in operation. But if the products are all to be integrated into Cisco's outsourced manufacturing process, then the products may wind up being manufactured by another outsourced vendor. In that case the acquired facility may no longer be needed. Additional items considered when making a closure decision include the impact of the closure on future R&D activities (which is very important to the Cisco model), any intrinsic high levels of expertise present in the established manufacturing facility that can be put to effective future use, and the financial impact of the closure. An assessment is made by both Cisco and acquired company personnel, who then form a recommendation to Cisco as to acquired plant disposition.

Direct labor personnel employed as part of the acquired manufacturing organization face what might be a difficult decision if plant closure is determined to be the optimal future course. Although Cisco strives hard to retain the acquired indirect labor force (including engineers, marketing personnel, and salespeople), it treats the retention of acquired manufacturing personnel as less critical and does not make their retention a driving criterion when making integration decisions.

Acquired direct personnel are able to work at the acquired plant for as long as it remains open. Upon closure, these personnel are offered opportunities, depending on the employees' skill sets, to work in another of the Cisco manufacturing plants, to move to another part of the Cisco organization, or simply to leave the company. If Cisco decides that it wants to retain the acquired direct labor personnel, it will offer cash incentives and bonuses to keep people interested and motivated until the time when the incentives are paid. Above all else, Cisco makes a distinct effort to be as open and honest as possible with acquired personnel about current and future plans.

CASE EXAMPLE—SUMMA FOUR (JULY 1998)

Cisco purchased Summa Four, a Manchester, New Hampshire–based provider of high-powered digital switching systems. Cisco has a remote R&D facility located in Chelmsford, Massachusetts, which supported over 1,000 Cisco employees. Summa Four had 210 employees, including 65 engineers and 23 manufacturing personnel.

At the time of the acquisition, Summa Four had several products in various stages of development and production. The production facility was determined to be solid, but the test systems were PC-based and not up to the Autotest or Cisco MRP standards. Existing products continued to be manufactured in the Manchester facility for several years after the acquisition. In addition, the new product initial post-R&D product runs were performed in Manchester and then transferred to the Silver Creek facility (near San Jose) for full production runs.

Existing products continued to be manufactured in the Manchester facility with the expectation that this manufacturing would be phased out when product demand dropped off in what was anticipated to be a two-to-three-year period.

Summa Four employees were offered a variety of incentives to remain on after the acquisition. In addition to stock options, employees were offered a "stay put" bonus that equated to a large percentage of salary if still employed two years after the acquisition.

The Summa Four bonus structure was also retained for a six-to-nine-month period after the purchase. The Cisco bonus structure was implemented at that point for key management employees. A little over one year later, as of February 2000, all but one of the prior Summa Four employees were still employed by Cisco Systems. The employee who left had an employment start date that did not qualify for many of the acquisition incentive benefits.

CISCO'S ASSUMPTIONS

Fundamental to the Cisco manufacturing and product development integration plan is the consistent assumption that Cisco should be the customer's one-stop-shopping point for its networking products needs. The rapid assignment of a Cisco part number and the immediate enabling of product ordering through the Cisco mechanisms both show to customers Cisco's commitment to being their one-stop supplier. The alternate approach of having customers order the target's products from the target company and Ciscos products from Cisco and eventually, maybe, combining the two is cumbersome when acquisitions are performed on a limited basis. This segmented product ordering strategy quickly becomes completely unwieldy from a customer's perspective when a company acquires as many companies annually as is done by Cisco Systems.

Cisco has also purposefully divided its management structure to enable entrepreneurship at the product development (intellectual property) level through decentralization while centralizing customer contact and company-wide support functions such as sales, finance, and manufacturing. Centralizing manufacturing when acquiring over 10 companies annually that all maintain their own MRP and quality processes would not only become a logistics nightmare but also seriously undermine the very economy of scale cost reductions Cisco intended with its centralized manufacturing. By placing a Cisco part number on products and the entire BOM, for longer-life products, Cisco minimizes the likelihood of the numerous acquisitions ballooning the MRP, inventory, and manufacturing processes into a se-

225

ries of unique activities that don't complement each other. Instead, Cisco's approach adds capabilities and volume buying power that can actually make Cisco more cost efficient with each added product and organization acquired.

The terms "cost efficient" and "acquisition" have a difficult time realistically meeting each other in a complementary way for most mergers. Cisco's approach of placing strong emphasis on up-front assessment, openness, and integration shows commitment to the acquisition and enables each one of the large number of acquisitions to be treated like another business process that makes Cisco stronger than it was before the acquisition.

Integral to this integration methodology is the belief that partnerships are a core value (strength) in the new global economy of the Internet. To foster these partnerships, Cisco makes extensive use of technology and integrates key operational areas through its MRP system. Once a company is acquired, Cisco makes every effort to integrate development and full production products completely into the established Cisco MRP system. The technology is used to lay the foundation on which partnerships with outsourced vendors, and also with acquired companies, are possible on a reliably, repeatable basis.

Geography becomes less important for the intellectual property generation aspect of the acquisition but remains important for the physical production of the products. By standardizing, through MRP and Autotest, Cisco takes much of the uncertainty out of a distance relationship and provides real-time feedback for both Cisco and its suppliers or acquired companies. This two-way feedback keeps all involved parties moving in a consistent and highly directed manner that ensures excellent quality control while optimizing the likelihood that remote partners will complement rather than interfere with each other's operation.

Can technology make obsolete the need for human involvement? This question will be answered over the coming years, but to date, in my opinion, the answer is "No" if the relationship is one of a non-routine nature. Routine products with well established designs and static performance specifications can be readily manufactured over a distance. But as the products and services become less routine, the interaction must provide real-time, two-way feedback that is ideally accomplished when the human being is physically close to the product being tested. The real-time nature of the Internet and its technologies makes the feedback richer and physical colocation less critical every year. Cisco places a great deal of emphasis on the cohesive power of a ubiquitous, standardized network that is embraced by its users. The seemingly unlimited expansion capability provided by this type of operational network can provide a company with an outstanding platform on which to base a virtual company that exists independent of geography. Although this seems to work in theory, and has worked for Cisco to date, only time will tell if technology can truly replace physical proximity when it comes to human interaction.

Of one thing we can all be sure: Advanced technology is ultimately only as effective as the people who use it. Cisco makes a point of putting the people and procedures in place that standardize the part numbers, consolidate product numbers, and totally Ciscoize acquired company processes. If you are going to make a strategic gamble, you might as well do it all the way since a halfhearted effort at anything is likely to meet with unsatisfactory results. And, so far, Cisco's full-power approach to integrating around its technological backbone has paid off.

PORTABILITY EVALUATION

Whether Cisco's approach to product integration can be applied to other industries is, in large part, dependent on the industry. It appears to have taken into account most possibilities but requires a universal commitment on the part of the buying company. If a target is purchased with the intent of later divesting it, then integration would not be an effective strategy. If the target is purchased for financial reasons and no operational synergies are expected, then this type of integration approach would not be feasible. If the acquired company provides products or services to a different industry from that of the buyer and operational consolidation provides no financial or operational benefits, then this high level of integration would not be justifiable, or even advisable. But if a company is purchased with the express intent of expanding product lines or other larger-scale operational capabilities, then this type of acquisition approach should be considered.

Just as Cisco does, it is recommended that a thorough assessment of the integration benefits be investigated during the prepurchase and due diligence stages. Once the purchase is finalized, the integration, if deemed advisable, should proceed at full throttle with specifically defined time frames, responsibilities, and performance checkpoints. Personnel from both the buyer and the seller should be involved with the integration planning and implementation so that the acquired personnel involved feel that they are a part of the process. This is particularly true when acquiring a small start-up firm where the employees may not just think of the company as their employer but may have emotional attachments similar to those felt toward a loved family member. It may be irrational, but it is true, nonetheless.

THE FINAL ANALYSIS

The ability to Ciscoize an acquired company is assessed as part of the prepurchase target evaluation process. Cisco makes no bones about its intention to meld the target's product development, ordering, manufacturing, and all other operational areas into the Cisco mold. Teams are established during the preacquisition stages to prepare for the purchase, and once the purchase is finalized, the teams swing into action. These teams, comprised of both Cisco and target personnel, have specific time frames within which integration milestones are to be reached. A major emphasis is placed on integrating the target's products into the Cisco MRP system in an effort to minimize the future complexity of the manufacturing operation. Another special effort is placed on integrating the quality control processes around the Autotest quality testing system.

The ultimate goal of the entire integration process is to have the acquired products look as though they always came from Cisco Systems with no indications of the product ever having been acquired from another company.

The overall manufacturing integration process germinates from Cisco's vision, business objectives, and goals. To support these goals a technology infrastructure and integration methodology was developed with the ability to expand as needed to meet acquisition integration requirements. This focused, systematic approach to acquisitions makes the Cisco method worthy of interest and study. It also demonstrates that dedication to a specific set of ideals and goals, and taking action commensurate with those goals, can turn separate organizations into a single business entity that is stronger as a result of the acquisition.

CHAPTER *14*

SETTING THE PURCHASE PRICE

We have the process down. We have a generic process. Sometimes in all this speed we end up paying too much. But the acquisitions are not financial—we don't do them because we can swing a good deal—they are strategic. We do them to grow the company in the right direction.[1]
—Mike Volpi, Senior Vice President, Cisco Systems

Price is always a factor in any acquisition, no matter what anyone, including Cisco, says. But some of the prices that Cisco has paid for an acquisition have been astronomical—and yet Cisco paid them. Assuming that any Cisco acquisition is conducted by competent businesspeople, with a fiscal responsibility to the company and its shareholders, they must have some justification for paying these prices. This chapter takes a closer look at the purchase price decision.

FIND THE RIGHT COMPANY FIRST

First and foremost in any Cisco acquisition is the uncovering of a worthy acquisition candidate. To be that candidate a firm must have great technology that rounds out the Cisco product mix in a way that customers have already indicated that they need. Secondly, it must meet at least four of the initial qualification criteria—vision, chemistry, short-term wins, long-term wins, geographic proximity, and, of course, no merger of equals. If the transaction gets this far, then Cisco will enter into concrete pricing discussions.

Notice that price is low on the totem pole with respect to items being considered. Truthfully, pricing a start-up company with minimal, if any, revenue and likely no profits is not a cut-and-dried process. It is going to be heavily based on the specifics of the transaction, and Cisco does not even enter into discussions until it is certain that this company, if acquired at all, would make a solid addition to the Cisco culture.

Just as one would not discuss prenuptial agreements with a person until sure that this person could be your spouse, so does Cisco avoid pricing discussions until it is certain that there is a fit on the major points.

FROM INSIDE CISCO

I think the most important decision in your acquisition is your selection process. If you select right, with the criteria we set, your probabilities of success are extremely high. . . . We spend a lot of time up front.[2]

> —*John Chambers, Cisco president and CEO, commenting on the importance of proper selection in making an acquisition succeed*

Once the initial purchase price is set during initial negotiations, the due diligence team moves in to verify that which was purported by the seller to be true. Once again the intent of due diligence is not to "find out where they lied" but to verify from Cisco's perspective that there is indeed the type of technology, product, culture, and management fit that everyone thinks is there.

Once the deal is closed, the sellers receive stock, options, cash, and other compensation as part of the sale.

BUY THE FUTURE—NOT THE PAST

Just as a stock price reflects the future performance of a company discounted back to the present, Cisco considers the value of a company not based on its current value, but rather on what it can provide when run through the Cisco mill. Cisco has a track record with some of its acquisitions of ramping up revenues over 50 times within a 12- to-18-month period. And it has an internal goal of the acquisition generating its purchase price in revenues within a three-year period to meet basic objectives. If done in two years, it is a home run. If achieved in 18 months or less, it is a grand slam.

Assume that Cisco revenues related to an acquired product increase 50 times and that Cisco maintains a 60 percent gross margin with respect to that product line–specific increased revenue. Sixty percent of 50 times revenue translates to a gross margin that is roughly 30 times (60 percent of 50 times) the sales of the acquired company at the time of purchase. This gross margin can then be used to pay Cisco's overhead. And all within an 18-month period. Do this on a regular basis and you are really making money!

Looking at it from a different perspective, Cisco stock trades at a multiple of its sales that ranges from five to eight. Loosely translated, this means that for every incremental dollar of sales generated by an acquisition resulting directly from revenue enhancement synergy, Cisco's overall market capitalization increases by between five and eight dollars.

John Chambers considers this a valid way of sizing up the success of an acquisition.

"Let me tell you, when we did our first acquisition in 1993, we caught unbelievable heat in the press. We paid $89 million [$95 million from other reports] for a company called Crescendo that had only $10 million in revenues. A lot of people thought we had lost our frugality and direction. Now [in 1997 at the time of this interview] that company contributes more than $500 million in revenues to Cisco. In terms of our market cap, selling for eight times sales, it's worth $4 billion to our shareholders," says Chambers. "And our acquisitions in local area network switching cost us $500 million and now contribute more than $1 billion in revenues—or more than $8 billion to our market cap. So the strategy has worked out well. But at the time, it was not so obvious." The switching division of Cisco that was a direct result of the Crescendo acquisition now generates around 40 percent of Cisco's revenues ($7.5 billion in switching sales in fiscal 2000) and is almost equal Cisco's router sales revenue.

A benchmark break-even analysis on a purchase, using stock to fund the purchase, might look something like this:

- Cisco purchases a company for $120 million in stock. Assume that this company is not yet profitable but had $10 million in annualized revenue just prior to purchase.

- Within 18 months, Cisco is generating 30 times incremental revenue ($300 million) from product sales directly related to this acquisition.

- From a gross margin perspective, Cisco is earning 60 percent average gross margin ($300 million × 60 percent = $180 million) from these sales.

- Assuming that Cisco market capitalization is only five times sales, which is historically low for Cisco as of early 2001, then the incremental revenue should, theoretically, add 5 × $300 million, or $1.5 billion in market cap, to Cisco's value.

- Obtaining $1.5 billion in market cap increase from a $120 million stock purchase within 18 months (12.5 times the purchase price) is a return on investment that I, and most of you, would take any day.

This analysis is only really focused on the first 18 months, and does not consider the benefits that may, and likely will, occur in years two, three, and maybe even four. The follow-on products developed and sold as a result of acquiring this development team can also be included in this analysis to make it far more attractive than it already is.

Looking at the pricing picture from this perspective, it is somewhat easier to understand Cisco's willingness to pay what appears to be high prices for its acquired companies. Contrary to most companies that purchase a target for its value today taking into account some type of cost-reduction synergy, Cisco is really not interested in the company's current value as a stand-alone entity. It is primarily interested in its value as an integrated part of Cisco, being fully leveraged through the Cisco sales, manufacturing, and finance machine. To Cisco, its shareholders, and the seller, this is the source of real value.

Finally, it should not be forgotten that Cisco has a strategic interest in any acquisition. Cisco would look at an acquisition only if it (1) believes that this is a product area it should offer, (2) has reasonable customer purchase visibility for the specific product family in question, (3) has determined that it cannot reasonably develop the technology internally in a way that meets market window requirements, and (4) thinks that it can leverage to a higher level the technology and personnel involved in the form of future products. Cisco has a belief that it must be the end-to-end supplier for its customers. If not offering a product area would provide a sizable entrance into a major

---

Inside the Valley

If Cisco wants something, it won't nickel and dime you.[3]

> —Tom Dyal, partner with Redpoint Ventures
> of Menlo Park, California, commenting on
> his experience with the StratumOne
> Communications acquisition (1999)

---

account by one of Cisco's competitors, Cisco would be likely to acquire the technology simply to avoid this potentially hazardous strategic sales situation.

In summary, what a company has done in the past on its own is an interesting benchmark to Cisco, but only the beginning of the value discussion. Of greater interest to Cisco is what that company's products, services, technologies, customers, and management can do in the future as an integral part of Cisco. Looking forward, while closely watching the strategic implications of a purchase, provides a much better framework for understanding the Cisco pricing model than taking a historical perspective.

THE COMPETITION: OTHER SUITORS AND AN IPO

No purchase happens in a vacuum. The networks industry is pretty small, primarily a result of the technology itself bringing people, companies, and geographies closer together. Plus, many of the people running today's networking companies have worked together in past lives and already have an established professional working relationship. This relationship is the first entrée when someone from Cisco calls a prospect or the prospect calls Cisco to open the acquisition door. It is easy to call up a friend or colleague to discuss things, including the possibility of an acquisition fit. Once a company is in play (for sale), the word often gets out and then other interested suitors will appear on the target's doorstep.

Competitive bidding typically drives up the purchase price of something—as anyone who has ever bid at an auction can verify. But there is another form of competition that has nothing directly to do with another company, but has directly to do with the state of the stock market in general and the initial public offering (IPO) market in particular.

The IPO market of the late 1990s and early 2000 was incredible. It seemed like everyone and their relatives had stock in an IPO of some type or other. It might have been a proven company like United Parcel Service (UPS) or a speculative start-up like koop.com, but they were there. And investors were not even necessarily interested in the company having any earnings. As long as it was in "tech" it was "good." Well, so much for that bubble, I regret to say since I also lost some of my portfolio in the bashing we all took when the bubble burst.

The IPO market has slowed to a crawl compared to those high-flying years, but it is still there and presents competition for any buyer interested in purchasing a company that is still in its pre-IPO stage. Most tech companies intend "going public" through an IPO as a major evolutionary goal and do not even want to consider being purchased. The investors who initially funded the start-up when it was still a high-risk venture did so with the likely intention of going public to recover their initial investment. Going public has been and still is a highly sought-after and very respectable way of obtaining additional funding for the next stage of company growth. Remember that when a company goes public, it still exists after the IPO. The company does not disappear as is the case with a Cisco acquisition. Entrepreneurs like to grow products and companies, and selling to a larger company often takes away that growth opportunity, not to mention the prestige of being an executive or board member with a highly sought-after start-up. Odd as it may sound, many start-ups do not relish the thought of being purchased by Cisco or any other company.

FROM INSIDE CISCO

Who's going to get rich out of this one?[4]

—John Morgridge, responding to the CEO of a target company during acquisition pricing negotiations

"We were planning to do an IPO," says Mario Mazzola, thinking back on his role as CEO of Crescendo before the Cisco purchase even came up in discussion. "Obviously, that was pivotal time. There were a few discussions already starting, looking for an IPO. But it would be, in a realistic time frame, not sooner than nine months." Then Cisco offered to purchase Crescendo for $95 million and Mazzola had to present the offer to his board of directors.

"Remember that my board members were not completely in agreement with me. They wanted to have more [money]. . . . They would like to go for an IPO and so on. I never understood what action was posturing and what action was real, you know. The final conclusion was that 'This is your company [Mario]. I'm sure that you have the support of the other people in the company. If you really want to sell, it's good what you're doing for us.'" And sell Crescendo did.

The acquisition of Grand Junction Networks (1995) presents another example of the interplay among Cisco, other suitors, and the IPO marketplace.

Grand Junction was on track to an IPO when Goldman Sachs called Charles Giancarlo, Cisco vice president of business development at the time, about the possibility of Cisco wanting to acquire Grand Junction. Mario Mazzola, now with Cisco as vice president of the switching products line, knew Howard Charney, Grand Junction CEO, and other members of his management team, and was interested in the purchase for Cisco. The purchase made strategic sense to Cisco since it needed a foothold in the marketplace that Grand Junction addressed, and this foothold would help to keep Bay Networks (floundering since its formation after the merger of Synoptics and Wellfleet), a major Cisco competitor, from recovering its market stature. Eventually, Cisco and Grand Junction got down to determining a reasonable purchase price.

Goldman Sachs thought that it could take Grand Junction public for around $300 million and that the stock could expect as much as a 15 percent bounce, or increase, on the first day, taking the first-day IPO valuation to $345 million. This was Grand Junction's initial asking price. Cisco offered $200 million, having previously been led to believe that this was the price that Grand Junction wanted. And the negotiations were on.

All types of things enter into negotiations when determining a purchase price, especially if an IPO is the major competition. Here are six things that affect a company and its shareholders when it goes public:

1. Persons who hold pre-IPO shares of stock cannot sell their stock immediately on the IPO date. They have to hold their stock for a six-month period after the IPO before they can sell. A new IPO stock can move around a great deal during that six-month period.

2. Officers of the company open themselves up to lawsuits when they are the visible executives of a post-IPO public company. People who purchase IPO stock may later feel that they were misled as part of the offering prospectus and sue the company and its executives should the IPO not turn out as presented or expected.

3. IPO companies' stock prices are highly unpredictable as they have no track record for investors to review when making the purchase. The upside potential of a high-flying IPO is immense, but the downside risk is also fairly substantial since the stock is basically extremely volatile.

4. Cisco's stock had track record that had continued to increase over the years. The company was solid financially and a darling child on Wall Street. Cisco stock might not exhibit the incredible upside potential of a Grand Junction IPO, but it would more be expected to consistently provide future appreciation gain, taking much of the risk out of the Cisco-purchase transaction.

5. There is sizzle attached to being part of a company going through a hot IPO. This sizzle and prestige is important to many people, and employees often sign on as employees specifically expecting to experience, once again, the thrill of going public. Being acquired has more risk associated with it

than sizzle and would require an excellent sales pitch to keep the highly qualified personnel who had been looking for an IPO around postpurchase.

6. A start-up company, even one funded by a successful IPO, does not have the sales, marketing, manufacturing, or financial muscle of a Cisco Systems—meaning that the start-up's products will take a longer time to acquire market share. It was likely that Cisco Systems would purchase another company to obtain a product that competed with Grand Junction's should the Grand Junction deal not come to closure. Grand Junction would then have an even more difficult time acquiring market share.

These reasons and others contribute to the reticence a target company CEO may encounter when presenting the board of directors with a purchase offer from Cisco Systems. At $200 million, the Grand Junction board was willing to take its chances with an IPO.

Cisco increased its offer to $225 million. Charney said, "No." The offer was then upped to $275 million. Once again, Grand Junction said, "No."

Once Grand Junction went into play, Bay Networks and two other computer companies started expressing an interest in purchasing Grand Junction, putting more pressure on Cisco to increase its offer. As it turned out, Cisco's stock price increase did a lot to help close the deal.

Chambers finally asked what it would take for the deal to close, and Charney replied, "Five million shares of Cisco stock." Chambers agreed. The stock was selling, at the time, for $65 per share, making the deal total $325 million. This offer got the attention of Charney and the Grand Junction board. Eventually, they put together a "standstill" agreement that sold Grand Junction to Cisco for 5 million shares priced at $69 per share. Cisco's stock was changing daily, and Charney wanted to eliminate any more uncertainty from the negotiations. When the acquisition actually occurred, the stock price had risen to the point that the total purchase valuation sat at $400 million!

What Grand Junction didn't know at the time was that Cisco's internal financial people had projected that Grand Junction's products, sold through the Cisco operation, would generate around $119 million in revenue in the first year after the purchase, around 17 times Grand Junction's sales for the year before. Using a market cap multiplier of eight, which Cisco's was at the time, meant that Grand Junction's incremental revenue opportunity would likely increase Cisco's valuation by $952 million. Looked at in this light, paying $400 million for a company that sold $7 million worth of product the prior year and estimated its next year's revenues at $32 million is a bargain!

FROM INSIDE CISCO

There were 40-plus millionaires created. We gained wider distribution channels. Cisco projected we'd do $119 million the first year. We did $124 million. We'd never have done that on our own.[5]

—Howard Charney, former CEO of Grand Junction Networks, commenting on the benefits of selling to Cisco in 1995

With all of this positive outcome from the Grand Junction sale, why were the board members and other Grand Junction personnel reticent to sell to Cisco, even at these great prices?

"At Grand Junction it was 'Ready, set, go.' Going from R&D to out-the-door took weeks," says Charney. "At Cisco, transferring a product from engineering to manufacturing is a big deal. There are international standards to be followed. There are integration issues to be concerned with. The software, the manufacturing—we have to give it all a common look and feel. . . . Any company that acquires you and says that you're going to stay autonomous, is giving you a crock."[6]

Charney continues and mentions what I feel is one of the most important aspects of being a high-technology entrepreneur: the ability and freedom to create.

"I've traded away things. There is an edge to creating something from nothing. There is excitement in the ebb and flow of a little company. There is beauty in getting one product to market. Cisco's product catalog is half an inch thick."

As I have said many times throughout this book, these entrepreneurs are a rare breed that are driven by a different set of motivations.

FROM INSIDE CISCO

I'm fortunate. Cisco is not really like a giant company. There's a start-up atmosphere here.[7]

—*Debra Pelsma, former Grand Junction employee, commenting on her move to Cisco after the 1995 acquisition*

WHAT NOW? DEALING WITH A DEVALUED CISCO STOCK PRICE

There is no question that Cisco's stock was a major factor in Cisco's ability to implement its acquisition strategy. Most of the acquisitions were paid for with Cisco stock, and employees were retained after the acquisition through stock options that vested over a number of years and a two-year noncompete agreement signed at the time of acquisition. That is a pretty powerful combination for keeping people around for at least two years. But keeping them around longer takes a stimulating work environment and a strong financial incentive. The Cisco stock was just that.

FROM INSIDE CISCO

It all comes back to one of the key assumptions, and that is the currency [stock and/or cash]. It is not only having a strong currency, but having growth in that currency. The reason why people have wanted to be acquired by Cisco is because the stock kept going up. And the reason why people hung around Cisco, the attrition rate on acquisitions is so small, is because the stock kept going up.[8]

—*Barry Eggers, former Cisco acquisitions leader and now venture capitalist, talking about the importance of Cisco's stock showing solid price performance increases*

What happens now that the stock is no longer the "Wall Street darling" that it has traditionally been? Does the stock's devaluation from $70+ dollars per share to the teens and 20s affect Cisco's ability to fund acquisitions with its stock? Oddly enough, the stock devaluation may actually play to Cisco's favor when it comes to acquisitions.

For starters, Cisco's stock did not drop off directly because of mismanagement on the part of Cisco personnel. The stock price dropped because the economy in general looked less promising going out into the future. The bad news is that the economic trend seriously dropped Cisco's projected future revenues, its shipments, and consequently its stock price, but the good news from an acquisitions perspective is that it also affected other potential target companies to the same extent and in many cases more seriously. Taken on a comparative basis, Cisco stock is now more valuable than the stock of the companies that it is likely to be interested in buying. This means that fewer Cisco shares will be needed to close the deal, and total deal valuations will be lower than historically seen and less dilutive on Cisco's stock. Let's face it; 5 million shares priced at $20 per share is $100 million instead of the $400 million paid for Grand Junction.

Related to the stock price, many people believe that Cisco stock, at the lower prices, actually has a much larger upside growth potential than it had at the $80 range. At $80 it was more likely to drop in price, but at $20 it is more likely to increase in value. For this reason, employees receiving Cisco stock options may perceive them as having a greater future value than they might originally have thought if their options were based on a much higher market price.

Secondly, the IPO market is much slower than it was in the 1990s. This makes Cisco a more desirable suitor for any start-up wanting to become liquid. Reduce the IPO threat, have Cisco's stock appear at least as strong as—if not stronger than—many of its competitors, have Cisco stock perceived with a much greater upside appreciation potential, and keep technology pushing forward as it always has, and you have what is potentially an excellent set of conditions for Cisco and its acquisition program.

In short, the drop-off in Cisco share prices was painful for people holding Cisco stock (me included), but it might well present an excellent opportunity for employees of future prospective acquisitions.

The Internet is not going away. IP technology is widely considered the technology of choice for future voice and data communications. Cisco is solidly entrenched in IP and Internet technology, and when this marketplace eventually rebounds—which it will—Cisco is in an excellent position to once again experience explosive growth, but with a management team that is far more seasoned than it was before the downturn.

THE FINAL ANALYSIS

The price of a share of a company's stock today is heavily tied to the future ability of that company to generate increased revenue and increased net income. When future sales growth estimates shrink, so typically does the stock price. But when future sales growth increases, the stock price increases with it. Nowhere is this more true than with Cisco Systems' method of setting a realistic purchase price for a company.

Cisco assumes that the target will be fully, successfully, integrated into its standard operation. From this assumption, Cisco then determines what it feels are realistic revenue numbers for the target company's products when sold and manufactured by Cisco. Knowing its gross margins and its market capitalization multiplier, Cisco can then make a reasonable determination as to what it considers a reasonable price for a company.

Paying 15 times sales for a start-up company sounds outrageous on the surface when you only consider today in your assessment. But if you are Cisco and you truly believe that you can increase sales of the target's products by anywhere from 17 to 50 times in a 12-month period, and by doing that you can increase your market cap by several times what you paid for the company in stock, then isn't it more ridiculous not to purchase the company?

The prices of companies, as with almost everything in our economy, are set by the market. Whatever someone is willing to pay for something is its price. Competition affects the boundaries of a reasonably priced deal, with IPOs and competitive pressures adding more sizzle to the process.

What is crucial to understand about any Cisco acquisition is that the transaction is first prompted by customer-required product or service needs. It is then appraised against the evaluation criteria to make sure that the company will assimilate into the Cisco mold. Finally, the acquisition is driven by the financial aspects of the target company. Once the company is assimilated into Cisco, its prior form and incarnation become irrelevant since the much larger Cisco culture and process will make what had been there obsolete.

CHAPTER *15*

CAN YOU REALLY GROW THROUGH ACQUISITION?

We are in the business of acquiring people. That is different from the automotive or financial industries where you are acquiring process, customer base, and distribution. So when we acquire something, we are not acquiring distribution capabilities or manufacturing expertise. We—Cisco—are very good at that. We are acquiring technology. In this business, if you are acquiring technology you are acquiring people.

—John Chambers, President and CEO, Cisco Systems

Can a solid growth strategy be based heavily on acquisition? The answer to this is "Yes" if the acquisitions do not stall the company in the postpurchase environment and "No" if every acquisition steals momentum from both the buyer's and the seller's organizations.

Adding to this already challenging set of affairs the distractions that come from a merger of equals from within the same industry or even two companies from separate industries with conflicting cultures, and you have a recipe for confrontation, heartburn, and intense distraction. Acquiring for acquisition's sake does not make much sense to me, and the statistics related to the success of major acquisitions bear out that they are risky ventures at best and highly debilitating activities at their worst. Regularly buying a company to promote growth and stalling the merged entity with each acquisition will eventually "grow" the buyer into a standstill. This, unfortunately, is the sordid history of corporate acquisitions.

It is difficult enough to grow a company without any distractions or hindrances. Competitors are always trying to take your share of the marketplace as they innovate into other areas. Any industry is challenging enough, but if you are in high tech you have to constantly be innovating because your competition is and your customers will demand it of you if you intend to stay their vendor.

Tom Peters presents some fairly sobering statistics in *Thriving on Chaos* that don't bear out a lot of optimism for large-scale acquisition success.

> When consultants McKinsey & Co. made an extensive study in 1986 of mergers between 1972 and 1983 that involved the two hundred largest public corporations, they determined that a mere 23 percent were successful (as measured by an increase in value to shareholders). The highest success rate (33 percent) was found with small acquisitions made in related fields, [and] the lowest (8 percent) resulted from the merger of large firms whose operations were in unrelated areas.[1]

Small acquisitions in related fields—sound like anyone we know?

But acquisition as a strategic tool to remain competitive in the face of a dynamic marketplace and increasing customer demands can and does make a lot of sense.

WHAT LIES BENEATH ...

If you can't do it yourself, you have to find someone who can or get out of the game. Period. End of story. And the first to market with a technology is the one to beat as others enter that marketplace. Customers in the networking area expect that next year's technology will be faster, smaller, more reliable, and less expensive than what they had purchased the year before. If you want to play in this game you simply have to adopt this set of playing rules.

Is it possible to develop advanced technology using exclusively internal resources? Certainly, but this approach has a set of liabilities intrinsic to its implementation: people and their habits. If a company insists on using only internally available resources and personnel, then the company is limited in its development efforts by the limits of those people and resources. Technology firms are heavily dependent on intellectual property that is derived almost exclusively from the minds of the people doing the design work. We have all seen incredibly creative people such as authors or movie directors who tend to find a formula that works and keep using that formula until it simply doesn't work any more—until it becomes stale and is no longer unique and of interest to the general public. It is tough to be creative consistently, and creating technology is no different. By adding new people, ideas and perspectives to a situation one can uncover ways of approaching that situation that are radically different, and often better, than the group had initially found on its own.

I see this all the time with my consulting work. People rarely bring in a business consultant when they have a simple problem. They usually bring in a consultant when they have a particularly troubling issue that seems to defy solution. They are looking for an expert to tell them what to do. Often I find that simply asking questions and presenting the situation in a different light, or from a different perspective, breaks the logjam being experienced. Once the ideas start to flow again, alternate solutions present themselves that these otherwise intelligent and experienced managers would have seen on their own had they simply looked at the problem from a different perspective, in this case the one that I brought to the table. This very reason is why highly creative people such as songwriters, musicians, authors, and screenwriters collaborate on projects. Collaboration adds another level of energy, creativity, and perspective to the creative process, usually making the end result highly different from what it would have been had either worked on the project on a solo basis. Collaboration works in the creative arts; why can't it be applied to the business art of technology creation? I say that it can, and the Cisco approach presents a way of systemizing that creation-integration process without betting the company on the results of the collaboration. Sometimes risky and creative ventures just don't result in a final outcome that is marketable. But the ones that do work have such huge market potential that the financial rewards reaped are large enough to more than offset the costs of those that didn't pan out.

From Inside Cisco

I think that the process, at a high level, is very portable—the process of identifying what your strengths are as a company, and, as we grow, which acquisition targets would be most likely to be successful with you, within you.[2]

—Barry Eggers, former Cisco acquisitions
leader and now venture capitalist

To determine the project areas on which to concentrate, the company should use its own expertise and history as a guidepost, but ultimately it is the customers' wishes that must come first. I love engineering as much as the next geek, but if it cannot be sold it is a hobby or pure research, not business. Businesses exist because they continue to present the products and services needed by their customer base. In short, any acquisition must support the ultimate goals of the customers. Or, to paraphrase a common political saying from recent elections, "In the end, it's the market, your customers, and what they need, stupid!"

Whether the required products should be internally developed or acquired is a case-by-case decision that depends heavily on the basic skill sets of the buyer, the companies available for purchase, the speed with which the marketplace is changing, and the ultimate cost of not making a timely entrance into the market. Microsoft missed the Internet opportunity in the late 1980s and early 1990s and paid dearly for the lapse as the marketplace exploded, finding Microsoft without a substantial Internet offering. Once Microsoft realized the error it focused intently on correcting the deficiency. I knew people at Microsoft during this period who told me that "You couldn't go to a meeting without having a few Internet-related product or service ideas in your pocket." The software giant had owned up to its mistake and went full-force to correct it. The good news with being a leading market giant is that you can substantially change a market by changing your focus. The bad thing is that blunders can become large mistakes with lasting repercussions, as is now seen with the browser-based antitrust case against Microsoft. Had Microsoft developed a browser earlier, or even purchased Netscape early on, could this whole fiasco have been avoided? Nobody knows for sure, but it certainly seems on the surface a likely possibility. By the way, don't forget that AOL's purchase of Netscape not only took the browser from Microsoft's camp but also put it into a competitor's. Independent of the final outcome of the lawsuit, Microsoft has been distracted from its core operation in defending itself, which has unquestionably cost it market opportunities.

Cisco missed its early chances with the optical networking market space and essentially bought itself a market presence. So far, this strategy has appeared to work, but the incredible price paid to catch up quickly has been construed by many as a sign of how desperate Cisco was to get a foothold in this optical marketplace before it passed Cisco by completely. Cisco might have been lucky this time, and the good news is that the Ciscos and Microsofts of the world do not make these kinds of product marketing mistakes very often. (See Chapter 2 for more information about the product and the strategic planning matrix used to determine Cisco's next market opportunity areas.)

ACQUIRING DOES NOT DEVELOP INTERNAL CAPABILITIES—OR DOES IT?

One criticism of the Cisco A&D approach is that it does not develop internal Cisco capabilities and, as a result, is a short-lived solution to the development problem. If Cisco left these acquired businesses as fully separate entities after acquisition, I think this could be a valid criticism. But Cisco makes every reasonable effort to fully assimilate the products, people, processes, and technologies into the Cisco fold so that future customers cannot tell where the acquired company stops and Cisco begins. In essence, Cisco promptly makes the acquired people part of Cisco. Nothing is lost through the acquisition and, in fact, a lot is gained since these new engineers can train the other Cisco engineers in their acquired areas of expertise. This knowledge then becomes part of the Cisco engineering culture. Instead of the expertise being something acquired, within a short period of time it is just another Cisco area of expertise.

FROM INSIDE CISCO

You have a large installed base. You have the need to provide innovation but in a way which is compatible [and] which creates the minimum type of distraction for the customers. So, to balance innovation with the compatibility, with the same look and feel, with the same semantics of things which are already installed is something that requires an extra effort.[3]

> —*Mario Mazzola, senior vice president, Cisco Systems, commenting on the need for a large organization to balance innovation with installed Cisco products, an effort that involves acquired engineers and existing Cisco engineers, both learning from the process*

So, by acquisition Cisco is expanding its internal expertise as well as the design capabilities of its engineering staff. Instead of potentially stagnating itself by restricting its developments to internally developed projects, Cisco renews itself through the infusion of new people, technologies, and ideas. Notice that contracting the development to a third-party company and then selling that product through the Cisco sales and marketing machine does not add expertise to Cisco and indeed can be construed as a liability for Cisco since it must now support a product for which it does not possess the needed technical talent as members of the Cisco payroll.

The more mature the acquired company, the larger its installed base of customers, and the greater its number of personnel, the greater the risk of the acquisition not working out. And, in such a case, the hassle factor associated with needing to maintain a customer-installed product family after the acquisition is deemed unsuccessful can become a resource drain on the merged entity. Once again, the Cisco approach of buying new companies with a minimal installed based keeps this potential customer service nightmare from becoming a Cisco reality.

Finally, notice that Cisco does not "bet the farm" on a particular acquisition working out. It typically acquires smaller companies and leverages their expertise throughout the Cisco organization. If it doesn't work out, as some reports indicate is true with the majority of Cisco acquisitions, then Cisco keeps on with minimal disruption. But if it works, the revenue enhancement opportunities are enormous. A large upside and a minimal downside sounds like a solid business strategy to me.

BEWARE THE TALK AND NO WALK

Acquisitions can work as an effective way to grow a business. And, in some ways, they may look like an easy remedy for a company looking to get into a market quickly. "After all, Cisco has pulled it off. We should be able to pull it off, too." This type of simplification of a business process has gotten more than one business manager with the best of intentions into trouble. It is one thing to want to adopt the Cisco A&D methodology. It is another entirely to make sure that your organization can handle that methodology, understand what must be

Inside the Valley

Seagate Technology in the early 1980s had to adopt a zero-defects manufacturing policy almost overnight. I worked for Seagate at that time as the national account manager responsible for the account making the demand. At the time, Seagate was experiencing high manufacturing returns, and one of our major customers had issued a mandate that we would comply with a zero-defects policy or likely lose their business. This company represented a huge portion of our business at the time, and—let's face it—a lower rejection rate would have been good for both Seagate and the customer.

Tom Mitchell, vice president of manufacturing at the time, held a meeting at a local hotel. To this meeting he invited all of Seagate's vendors. In front of each of them was a binder outlining the new Seagate zero-defects program. Anticipation was in the air as Mitchell walked into the room and stepped before the podium.

"In front of you all is the new Seagate zero-defects program. It outlines how your particular products will be evaluated from a zero-defects perspective. Things now are different than they were. Those of you not in compliance with the program requirements within the time frames specified will no longer be Seagate approved vendors. Thank you for your cooperation and willingness to make these changes," said Mitchell. He then turned and walked from the room. He was done. The meeting was over. You either comply or you are out. Period. By the way, it worked, and we made it to zero defects so quickly that it made many or our heads spin. This was one of many Tom Mitchell mini-miracles that I witnessed in my time at Seagate.

I am not suggesting that this is the only approach to changing a culture, but this particular one was the right one for Tom Mitchell, Seagate, and its vendors at the time. It worked, and Seagate's culture changed, albeit painfully, in what seemed almost an overnight time frame. Where defects were previously simply a part of the process, they were no longer accepted and needed to be eliminated. If you were not aboard the "eliminate defects" wagon you were in the way. Remain in the way long enough and you could be out. To this day I think back on that time and know in my heart that organizations can change. It takes an executive management team committed to making the change happen. It takes a team with vision that provides the organization's constituencies with enough motivation to want to make it happen and who then set the example themselves to be followed by those around them. Talk is good, but be sure to walk the talk.

done or adapted to make it work, and then make the corporate-wide commitment to actually implement the entire strategy needed to make it, or its derivative, work.

Trying to adopt the methodology without making the cultural and systemic changes needed to make the entire process work, from target selection to target assimilation, will likely meet with dismal failure. These types of failures involve a lot of personalities, projects, technologies, and products, and as a result investors get hurt.

The one thing that Cisco has going for it with respect to making the A&D strategy work is that its entire culture, history, and operational structure are designed around assimilating products, people, and customers into the Cisco culture. Cisco has consciously made A&D an integral part of its development strategy and has invested the time, money, people, facilities, processes, and management support behind making it work. Just as any company would finely hone its chosen research strategy, Cisco has finely honed its A&D strategy. Acquisition is simply the way things are done at Cisco. Any organization that chooses to adopt a similar strategy cannot tell part of its organization that it will pursue an A&D strategy while in the next breath telling the rest of the organization that in-house development remains a primary focus of management. Perhaps employees won't say anything at the meetings, but they will surely think about the discrepancy on their own time or back at their personal offices.

If the buyer's culture looks at acquired personnel as "intruders" or "threats" an A&D strategy will suffer and much financial and career fallout may result. If, on the other hand, management ensures a solid cultural fit, ensures that the products acquired have a high likelihood of producing an incremental revenue grand slam, ensures that the acquired personnel have a transition team there to smooth their way from the target's to the buyer's culture and feels that they are not just a short-term addition but truly a longer-term part of the buyer's family, then the initial acquisition will probably not be a disaster and may even turn out to be a huge success—just as Crescendo was a huge success for Chambers and Cisco in 1993 and the years immediately afterward. With that success comes more confidence for the next ones along with a track record for making acquisitions succeed. Just as people now expect a Cisco acquisition to work out as planned, so will prospective targets begin to expect the acquisition by their particular A&D buyer to be successful.

There is, however, no way of getting into the Cisco type of acquisition program without having a total commitment from the executive level down to the line personnel. A clear focus on the purchase itself not being the goal but successful integration being the celebration point helps to keep things in perspective. If you want to talk the talk, make sure that you are also ready to walk the walk; otherwise you may find yourself walking away from your current employer.

INDUSTRY AND COMPANY LIMITATIONS

There are certain industries that do not immediately lend themselves to the Cisco A&D approach and by their nature conflict with many of the underlying assumptions that have worked so well for Cisco.

Large manufacturing concerns that are heavily capital equipment intensive are an excellent example. If my company is looking to purchase a refinery in a specific geographic area of the world, I may not have a lot of choices as to which company I can purchase. In this case, this particular deal must be structured in such a way that the cultural, financial, and operational areas of prime importance are protected, and we must be willing to have things rocky for a while. Why? Because the refinery itself will be a large investment and will, by its very nature, involve a culture that is different from my company's. Cisco would under these circumstances tend to pass on this type of acquisition and look for another company with great technology to purchase. My refining company cannot do this if access to this part of the world is important, since this may well be the only refinery available in the region. Simply stated, we may have to determine a way to make it work in spite of our differences and the intrinsic acquisition challenges.

FROM INSIDE CISCO

Anyone who takes risks and does not make mistakes is kidding themselves—you're not taking a risk. And companies who say, "We're risk takers" and then you ask key employees what happens if you miss and they say, "I get shot," they aren't risk takers, either.

> —John Chambers, commenting on the need
> to accept risk in an organization and
> not to punish if the risks do not work out
> as planned

Assume that I work for a wireless carrier that intends to purchase other wireless carriers and combine them into a single large network. When looking at a given geographic area I may find that my choices of wireless carriers will be limited by statute. There is likely to be a single wireless and another wireline carrier in a given area. If only one is for sale, then that certainly limits my options. The one available is the one to buy, or else pass on the opportunity. If the market dictates that my company should make a purchase in this geography, then somehow it must be made to work. Performing a comparison between my company and the target so that complementary areas and those that conflict can be determined up front is a great idea and should be part of the due diligence. Placing a special focus on the cultural differences will help the transition teams to smooth the subsequent integration steps that will have to happen. Knowing if key people will leave after the purchase is critical to the transaction proceedings and will affect the offering price. Finding ways to keep these key people will take center stage and will require the cooperation of both buyer and seller. Placing executives or other influential people within the buyer's organization will indicate to acquired personnel that they are not simply at the whim of the buyer and that their own people have a say in how things are run.

In short, all of the conventional wisdom about combining organizations must be put to work in this type of acquisition situation. By its basic structure, this deal is one that Cisco would walk away from or not encounter due to its particular industry situation. But if this is your industry and particular situation you must deal with it, and deal with it you will. Looking for ways to apply the cultural, assimilation, and other lessons from the Cisco approach will help you in making your particular acquisition a success.

There are numerous other examples of industries and companies that will not find the Cisco A&D approach, in total, directly applicable to their situations. People in these situations should remember, though, that people are people and much of the Cisco approach is oriented toward making the transition for the people as fruitful as possible. I feel that Cisco's lessons in this regard should be heavily considered by any acquisition manager in any industry.

THE FINAL ANALYSIS

There are dangers associated with using an A&D approach to product development. Acquiring the talent and then keeping that talent segregated from the buying organization prevents the passing on, or assimilation, of the expertise of the acquired organization. This technique limits the future benefits that the buyer can expect to reap from the purchase since minimal development synergy will result from this type of arrangement. Fully assimilating acquired personnel, on the other hand, transfers their knowledge to the buyer's personnel and thereby makes the buying organization that much stronger from the purchase. Even if this particular set of products does not perform up to expectations, the knowledge transfer from seller to buyer expands the development expertise and viewpoint of the buying organization.

Making sure that the buyer's culture will accommodate the acquired personnel in a welcoming way is a key challenge to buyer management. And this level of acceptance starts at the top, continuing its way down the operational ladder to the line personnel. If it is believed by buyer personnel that this acquisition represents a risk to their jobs or cultural norms, then they may treat the acquired personnel with distrust or worse, no matter the level of encouragement given by management. Cultures do not change overnight, and a solid commitment must be there from top management on down to reinforce the changes at every possible opportunity. Top management of companies looking to migrate their culture to one of "business immigrants" as a method of revitalizing must be prepared to feel a lot like an evangelist preaching the assimilation gospel.

If you can make the transition, I contend that your company will be stronger and more resilient for it. But expect that there will be some bumps along the way as your existing culture adapts to and even adopts some of the cultural norms of the acquired company.

A small acquisition can plant a seed from which a larger company transformation can occur, but it will not happen overnight. It can happen if management believes it can and if management can make a solid case to shareholders, employees, customers, and vendors that it is in everyone's best interest that they also cooperate.

If A&D is what your organization wants to do, then you can. Simply be prepared for the changes that implementing this decision will have on you and your organization, and then make it so.

CHAPTER *16*

SO HOW GOOD REALLY IS THE CISCO A&D APPROACH?

Clearly the assumption of a strong currency is important—either cash or stock. [Next is] the assumption that there is a strong set of either privately funded companies or smaller publicly funded companies that are targets. [There is also] the assumption that Cisco's sales machine remains as strong as it is. And the last assumption is customer demand: that customers continue to demand new and different products from Cisco in new areas.[1]

—Barry Eggers, Former Cisco Acquisition Leader
and Current Silicon Valley Venture Capitalist

Cisco reminds me of the United States in a lot of ways. It encourages diversity of thought with a requirement that we all eventually rally around a single course. It rewards risk taking. It thinks that it is the best possible place on earth to work. It is designed to accept and integrate companies just as the United States has accepted and integrated other cultures. The United States is a nation of immigrants and stronger for it. Cisco is in its own way a company of "business immigrants" and, arguably, stronger for it.

Winston Churchill while visiting New York in the early 1900s wrote a letter to his younger brother, Jack, wherein he described his impression of America.

This is a very great country my dear Jack. Not pretty or romantic but great and utilitarian. There seems to be no such thing as reverence or tradition. Everything is eminently practical and things are judged from a matter of fact standpoint. Take for instance the Court house. No robes or wigs or uniformed ushers. Nothing but a lot of men in black coats and tweed suits. Judge, prisoner, jury counsel & warders all indiscriminately mixed.[2]

I included this quote for two reasons: (1) I am a Churchill fan, and (2) in many ways it makes me think of Cisco Systems.

Let's face it, there is nothing pretty or romantic about networks in general, and routing in particular. Heck, most people don't even know that routers exist, and if they do they haven't really a clue about what they do. This even goes for people who have made lots of money from Cisco's stock over the years. Now, add asynchronous transfer mode (ATM), frame relay, ISDN, and the rest of the acronyms to the mix, and most people say in defeat, "Cisco makes the Internet work, right?" Follow with me to understand the basis for my paralleling of the United States and Cisco Systems.

FROM INSIDE CISCO

The first thing was to really empower teams. We went through an evolution from a very tight central management group with the top four or five people making all the decisions to the empowerment of groups. Our aim was to drive our strategy down through the company.[3]

—*John Chambers, commenting on steps taken to decentralize Cisco*

Is Cisco a great company? Undoubtedly! It is truly one of the most successful and enlivening start-up stories of our time right next to Microsoft, Intel, Sun, Oracle, AOL, and a handful of other incredible technology success stories. I think that the same statement can be made about the United States in that, after all, the Pilgrims were probably the greatest entrepreneurs America has ever seen, and I certainly think that they spawned a successful start-up.

Utilitarian? If you have ever seen Cisco's offices you would have no doubt about this fact, either. Cisco's offices, even those of senior vice presidents are modest at best. They are no larger than an average spare bedroom in a house, with much clutter, few adornments of power, and even less formality. Assistants to the executives have small cubicles that are adjoining other cubicles. Little space is wasted, and frills are almost nonexistent—except when it comes to drinks and coffee. I did find a few espresso machines in the coffee areas, but rumor had it that one of the engineering managers purchased and brought in his own espresso machine for everyone, including himself, to use. Caffeine in Silicon Valley is right up there with air, and since the air quality continues to erode, you might as well make sure that the coffee is the best.

If there is reverence at Cisco it is for the customer, and (unfortunately) for John Chambers, which I think he himself would like to minimize if he could. It is difficult, however, not to think highly of a man who not only is an excellent manager but who also helped to make you wealthy! Anyone who makes me a multimillionaire would be high on my list as well, so Chambers may just have to suffer the burden that many people think of him so highly.

There is also a reverence for technology. Not any particular technology, mind you, but for technology in general. For these people, more than most, understand that the technology of today is a miracle and we are only at the first stages of wherever this technology will take us. There is also a reverence for the culture and the values associated with that culture. Just as we Americans have a reverence for the Constitution and the Declaration of Independence, which represent the finest ideals we strive toward, Cisco treats its values, culture, mission, and vision with a type of overarching reverence that truly does dictate the daily actions of its employees.

FROM INSIDE CISCO

We moved from our "religious" technology mind-set, first of all. We were router bigots. We thought routers were the future, switching was wrong. . . . So we moved out of that into a nonreligious view about technology. We also began to think a couple of years out about what could happen. Before that, we never thought beyond a year.[4]

—*John Chambers,* commenting on Cisco's becoming a technology agnostic

Tradition, at Cisco, exists within the culture but not within the technology itself. Being a technological agnostic has, in my opinion, kept Cisco on the cutting edge as its competitors tried to protect their existing positions. Adhering to the tradition of listening to customers in making future product direction decisions while not adhering to any particular technology as the "best" way to service that customer is a blending of holding to values while staying dynamic with the marketplace. Cisco seems to have mastered this dance and thrives because of it. In essence, everything is, as Churchill said, "eminently practical and . . . judged from a matter of fact standpoint." Couldn't have said it better myself.

There is not a necktie to be found at Cisco, except at the executive levels when they are dealing with the outside world. If you simply walked around Cisco you would not be able to tell most of the executives from the line workers. There are "No robes or wigs or uniformed ushers." When you meet someone in passing at Cisco you really have no idea of what the person does simply by his or her appearance. The dress code is almost always business casual.

Later in the same article Churchill makes another reference to America that I think also applies to Cisco, much to the chagrin of some

264

more established companies such as IBM or Nortel Networks of Canada. Churchill is referring to the American press, but it struck me that this description also describes Cisco in many ways: "[a] great, crude, strong, young people" who act "with a good hearted freshness which may well be the envy of older nations of the earth."[5] Envy could be replaced with a mixture of respect and fear when referring to the attitude that most of Cisco's competition has toward Cisco deciding to enter its marketplace. To present a realistic example of this reality, take a look at this quotation from a March 2001 Interactive Week article.

"According to research firm RHK, Cisco grabbed 29 percent of the $2.2 billion North American market for OC-48 SONET equipment in 2000, to Nortel's 27 percent, NEC's 21 percent, and Lucent's 18 percent. A year earlier, Cisco had just 1 percent of the market for OC-48 products."[6]

Cisco acquired StratumOne Communications (78 employees) in June 1999 for $435 million. It also acquired Cerent Corporation (130 employees) and Monterey Networks (132 employees) in August 1999 for a combined $7.4 billion. All of these companies provided products that helped Cisco to enter this OC-48 and higher-speed space quickly. If Cisco had to develop this technology using internal resources alone, it would have undoubtedly taken years before Cisco would have had a viable product with which to enter this marketplace. By the way, the combined employee additions to Cisco's payroll from these three acquisitions totaled 340.

Notice that 29 percent of $2.2 billion is $638 million, which is far below the amount paid by Cisco for these three companies alone. Cerent's sales to date at the time of the acquisition were $10 million. I had a hard time finding sales information on StratumOne and Monterey, but it is safe to assume that they were less than Cerent's since Cerent represented the lion's share of the purchase price and all three companies were about the same age at the time of purchase. But still, there is an amazing increase in sales experienced from this set of acquisitions if you assume generously, and hypothetically, that the combined sales to date at the time for all three was $20 million. Cisco ramped those sales from $20 million to $638 million in a little over a year! That is an almost 32-fold increase in sales! Tie that in with a six times sales-to-market valuation and you expect that the company's valuation increased by $3.8 billion. There is still a ways to go to recover the total $7.8 billion ($4 billion), but if Cisco has shown that it can aggressively increase sales and if it can also increase its market cap multiplier in the process, it can recover the incredible purchase price within a few years, as amazing as it sounds!

FROM INSIDE CISCO

We can allow this same platform to play in the 10-gig market. In one year we came out of nowhere to take the number one share of OC-48. I suspect we'll be going forward with that same type of success.[7]

—*Robert Koslowsky, Cisco vice president*

There is an energy at Cisco that is friendly, professional, and vibrant. There is a can-do attitude that permeates the place that is positive and upbeat. If it needs doing, they will do it. If you are not contributing your share to the effort, they will let you know. If you deviate from the cultural norm, they will let you know. There is a freshness that comes from having a constant infusion of new people, with new ideas, while working right next to someone else who is also a "business immigrant." A friend who is also a Cisco employee contends that the internal mood is still predominantly one of optimism and that few are blaming Chambers and other top management for the set of undesirable conditions present in mid-2001.

Your visa into Cisco is a team spirit, an interest in great technology, and a desire to change things—to do things differently than they were done before. This is to me the essence of what made the United States great, and I contend it was also what has made Cisco great. Whether the company can maintain this vitality in light of becoming the industry leader, and in many ways a world leader, is yet to be seen. But just as the country has kept itself fresh by adapting to new peoples, ideas, and a changing world climate, so will Cisco be able to maintain its prominence by sticking to all that has made it great in the past. For designing to accommodate change is arguably the best way to predict, adapt to, and thrive from change.

Tom Peters, the management guru, contends in his book *Thriving on Chaos* that the world as we have traditionally known it is "turned upside down." Here are few points that he presents for dealing with this new, chaotic world.

> (1) An obsession with responsiveness to customers, (2) constant innovation in all areas of the firm, (3) partnership—the wholesale participation of and gain sharing with all people connected with the organization, (4) leadership that loves change (instead of fighting it) and instills and shares an inspiring vision, and (5) control by means of simple support systems aimed at measuring the "right stuff" for today's environment.[8]

Huh? Sound like any company you know or have been reading about for the last umpteen chapters? I don't know whether Tom Peters has been involved with Cisco management in developing its overall business model, but there is certainly a lot of synergy between the two.

Peters presents the following assertion early in his book, and it seems to apply to the Cisco model as well.

> If the word "excellence" is to be applicable in the future, it requires wholesale redefinition. Perhaps: "Excellent firms don't believe in excellence—only in constant improvement and constant change." That is, excellent firms of tomorrow will cherish impermanence—and thrive on chaos.[9]

So, you may be asking yourself, how does all of this apply to Cisco's A&D methodology? Simple. Cisco keeps itself fresh by constantly infusing new technology, people, and products into its organization in response to customer-mandated changes. The marketplace tells Cisco where it should be going next, not the reverse! The acquired companies and personnel are not separated off in a little corner, basement, or remote site and occasionally brought in for a meeting. They are assimilated into the Cisco culture. In the terms of the Borg and *Star Trek*, they are added to the collective consciousness of the organization such that their addition changes the organization as a whole. The acquired personnel are certainly changed by Cisco, but Cisco, itself, cannot help being changed by the acquired personnel as well.

Mario Mazzola and his engineering team are an excellent example of this change process. Mazzola was brought into Cisco with the Crescendo purchase in 1993. Mazzola is a solid engineer, a proven business manager, an entrepreneur at heart with several start-ups under his belt, and a person who likes to grow things. He managed the switching side of Cisco's business up until the 2000 time frame, when he transferred to heading up the new business ventures area of Cisco. Switching was a $7 billion business when Mazzola passed the reins.

Randy Pond, another Crescendo employee brought in with the purchase, is now the senior vice president of operations for Cisco. Judith Estrin, former president and CEO of Precept Software, acquired by Cisco in 1998, became Cisco's chief technology officer. Prem Jain, another engineer brought in with the Crescendo purchase, is a vice president with Cisco in its enterprise line of business. The list goes on and on. These are all high-powered, professional individuals who make a contribution to Cisco and through their leadership change the way Cisco operates. They are not Cisco-homegrown, and all have a strongly entrepreneurial spirit that, like it or not sometimes, will keep Cisco on its toes. Couple this with Chambers' "more paranoid than Andy Grove" mentality, and you have a company that, despite its size, may actually be able to beat the odds and remain nimble while an industry behemoth.

CISCO, LIKE THE SELLER, FULLY COMMITS

When Cisco purchases a company there is little hesitation about the purchase once the purchase decision is made. The target has already passed the disqualification criteria and due diligence, and the people are employees that Cisco would want, anyway. A great tribute to the Cisco acquisition process is that it is up front with acquired employees about their fates and, once they become Cisco employees, is fully committed to making them productive and personally rewarded by working for Cisco. This means more than providing a stock option, which is no trivial offering in itself. It extends to finding the right person for the right Cisco job. In summary, Cisco commits to the employees just as the employees are fully committing to Cisco by agreeing to the purchase. Once the target is sold it is gone, seamlessly assimilated into Cisco. Cisco provides this same level of commitment back to the selling employees, making every possible effort to welcome them. Instead of waiting to train acquired employees on the buyer's ways, allowing them to flounder and creating resentment in the process, Cisco proactively works with acquired employees to Ciscoize them as quickly as possible, often within 90 days. The low turnover rate for acquired employees is a tribute to the effectiveness of the personnel integration aspect of Cisco's acquisitions.

These people stay for any number of reasons, some of which are financial, but my experience is that if people stay for the money but are unhappy with their jobs, employee effectiveness will suffer. Cisco does not seem to have that problem.

FROM INSIDE CISCO

The mathematics of this is interesting. If you grow at 50 percent per [year] for 18 months . . . it requires you to double your leadership team every 18 months . . . just to stay where you were before.[10]

—*John Chambers on the importance of hiring and keeping excellent management talent while growing*

Take a look at Table 16.1 to get an idea about the number of employees added per fiscal year by acquisition and those added as a direct result of growth requirements. There is no question from this chart that the majority of Cisco's personnel growth has been from sources other than acquisition. From fiscal 1993 to fiscal 2000, Cisco's number of employees has increased by around 33,000 employees; acquisitions accounted for around 5,900 of these added employees, or a difference of around 27,000 obtained from nonacquisition sources.

When a company is undergoing this type of incredible revenue growth it has a huge need for employees and simply cannot afford to lose too many. Cisco has, by many measures, held on to its employees well. Turnover estimates are in the 4 percent to 6 percent per year range in an industry that typically experiences anywhere from 20 percent to 40 percent turnover per year. Obviously, Cisco is doing something right.

Table 16.1 Cisco Revenue and Employee Information by Fiscal Year

Year	Revenues	Number of Employees	Revenue per Employee	Added Employees from Acquisitions	Employees Added from Growth
1990	$69,000,000	254	$271,654	0	N/A
1991	$183,000,000	506	$361,660	0	252
1992	$340,000,000	882	$385,488	0	376
1993	$649,000,000	1,451	$447,278	0	569
1994	$1,243,000,000	2,262	$549,514	120	691
1995	$1,979,000,000	3,479	$568,842	210	1,007
1996	$4,096,000,000	8,259	$495,944	1,248	3,532
1997	$6,440,000,000	10,728	$600,298	291	2,178
1998	$8,459,000,000	14,623	$578,472	369	3,526
1999	$12,154,000,000	20,657	$588,372	1,223	4,811
2000	$18,928,000,000	34,617	$546,783	2,394	11,566
2001	$22,293,000,000	30,000	$743,100	625	−5,242
Total Employees Added:				5,855	

THE CHAMBERS EFFECT

The methodology is one thing, but it is difficult to separate the success of Cisco's acquisition activities from the people responsible for their implementation. After all, these business development managers are some of the most experienced in the field and have learned lessons from mistakes made along the way that might still have to be learned by someone new to the process. On the other hand, Cisco has a highly refined process that seems to work. It has taken a lot of the experimentation out of acquisitions and provided a framework within which those acquisitions can successfully occur.

The question is whether the process is independent of the personnel and robust enough to be replicated by non-Cisco personnel.

FROM INSIDE CISCO

The only thing that is not portable are some of the key people there that have the knowledge. I hired Mike Volpi, and on the first couple of acquisitions he was learning. He has developed into the best-practices, best-in-class BD [business development] guy. And you have Dan Scheinman on the legal side. Both of those guys are very high quality. They know what they are doing and learned from early mistakes.[11]

—Barry Eggers, former business development leader with Cisco Systems and now Silicon Valley venture capitalist, commenting on the value of experience

Starting at the top, I think that John Chambers and the culture that he cocreates with the others at Cisco an integral part of Cisco's success. His consistency and leadership are important to Cisco's success, and Cisco's acquisition programs are integral to that success. The freedom and trust that Chambers gives to the business development team is a strong tribute to them professionally and to him as a leader. Acquisitions do not happen in a vacuum but are also not controlled by upper management to the point that they may be stifled. Put another leadership style in Chambers' chair, and probably the acquisitions programs would also change. Remove Mike Volpi, Dan Scheinman, or Ed Kozel from Cisco, and their expertise goes with them. That expertise is important not only when things are going well, but mostly when things are outside of the norm. When an acquisition is having unforeseen problems, these must be overcome for the purchase not only to consummate but also to succeed in the postpurchase environment.

The good news is that Cisco's people did not have a lot of experience either when they started and certainly did not have as refined a process as they do today. In fact, most people at the time thought that the Cisco A&D approach was folly, which we now know to be inaccurate. Acquisition managers today have the benefit of using Cisco's expertise as presented in this book and other sources. New acquisition managers do not have to start from scratch, as Cisco did, in creating their particular methodology. The acquisition managers of today may have the experience of a 1993 Cisco business development manager but they have a knowledge base to start from that incorporates more than 70 successful acquisitions by Cisco Systems. That puts the new acquisition manager on a much better footing than Cisco had in 1993.

THE FINAL ANALYSIS

I contend that the Cisco acquisition process succeeds because Cisco and its personnel know what they expect from an acquisition. They talk seriously only to target companies that have the technology and products needed to expand Cisco in the direction its customers require. It then only proceeds to due diligence with companies that have a solid intangible fit with Cisco's culture and overall business direction. Cisco then considers pricing as a final point instead of the first point of a discussion. In essence, Cisco is willing to pay top dollar for quality, with quality being defined by the specific aspects of the Cisco acquisition methodology for this particular target and its value components.

So how successful are Cisco's acquisition practices? Very effective, as demonstrated by the flattering copying of the procedure by some of its competition.

Jon Bayless, a general partner at Sevin Rosen Funds of Dallas, a venture capital fund that helped negotiate the 1999 acquisition of optical Internetworking company Monterey Networks, says this about the Cisco methodology: "I haven't found anyone in any industry that has a process that is as tuned."[12]

When you have people like Charles Giancarlo, currently a senior vice president at Cisco but previously CEO of Kalpana, remaining with Cisco after the acquisition, you have a lot of good things happening for Cisco. It is always exciting to work in a dynamic environment with dynamic people on a mission to change things for the better.

"Cisco is able to hold on to people like me," says Giancarlo. "They gave me a chance to play a major role." That is a big deal to successful entrepreneurs—how to play a bigger role in an industry that they love while having fun along the way. After all, for many of these people, it is no longer about the money. Cisco's buying them and then appreciating its stock value took care of their financial problems.

So how good is the Cisco acquisition methodology? When you can keep a $20+ billion revenue company from stagnating, keep attracting and holding good people, and still have the industry treating you like you are the guys to beat, you are a success in almost any book. Cisco's A&D methodology is without question an integral part of that success. By that measure, the Cisco A&D methodology has been a huge success.

APPENDIX *A*

DUE DILIGENCE STARTING CHECKLIST

Due Diligence General Investigation Areas
General Background
 Buyer
  Contact Personnel
 Seller
  Contact Personnel
 Time Frame for Completion
 Buyer Intended Objectives with Acquisition
Deal Stoppers (Deal Specific)
Areas of Investigation (High-impact list provided at beginning of each major investigation area)
 Legal
  High-Impact Items
  Corporate Structure, Bylaws, Charter, and So On
  Ownership
  SEC Filings and Relationship
  Board of Directors

Source: From *The Technology M&A Guidebook*, by Ed Paulson with Court Huber (New York: John Wiley & Sons, 2001), pp. 405–408. Reprinted with permission.

Pending Litigation
Intellectual Property Ownership
Regulatory Issues
Accounting and Finance
High-Impact Items
Past Accounting Procedures
Verification of Financial Statements
Internal Policies and Procedures
Automation
Auditing of Statements
Publicly Traded Stock Performance
Banking and Investor Relations
Financial Structure
In-Depth Ratio Analysis
Forecasts
Tax Situation
Research and Development Engineering
High-Impact Items
Internally Developed Technology
Purchased Technology
Unique Design Strategies and Techniques
Adherence to Standards
Independent Certification Testing as Applicable
Patent Review
Key Engineering Developments and Personnel
Verification of Product Performance to Specifications
Design Verification Procedures
New Technologies under Development
Success in Meeting Design Goals
Research Alliances
Marketing and Sales
High-Impact Items
Customer Base Analysis
Distribution Channel Analysis
Product Definition Process

    Pricing and Demand Analysis
    Market Analysis
    Advertising and Promotion
    Regulatory Issues
    Segmentation Analysis
    Positioning
    Future Strategies
    Historical Trends by Product and Region
    Personnel Review
Production
    High-Impact Items
    Manufacturing Locations
    Yields and Performance
    Proprietary Processes
    Cost Breakdown By Product
    Personnel
    Union Issues
    Environmental Impact Issues
    Material Planning
    Purchasing
    Automation Levels
Human Resources
    High-Impact Items
    Policies
    Retirement Plans
    Benefit Package
    Stock Options
    Employee Contracts
    Employee Turnover Rates
    Pending Personnel-Related Litigation
    Sources of Employees
    Overall Cultural Assessment
Internet Usage
    High-Impact Items
    Internal Usage

External Usage
Technology in Use
Future Strategy
Management
    High-Impact Items
    Management Style
    History of Executive Managers
    Promotion Strategy
    Corporate Culture Requirements
    Overall Use of Technology (May warrant a dedicated section.)
    Reporting and Evaluation Procedures
    Employee Development Policies

VARIOUS COMPANY BUYER TYPES AND THEIR MOTIVATIONS

Buyer Type	Attributes and Motivations
Financial buyer	Buyer that is primarily interested in the target company as a financial investment. May purchase the company to split it into smaller units or to bundle with other owned companies for resale.
Bottom fisher	Buyer that looks for highly undervalued companies so that the target can be purchased at a reduced price, which translates into reduced risk. Companies that grow too quickly and develop financial problems are excellent bottom fisher acquisition target companies.
Strategic buyer	One looking for an important technology, marketing, or other benefit that the buyer does not yet have. By adding, through purchase, this capability, the buyer hopes to acquire synergies that make the new combined company stronger and more valuable than the individual parts.
Product line or market share expansion buyer	One interested in purchasing a company that provides a product line or market presence that expands the buyer's. Buying the presence is often cheaper and faster than developing it from scratch.

(Continued)

Appendix B Various Company Buyer Types and Their Motivations

Buyer Type	Attributes and Motivations
Tire kicker	One that looks around for acquisition deals, takes up the seller's time, and then never makes a purchase.
Employee stock ownership plan (ESOP), management buyout, or leveraged buyout	Related to the financial buyer except that the buyers might be the current company management or employees themselves. This is sometimes called "taking a company private."

Source: From *The Technology M&A Guidebook*, by Ed Paulson with Court Huber (New York: John Wiley & Sons, 2001), p. 25. Reprinted with permission.
Note: Cisco Systems is a combination of strategic buyer and product line expansion buyer.

APPENDIX C

TYPICAL MOTIVATIONS FOR BUYING A COMPANY

The chapters in this book present the Cisco-specific reasons for purchasing a company. This appendix is provided as background information for buyers from other companies or industries to understand some of the typical motivations for purchasing a company that may differ from those of Cisco Systems.

BUYING VERSUS INTERNAL DEVELOPMENT (LIKELY CISCO MOTIVATION)

70 percent of Cisco's products are developed internally, while the other 30 percent are acquired with company purchases. So, determining which products should be internally developed and which should be acquired is an ongoing and highly evolved process of evaluation within Cisco.

Once a company determines its required capability enhance-

Source: The Technology M&A Guidebook, by Ed Paulson with Court Huber (New York: John Wiley & Sons, 2001), pp. 28–30 and 33–36. Reprinted with permission.

ments, it must then decide whether its interests are better served by developing the enhancements using internal capabilities or whether purchasing the enhancements is a better approach. A number of factors should be considered when making this determination, especially when dealing with a technology-related issue.

First, how quickly is the technology market window moving? If the technology is rapidly evolving in a quickly expanding marketplace, then purchasing the required capability might be the wisest approach along with being the most financially appealing.

Assume that you can develop the technology in an 18-month period for a cost of $3.5 million, after which time you will begin to acquire market share related to that particular technology. Assume that it will take you six months to purchase a company with a 15 percent market share and established technology for around $5 million, which also happens to be the same as its sales numbers. Assume also that the company has a net income of 15 percent of $5 million, or $750,000. Total sales in this company's market are assumed at around $33.3 million ($5 million divided by 15 percent market share).

The fact that the $3.5 million is less the $5 million might make developing the technology a more attractive option on the surface. But notice also that the decision to purchase gets you to the marketplace 12 months sooner and also makes you $750,000 in net income that would otherwise have been lost. Instead of dealing with a $1.5 million spread between the two options, you are now dealing with only $750,000 ($1.5 million minus $750,000 net income).

If your 18-month development schedule is short by a six-month period (which is not uncommon) then you are now looking at only a $375,000 differential. The strategic benefits of getting into the industry more quickly and gaining a 15 percent market share early in a growing market might easily offset this $375,000 additional cost and even turn it into a profit. If the marketplace itself is growing at a 15 percent annual rate, which can happen for a limited period of time for some technology areas, then the market will grow to $38.3 million in a single year, and the target company's sales revenues (remaining at a 15 percent market share) will grow to $5.75 million. If the net income remains at 15 percent, it now also climbs to $860,000, whittling the $375,000 differential found with the extended development schedule to only $210,000 ($1.5 million minus $860,000, minus $860,000 divided by 2). This $210,000 differential might be easily justified on a strategic basis only or accounted for in the financial activities associated with the company purchase. Remember that companies are purchased with combinations of debt, stock, and other financial techniques. R&D is usually treated as a simple company expense that affects the purchasing company's financial statements in a negative way, driving down earnings and stock prices and making this an unattractive option to most financially motivated managers.

I admit that this is a simplified example using a specially created set of circumstances to keep the math simple, but the general concept is sound with respect to determining the major reasons why you would purchase instead of develop a specific technology. Just because internal development looks less expensive from an accounting standpoint, it might not be less expensive when reviewed from a business perspective that includes opportunity and market exposure costs.

MARKET WINDOW CONSIDERATIONS (TYPICAL CISCO MOTIVATION)

Technology markets change quickly; today's hottest technology becomes obsolete in anywhere from a few months to a few years. Many of the technology advancements of today would simply not have been possible as few as five years ago, and they would certainly not have been possible at today's lower prices. This rapidly changing technological pace destroys older markets and generates new ones, also creating M&A opportunities in its wake.

Gordon E. Moore, cofounder of Intel and key developer of the microprocessor, contends that a new microprocessor chip is introduced every 18 to 24 months, and each chip has roughly twice the capacity of its immediate predecessor. This translates into an exponential increase in processing capacity when plotted over a number of years. According to the Intel web site (www.intel.com): "In 26 years the number of transistors on a chip has increased more than 3,200 times, from 2,300 on the 4004 in 1971 to 7.5 million on the Pentium® II processor." Putting this increased processing capacity on a single processor chip enables huge increases in processing power while also substantially decreasing manufacturing cost. The fact that we can purchase the processing power of today at a price that is a fraction of initial IBM PC prices is truly one of today's business and technology miracles and one unique to the technology industries.

Each increase in processing power and decrease in cost spawns secondary markets that take advantage of that processing power in the form of embedded controllers, dedicated processors, real-time processing, and monitoring activities. Software applications are also developed to support the application needs of these smaller, more powerful hardware devices.

Notice that Moore's Law presents a market window, or time frame, within which existing technologies can be applied on the leading edge. If you add to this time frame the staged introduction of Microsoft's operating systems and office products, which have an undisputed dominance in their respective market segments, you find a frequently changing technological landscape.

The incredible dominance of the consumer software marketplace by Microsoft has caused M&A activity. One notable example is that of Novell's early 1990s purchase (merge) of WordPerfect in an attempt to provide its customers with not only a network but also the applications that run on that network. It didn't work out as planned, though, and the WordPerfect application suite was sold to Corel Corporation so that Corel could round out its graphic design product offerings with a comprehensive desktop office suite. Novell went back to working on its networking products, and Corel started working to turn WordPerfect back into a desktop application powerhouse.

WordPerfect Corporation was not a company in need of repair. It was doing well prior to its acquisition by Novell, although only conjecture can determine what would have happened to WordPerfect had Novell not purchased it. Where as WordPerfect was once the standard for PC-based word processing, it now has a very small market share and has been almost completely replaced by Microsoft Word as the de facto industry standard.

The IBM purchase of Lotus Development was a similar defensive move by IBM against Microsoft's dominance of the desktop. Lotus Development was clearly a pioneer in the technology industry and brought strong resources to IBM when purchased. But where the desktop application arena was once dominated by WordPerfect and Lotus 1-2-3 with Microsoft being an operating system provider, we now find Microsoft the powerhouse (at 92 percent market share for office suite products) with WordPerfect and Lotus Development in an also-ran position. Things change in nanoseconds for technology industries.

ACQUIRING PROPRIETARY TECHNOLOGY (POSSIBLE CISCO MOTIVATION)

Imagine that you are a major technology products vendor who just found out about a smaller company with a new technology that could make a major portion of your product line obsolete. To add to the excitement, assume that this smaller company has solid legal protection in the form of a patent that cannot be easily circumvented. Would you want one of your competitors to get hold of this technology instead of you? Probably not. And think about the strategic advantage your company would have if this technology were placed under your corporate umbrella along with the engineers who created the competitive technology in the first place.

This type of scenario plays itself out daily in the Silicon Valleys, Austins, and other technology hotbeds around the country. Smaller companies are always looking for entrepreneurial methods of solving major technology problems that have usually been created by, and ignored by, the major providers. Once that technology is brought to a reasonable state of readiness, the smaller companies often become acquisition targets so that the larger companies can purchase the technology rights or personnel, or both.

Typically, the smaller company is happy to be bought since it does not have the marketing or financial muscle to capitalize fully on its idea without outside help. And any existing patent protection has a limited life, after which others can copy the idea and infringe on what was previously an exclusive market. Many companies can survive long enough to fund their next stage of growth with a public stock offering. This has been the case with Cisco, Yahoo! Seagate, Dell, Microsoft, and countless others.

There are still other companies, such as Net Guru Technologies (NGT), creator of the industry standard Certified Internet Webmaster (CIW) certification, which chose to sell to Prosoft as a way of more rapidly expanding the influence of its certification process.

Yahoo!'s purchase of Broadcast.com (1999) is another example of a smaller company's technology being bought by a larger one with a more established means of marketing that technology. Broadcast.com has had a leadership position in streaming media, which is the ability to provide audio and video content over the Internet. Yahoo! is continually looking for ways to enhance the value of its site to its users. Any feature that increases usage makes Yahoo!'s site more valuable. It had to either purchase the technology, as it did with Broadcast.com, or develop it internally. The transaction trades 0.7722 shares of Yahoo! stock for each share of the outstanding 36 million shares and 7 million stock options of Broadcast.com stock. Both companies were traded on the Nasdaq. The marketplace obviously approved, since the announcement caused Yahoo! share prices to increase $11.37 (7 percent) to $179.75 and Broadcast.com share prices to increase $11.81 (10 percent) to $130 (April 1, 1999).

When the underlying technology or proprietary content is the motivation for purchase, the selling company is in a unique position with respect to the buyer in that there is really no comparable competitor. This often means that the smaller company can command a higher price than its standard book value, and if the company is not publicly traded there is no market valuation upon which the sale price must be based. This might present an excellent purchasing opportunity for the buyer if the seller is motivated to sell, but might present an excellent opportunity for the seller if a bidding war between larger competitors can be started who might bid up the price of the to-be-purchased company simply to keep the other competitor from obtaining the underlying technology and its associated competitive advantage.

Remember that this type of purchase often has a strategic component to it that might completely dominate the financial aspects of the transaction. This is usually good news for the selling company since purchase price ceilings would now take a backseat to the strategic components.

BUYING MARKET SHARE AND PRESENCE (POSSIBLE CISCO MOTIVATION)

Purchasing a company is a quick way to gain market presence in a new or emerging marketplace. Once again, a company can invest the time and money in creating that market presence itself, but might be able to accomplish the same goals with less money and risk by purchasing an existing company in that marketplace.

The April 1999 purchase of Livebid.com by Amazon.com falls into this category.

Amazon.com is a major Internet retailer that started out offering books online and is now leveraging its high name recognition into other Internet retail marketing areas. Livebid.com offers technology and Internet presence that enable live Internet-based auctions. Livebid.com handled the auction of the only known completely intact passenger ticket for the *Titanic*. Through its purchase of Livebid.com, Amazon.com quickly moves into the live Internet auction business, which helps it compete more favorably with companies such as eBay.

Cisco Systems' 1999 purchases of Cerent Corporation and Monterey Networks are other examples of a major company purchasing technology instead of developing it internally. Cisco understands that it must move into optical fiber technology to remain ahead of its competition and justifies the purchase as being attractive for its shareholders, according to Cisco chief executive John Chambers.

"We who understood our market understood that optical transport was going to explode and so our shareholders as well as industry analysts have been asking us for a while what we're going to do." It looks like Cisco just answered that question with this $7.36 billion stock transfer transaction. (Reuters as reported in the *Chicago Tribune*, August 27, 1999, Section 3, p. 3.)

Notice that these types of purchases only make sense when the purchasing company understands its marketplace and its strategic position within that marketplace. In addition, the purchasing company has a much easier time funding the purchase if its own core operations are intact and profitable. The higher the market valuation of the purchasing company's stock, the more purchasing power that stock commands on the M&A market.

As the stock market continues to increase in value, the more you can expect M&A activity to increase along with it. Most major companies have staffs of people who are continually on the lookout for attractive acquisition targets or companies that might be potential acquirers. The most likely candidates are determined and monitored so that when the right timing presents itself the preliminary legwork has already been done and productive conversations can be held from the beginning.

BUYING PEOPLE WITH THE PURCHASE (HEAVY CISCO MOTIVATION)

It is also common for an acquisition to become attractive due in large part to the executive management team also being acquired. Many companies do not have an obvious heir apparent to the top management slots. An acquisition presents a technique not only for rounding out the company's operation and/or financial condition but also for acquiring the personnel needed to fill key personnel slots. Don't ever forget that corporations are legal shells within which people work, and the personalities of the people involved are key to success of failure.

Looking back at the Viacom–CBS merger, you find that the acquisition of Mel Karmazin appears to have been an important consideration in the transaction. Sumner Redstone, CEO of Viacom, was 76 years old in 1999 when the transaction occurred. Mel Karmazin, 55, will act as president and chief operating officer with an agreement to take over as CEO when Redstone leaves at an undetermined future date.

Larger companies often acquire smaller companies not only in an attempt to capture innovative technologies, but also with the intention of instilling an entrepreneurial spirit into the much larger organization. Although the intent might be noble, my experience has shown that entrepreneurs don't work well within the highly bureaucratic environments that usually accompany larger organizations. (I know several who sold their companies to larger firms only to find themselves dissatisfied and irritated at how the company was subsequently run.) Their dissatisfaction often increases to the point that leaving is more attractive than staying.

If a major intention of the acquisition is to acquire the management talent, then a careful evaluation of the fit between the acquired management team and the existing culture of the purchasing company must be made. In essence, the acquired management team should be interviewed just as though they were being evaluated for a job, since that is the basic intent. How this is handled during negotiations is a matter of individual personalities and circumstances, but taking this step slowly and with open eyes is critical if the transaction is to produce the intended final results. It is a lot easier to integrate technology into a company than it is to mesh the strong personalities that exist at executive levels in successful corporations.

APPENDIX

SUMMARY OF CISCO'S ACQUISITIONS

Trans. Number	Company Name	Acquisition Announcement Date	Total Transaction Valuation	Number of Employees	Price per Employee
1	Crescendo Systems	9/21/1993	$95,000,000	65	$1,461,538.46
2	Newport Systems Solutions	7/12/1994	$93,000,000	55	$1,690,909.09
3	LightStream Corporation	10/8/1994	$120,000,000	60	$2,000,000.00
4	Kalpana, Inc.	10/24/1994	$240,000,000	150	$1,600,000.00
5	Combinet	8/10/1995	$132,000,000	100	$1,320,000.00
6	Internet Junction	9/6/1995	$6,000,000	10	$600,000.00
7	Grand Junction Networks, Inc.	9/27/1995	$400,000,000	85	$4,705,882.35
8	Network Translation	10/27/1995	$32,000,000	10	$3,200,000.00
9	TGV Software	1/23/1996	$138,000,000	130	$1,061,538.46
10	StrataCom	4/22/1996	$4,666,000,000	1,200	$7,465,600.00
11	Telebit Corporations MICA Technologies	7/22/1996	$200,000,000	288	$694,444.44
12	Nashoba Networks	8/6/1996	$100,000,000	40	$2,500,000.00

(Continued)

Trans. Number	Company Name	Acquisition Announcement Date	Total Transaction Valuation	Number of Employees	Price per Employee
13	Granite Systems	9/3/1996	$220,000,000	50	$4,400,000.00
14	NETSYS Technologies	10/14/1996	$79,000,000	50	$1,580,000.00
15	Metaplex Inc.	12/1/1996	$2,000,000	20	$100,000.00
16	Telesend	3/26/1997	$6,000,000	N/A	$6,000,000.00
17	Skystone Systems Corporation	6/9/1997	$102,000,000	40	$2,550,000.00
18	Ardent Communications Corporation	6/24/1997	$156,000,000	40	$3,900,000.00
19	Global Internet Software Group	6/24/1997	$40,000,000	20	$2,000,000.00
20	Dagaz	6/28/1997	$126,000,000	30	$4,200,000.00
21	LightSpeed International	12/22/1997	$194,000,000	70	$2,771,428.57
22	WheelGroup Corporation	2/18/1998	$124,000,000	75	$1,653,333.33
23	NetSpeed, Inc.	3/10/1998	$265,000,000	140	$1,892,857.14
24	Precept Software	3/11/1998	$84,000,000	50	$1,680,000.00
25	Class Data Systems	5/4/1998	$51,000,000	34	$1,500,000.00
26	Summa Four	7/28/1998	$118,000,000	210	$561,904.76
27	American Internet Corporation	8/21/1998	$35,600,000	50	$712,000.00
28	Clarity Wireless Corporation	9/15/1998	$157,000,000	39	$4,025,641.03
29	Selsius Systems	10/14/1998	$145,000,000	51	$2,843,137.25
30	PipeLinks	12/2/1998	$126,000,000	73	$1,726,027.40
31	Fibex Systems	4/8/1999	$445,000,000	100	$4,450,000.00
32	Sentient Networks, Inc.	4/8/1999	N/A	102	N/A
33	GeoTel Communications Corporation	4/13/1999	$2,000,000,000	310	$6,451,612.90

Summary of Cisco's Acquisitions

Trans. Number	Company Name	Acquisition Announcement Date	Total Transaction Valuation	Number of Employees	Price per Employee
34	Amteva Technologies, Inc.	4/28/1999	$170,000,000	144	$1,180,555.56
35	TransMedia Communications	6/17/1999	$407,000,000	66	$6,166,666.67
36	StratumOne Communications	6/29/1999	$435,000,000	78	$5,576,923.08
37	Calista	8/16/1999	$55,000,000	20	$2,750,000.00
38	MaxComm Technologies	8/18/1999	$143,000,000	35	$4,085,714.29
39	Monterey Networks	8/26/1999	$500,000,000	132	$3,787,878.79
40	Cerent Corporation	8/26/1999	$6,900,000,000	130	$53,076,923.08
41	Cocom A/S	9/15/1999	$66,000,000	66	$1,000,000.00
42	Webline Communications Corporation	9/22/1999	$325,000,000	120	$2,708,333.33
43	Tasmania Network Systems	10/26/1999	$25,000,000	16	$1,562,500.00
44	Aironet Wireless Communications	11/9/1999	$799,000,000	131	$6,099,236.64
45	V-Bits	11/11/1999	$128,000,000	30	$4,266,666.67
46	Worldwide Data Systems	12/16/1999	$26,000,000	N/A	$26,000,000.00
47	Internet Engineering Group, LLC	12/17/1999	$25,000,000	13	$1,923,076.92
48	Pirelli Optical Systems	12/20/1999	$2,150,000,000	701	$3,067,047.08
49	Compatible Systems	1/19/2000	N/A	68	N/A
50	Altiga Networks	1/19/2000	$567,000,000	76	$7,460,526.32
51	Growth Networks, Inc.	2/16/2000	$355,000,000	53	$6,698,113.21
52	Atlantech Technologies Ltd.	3/1/2000	$180,000,000	120	$1,500,000.00

(Continued)

Trans. Number	Company Name	Acquisition Announcement Date	Total Transaction Valuation	Number of Employees	Price per Employee
53	Jetcell, Inc.	3/16/2000	$200,000,000	46	$4,347,826.09
54	InfoGear Technologies Corporation	3/16/2000	$301,000,000	74	$4,067,567.57
55	PentaCom Ltd.	4/11/2000	$118,000,000	48	$2,458,333.33
56	Seagull Semiconductor Ltd.	4/12/2000	$19,000,000	17	$1,117,647.06
57	ArrowPoint Communications	5/5/2000	$5,700,000,000	337	$16,913,946.59
58	Qeyton Systems	5/12/2000	$800,000,000	52	$15,384,615.38
59	HyNEX, Ltd.	6/5/2000	$127,000,000	49	$2,591,836.70
60	Netiverse	7/7/2000	$210,000,000	34	$6,176,470.59
61	Komodo	7/25/2000	$175,000,000	25	$7,000,000.00
62	NuSpeed	7/27/2000	$450,000,000	56	$8,035,714.29
63	Ipmobile	8/1/2000	$425,000,000	81	$5,246,913.58
64	PixStream, Inc.	8/31/2000	$369,000,000	156	$2,365,384.62
65	IpCell Technologies, Inc.	9/28/2000	$369,000,000	110	$3,354,545.45
66	Vovida Networks, Inc.	9/28/2000	$369,000,000	65	$5,676,923.08
67	CAIS Software Solutions	10/20/2000	$170,000,000	65	$2,615,384.62
68	Active Voice Corporation	11/10/2000	$266,000,000	N/A	N/A
69	Radiata, Inc.	11/13/2000	$295,000,000	53	$5.566.037.74
70	ExIO Communications, Inc.	12/14/2000	$155,000,000	38	$4,078,947.37
71	AuroraNetics, Inc.	7/11/2001	$150,000,000	52	$2,884,615.38
	Totals		$34,621,600,000	7,104	

Note: The announcement date and the actual acquisition date will generally not be the same and usually only separate each other by a few months. All announced acquisitions included in this list actually culminated in purchases.

Source: A consolidation of information provided from various sources such as the Cisco Systems web site (www.cisco.com), published press releases, news articles, analysis reports, and various other publicly available sources.

NOTES

Chapter 1 So What's the Big Deal?

1. Standard & Poor's Industry Reports, "Computers: Networking," by Megan Graham-Hackett, computer networking analyst, September 14, 2000, p. 4.

2. "The Network Effect: Cisco, only 10 years old, is emerging as the world's most valuable firm. Welcome to the post-PC market," by Karl Taro Greenfeld, *Time*, April 10, 2000, vol. 155, no. 14, Visions 21, p. 48.

3. *Making the Cisco Connection: The Story behind the Real Internet Superpower*, by David Bunnell with Adam Brate (New York: John Wiley & Sons, 2000), p. 77.

4. "Growth by Acquisition: The Case of Cisco Systems," Second Quarter, 1997, Thought Leaders, Strategy and Business, Booz, Allen and Hamilton (www.strategy-business.com/thoughtleaders/97209/page6.html).

5. "John Chambers: The Art of the Deal," Interview with John Daly, Business 2.0, October 1999 (www.business2.com/articles/1999/10/text/chambers.html), page 6/8.

Chapter 2 Buying the Cisco Way

1. "Cisco's Secrets," by Henry Goldblatt, *Fortune*, November 8, 1999, vol. 140, no. 9, p. 177+.

2. "Growth by Acquisition: The Case of Cisco Systems," Second Quarter, 1997, Thought Leaders, Strategy and Business, Booz, Allen and Hamilton (www.strategy-business.com/thoughtleaders/97209/page1.html).

3. "John Chambers: The Art of the Deal," Interview with James Daly, Business 2.0, October 1999 (www.business2.com/articles/1999/10/text/chambers.html).

4. www.cisco.com/warp/public/750/corpfact.html.

5. "John Chambers: The Art of the Deal."

6. "Growth by Acquisition: The Case of Cisco Systems," p. 3.

7. Cisco press release, April 22, 1996.

8. "John Chambers: The Art of the Deal," p. 3/8.

9. *Cisco Systems, Inc.*, by Richard L. Nolan (Boston: Harvard Business School Publishing, 2000; Case Number: 9-398-127, October 5, 2000), p. 8.

10. "Growth by Acquisition: The Case of Cisco Systems," p.10.

11. Ibid., p. 9/12.

CHAPTER 3   The Company That Sandy, Len, Don, John, and John Built

1. Interview with Ed Paulson, March 2001.

2. "High Tech Wealth," by Robert X. Cringely, *Forbes*, July 7, 1997 (www.forbes.com/forbes/97/0707/6001296a.html).

3. "Cisco Unauthorized: Inside the High-Stakes Race to Own the Future," by Jeffrey S. Young, Copyright 2001 by Jeffrey S. Young, Forum-Prima, Roseville, CA 95661, p. 169.

4. *Making the Cisco Connection: The Story behind the Real Internet Superpower*, by David Bunnell with Adam Brate (New York: John Wiley & Sons, 2000), p. 11.

5. Ibid., p. 29.

6. *Making the Cisco Connection*, p. 24.

7. Ibid., p. 23.

8. "Cisco Unauthorized," p. 45.

9. "Growth by Acquisition: The Case of Cisco Systems," Second Quarter, 1997, Thought Leaders, Strategy and Business, Booz, Allen and Hamilton (www.strategy-business.com/thoughtleaders/97209/page4.html).

10. "Q&A: The Star Chambers," by Leonard Heymann, Jeremiah Caron, and Michelle Rae McLean, *LAN Times*, July 1996 (www.lantimes.com/96jul/607a001b.html).

11. *Making the Cisco Connection*, p. 48.

12. Interview with Ed Paulson, March 2001.

CHAPTER 4   Vision Compatibility Must Exist

1. "John Chambers: The Art of the Deal," Interview with John Daly, Business 2.0, October 1999 (www.business2.com/articles/1999/10/text/chambers.html), p. 2/8.

2. Interview with Ed Paulson, March 2001.

3. "Growth by Acquisition: The Case of Cisco Systems," Second Quarter, 1997, Thought Leaders, Strategy and Business, Booz, Allen and Hamilton (www.strategy-business.com/thoughtleaders/97209/page6.html), pp. 6 and 12.

CHAPTER 5   Win in the Short Term

1. "Growth by Acquisition: The Case of Cisco Systems," Second Quarter, 1997, Thought Leaders, Strategy and Business, Booz, Allen and Hamilton (www.strategy-business.com/thoughtleaders/97209/page9.html).

2. "Cisco to Scale Back Acquisitions," *Network World*, June 25, 2001, page 8, News Briefs.

3. "Growth by Acquisition: The Case of Cisco Systems," p. 10.

4. "Cisco Unauthorized: Inside the High-Stakes Race to Own the Future," by Jeffrey S. Young, Copyright 2001 by Jeffrey S. Young, Forum-Prima, Roseville, CA 95661, p. 61.

CHAPTER 6   Good Vibrations

1. *Organizational Behavior*, 5th Edition, by Don Hellreigel, John W. Slocum Jr., and Richard W. Woodman (St. Paul, MN: West Publishing Company, 1989), Chapter 11.

2. *Hidden Value: How Great Companies Achieve Extraordinary Results with Ordinary People,* by Charles A. O'Reilly III and Jeffrey Pferrer (Boston: Harvard Business School Press, 2000), p. 55.

3. "John Chambers: The Art of the Deal," Interview with John Daly, Business 2.0, October 1999 (www.business2.com/articles/1999/10/text/chambers.html), p. 5/8.

4. *Hidden Value*, p. 55.

5. *Cisco Systems: Are You Ready? (A)*, by John P. Morgridge and James L. Keskett (Boston: Harvard Business School Publishing, 2000; Case Number: 9-901-002, Rev. October 17, 2000), p. 25.

6. Ibid.

7. Ibid.

8. Ibid., p. 26.

9. "Q&A: The Star Chambers," by Leonard Heymann, Jeremiah Caron, and Michelle Rae McLean, *LAN Times*, July 1996 (www.lantimes.com/96jul/607a001b.html).

10. "John Chambers: The Art of the Deal," p. 5/8.

11. *Cisco Systems: Are You Ready? (A)*, p. 3/26.

12. "The Best CEOs," *Worth*, May 2000, p. 129.

13. "Annual Meeting Announcement to Shareholders," September 29, 2000, by Cisco Systems, Inc., p. 11.

14. "Cisco's Secrets," by Henry Goldblatt, *Fortune*, November 8, 1999, vol. 140, no. 9, pp. 178–180.

15. Ibid., p. 178.

CHAPTER 7 Make It a Long-Term Win, Too

1. "Cisco Systems: The Acquisition of Technology Is the Acquisition of People," by Charles O'Reilly, Stanford University, Case # HR-10, October 27, 1998, p. 15.

2. Ibid., p. 13.

3. "John Chambers: The Art of the Deal," Interview with John Daly, Business 2.0, October 1999 (www.business2.com/articles/1999/10/text/chambers.html), p. 2/8.

4. Ibid., p. 4/8.

5. "Growth by Acquisition: The Case of Cisco Systems," Second Quarter, 1997, Thought Leaders, Strategy and Business, Booz, Allen and Hamilton (www.strategy-business.com/thoughtleaders/97209/page7.html).

6. *Making the Cisco Connection: The Story behind the Real Internet Superpower,* by David Bunnell with Adam Brate (New York: John Wiley & Sons, 2000), p. 73.

7. "Grand Junction Networks: In September 1995, Grand Junction Networks Was Growing out of Its Skin," *Fast Company*, February 1998, issue 13, p. 88.

8. Schwab research site data acquired February 27, 2001.

9. "Growth by Acquisition: The Case of Cisco Systems," p. 12.

10. *Cisco Systems: Are You Ready? (B),* by John P. Morgridge and James L. Keskett (Boston: Harvard Business School Publishing, 2000; Case Number: 9-901-003, July 31, 2000), p. 1.

CHAPTER 8   Closer Is Better

1. "Growth by Acquisition: The Case of Cisco Systems," Second Quarter, 1997, Thought Leaders, Strategy and Business, Booz, Allen and Hamilton (www.strategy-business.com/thoughtleaders/97209/page9.html).

2. Ibid.

3. "John Chambers: The Art of the Deal," Interview with John Daly, Business 2.0, October 1999 (www.business2.com/articles/1999/10/text/chambers.html), p. 3/8).

4. "Cisco Unauthorized: Inside the High-Stakes Race to Own the Future," by Jeffrey S. Young, Copyright 2001 by Jeffrey S. Young, Forma-Prima, Roseville, CA 95661, p. 184.

5. Interview with Ed Paulson, March 2001.

6. *Cisco Systems, Inc.: Acquisition Integration for Manufacturing (B),* by Nicole Tempest and Charles A. Holloway (Boston: Harvard Business School Publishing, 2000; Case Number: 9-600-016, Febuary 2000), p. 1.

7. "Brainstorming Is Best Face-to-Face," by Alan Warms, *Chicago Tribune*, February 5, 2001 (www.chicagotribune.com/tech/diary/ws/item/0,1308,48826-48827-49593,00.html).

CHAPTER 9   No Merger of Equals

1. "Cisco's Secrets," by Henry Goldblatt, *Fortune*, November 8, 1999, vol. 140, no. 9, p. 184.

2. Ibid.

3. "Growth by Acquisition: The Case of Cisco Systems," Second Quarter, 1997, Thought Leaders, Strategy and Business, Booz, Allen and Hamilton (www.strategy-business.com/thoughtleaders/97209/page7.html), pp. 7–9.

4. Interview with Barry Eggers conducted by Ed Paulson, March 2001.

5. Ibid.

6. *Winning at Mergers and Acquisitions: The Guide to Market-Focused Planning and Integration*, by Mark N. Clemente and David S. Greenspan (New York: John Wiley & Sons, 1998), p. 302.

7. "Synoptics, Wellfleet to Merge: Consolidation of 2 Big Networking Players Will Give Cisco a Rival," by Steve Kaufman, *Mercury News, Business and Stocks*, July 6, 1994 (www.mercurycenter.com/business/sv15098/synopwellfleet.htm).

8. Ibid.

9. "Networking Industry: A New Way to Listen to the Music: ROIC," by Paul Silverstein et al., Institutional Research, Robertson, Stephens & Company, December 17, 1996.

CHAPTER 10   Target Practice

1. "Growth by Acquisition: The Case of Cisco Systems," Second Quarter, 1997, Thought Leaders, Strategy and Business, Booz, Allen and Hamilton (www.strategy-business.com/thoughtleaders/97209/page7.html), pp. 7–9.

2. "Cisco Defies Odds with Mergers That Work," by Scott Thurm, *Wall Street Journal*, March 1, 2000 (www.benchmarkingreports.com/articles/wsj_merger_article/wsj_merger_article.htm).

3. "Whiz Kid: Young Deal Maker Is the Force Behind a Company's Growth," by Laura M. Holson, *New York Times* on the Web, November 1998,www.cisco.com/warp/public/750/acquisition/articles/volpi.html), p. 4/6.

4. Ibid.

5. "Can Mike Volpi Make Cisco Sizzle Again?" by John Shinal, *Business Week*, February 26, 2001 (www.businessweek.com/datedtoc/2001/0109t.htm).

6. Interview with Ed Paulson, March 2001.

7. "Whiz Kid," p. 5/6.

8. Interview with Barry Eggers by Ed Paulson, March 2001.

9. Interview with Dave Newkirk by Ed Paulson, March 2001.

10. Ibid.

CHAPTER 11   The Cisco Due Diligence "Sniff Test"

1. From an interview with Ed Paulson, March 2001.

2. All quotes in this section from Mario Mazzola interview by Ed Paulson, March 2001.

3. Cisco's Secret: Entrepreneurs Sell Out, Stay Put, by Hal Plotkin, *Inc.*, March 01, 1997 http://www.inc.com/incmagazine/article10,art1180,co.html.

CHAPTER 12   Personnel Integration à la Cisco—Bam!

1. "John Chambers: The Art of the Deal," Interview with John Daly, Business 2.0, October 1999 (www.business2.com/articles/1999/10/text/chambers.html), p. 2/8.

2. "Growth by Acquisition: The Case of Cisco Systems," Second Quarter, 1997, Thought Leaders, Strategy and Business, Booz, Allen and Hamilton (www.strategy-business.com/thoughtleaders/97209/page4.html).

3. Ibid., p.10.

4. *Making the Cisco Connection: The Story behind the Real Internet Superpower,* by David Bunnell with Adam Brate (New York: John Wiley & Sons, 2000), p. 85.

5. Interview with Ed Paulson, March 2001.

6. Ibid.

7. "John Chambers: The Art of the Deal," p. 3/8.

8. "Cisco Systems: The Acquisition of Technology Is the Acquisition of People," by Charles O'Reilly, Stanford University, Case # HR-10, October 27, 1998, p. 6.

9. "Cisco's Secrets," by Henry Goldblatt, *Fortune*, November 8, 1999, vol. 140, no. 9, p. 184.

10. "Growth by Acquisition: The Case of Cisco Systems," p. 4/12.

11. "John Chambers: The Art of the Deal," p. 1/8.

12. "How to Drive an Express Train: At Fast-Moving Cisco, CEO Says: Put Customers First, View Rivals as 'Good Guys,'" by Scott Thurm, *Wall Street Journal*, June 1, 2000, Boss Talk, p. 1.

13. "Cisco Defies Odds with Mergers That Work," by Scott Thurm, *Wall Street Journal*, March 1, 2000, p. 5/8.

14. "Cisco Systems: The Acquisition of Technology Is the Acquisition of People," p. 6.

15. Ibid., p. 7

16. "Cisco's Secrets," p. 178.

17. Ibid., pp. 180–184.

18. Interview with Ed Paulson, March 2001.

19. Ibid.

20. Interview with Barry Eggers by Ed Paulson, March 2001.

21. "Cisco Defies Odds," p. 6/8.

22. "Cisco's Secrets," p. 180.

23. Interview with Dave Newkirk by Ed Paulson, March 2001.

24. "Cisco Systems: The Acquisition of Technology Is the Acquisition of People," p. 5.

25. "Growth by Acquisition: The Case of Cisco Systems," Second Quarter, 1997, Thought Leaders, Strategy and Business, Booz, Allen and Hamilton (www.strategy-business.com/thoughtleaders/97209/page4.html).

26. "Cisco Systems: The Acquisition of Technology Is the Acquisition of People," p. 5.

27. "John Chambers: The Art of the Deal," Interview with John Daly, Busi-

ness 2.0, October 1999 (www.usiness2.com/articles/1999/10/text/
chambers.html), page 4/8.

28. Ibid.

Chapter 13   Integrating Products and Production

1. "Cisco Systems, Inc.: Acquisition Integration for Manufacturing," by
Nicole Tempest, Stanford University, Case #OIT-26, January 1999.
2. Ibid., pp. 4–5.
3. Ibid., p. 15.

Chapter 14   Setting the Purchase Price

1. *Hidden Value: How Great Companies Achieve Extraordinary Results
with Ordinary People*, by Charles A. O'Reilly III and Jeffrey Pfeffer
(Boston, MA: Harvard Business School Press, 2000), p. 65.
2. "Growth by Acquisition: The Case of Cisco Systems," Second Quarter,
1997, Thought Leaders, Strategy and Business, Booz, Allen and Hamilton (www.strategy-business.com/thoughtleaders/97209/page10.html).
3. "Cisco's Secrets," by Henry Goldblatt, *Fortune*, November 8, 1999,
vol. 140, no. 9, p. 180.
4. *Making the Cisco Connection: The Story behind the Real Internet Superpower*, by David Bunnell with Adam Brate (New York: John Wiley &
Sons, 2000), p. 23.
5. "Grand Junction Networks: In September 1995, Grand Junction Networks Was Growing out of Its Skin," by Pat Dillon, *Fast Company*, February 1998, issue 13 (http://pf.fastcompany.com/online/13/junction.
html), p. 88.
6. Ibid.
7. Ibid.
8. Interview with Ed Paulson, March 2001.

Chapter 15   Can You Really Grow through Acquisition?

1. *Thriving on Chaos: Handbook for a Management Revolution*, by Tom
Peters (New York: Knopf, 1987), p. 7.

2. Interview with Ed Paulson, March 2001.

3. Ibid.

CHAPTER 16   So How Good Really Is the Cisco A&D Approach?

1. Interview with Ed Paulson, March 2001.

2. "Winston Churchill in America," by John H. Chettle, *Smithsonian*, April 2001, p. 82.

3. "Growth by Acquisition: The Case of Cisco Systems," Second Quarter, 1997, Thought Leaders, Strategy and Business, Booz, Allen and Hamilton (www.strategy-business.com/thoughtleaders/97209/page6.html).

4. Ibid.

5. "Winston Churchill in America," p. 82.

6. "Cisco Wins One in Battle with Nortel," by Bill Scanlon, *Interactive Week*, March 12, 2001 (www.zdnet.com/intweek/stories/news/0,4164,2694875,00.html).

7. Ibid.

8. *Thriving on Chaos: Handbook for a Management Revolution*, by Tom Peters (New York: Knopf, 1987), p. 36.

9. Ibid., p. 4.

10. "How to Drive an Express Train: At Fast-Moving Cisco, CEO Says: Put Customers First, View Rivals as 'Good Guys,'" by Scott Thurm, *Wall Street Journal*, June 1, 2000, Boss Talk, p. 1.

11. Interview with Ed Paulson, March 2001.

12. "Cisco's Secrets," by Henry Goldblatt, *Fortune*, November 8, 1999, vol. 140, no. 9, p. 178.

INDEX